Urban Public Finance

FUNDAMENTALS OF PURE AND APPLIED ECONOMICS

EDITORS-IN-CHIEF

J. LESOURNE, Conservatoire National des Arts et Métiers, Paris, France
H. SONNENSCHEIN, Princeton University, Princeton, NJ, USA

ADVISORY BOARD

K. ARROW, Stanford, CA, USA
W. BAUMOL, Princeton, NJ, USA
W. A. LEWIS, Princeton, NJ, USA
S. TSURU, Tokyo, Japan

SECTIONS AND EDITORS

BALANCE OF PAYMENTS AND INTERNATIONAL FINANCE
W. Branson, Princeton University

DISTRIBUTION
A. Atkinson, London School of Economics

ECONOMIC DEMOGRAPHY
T.P. Schultz, Yale University

ECONOMIC DEVELOPMENT STUDIES
S. Chakravarty, Delhi School of Economics

ECONOMIC FLUCTUATIONS: FORECASTING, STABILIZATION, INFLATION, SHORT TERM MODELS, UNEMPLOYMENT
A. Ando, University of Pennsylvania

ECONOMIC HISTORY
P. David, Stanford University and M. Lévy-Leboyer, Université Paris X

ECONOMIC SYSTEMS
J.M. Montias, Yale University and J. Kornai, Institute of Economics, Hungarian Academy of Sciences

ECONOMICS OF HEALTH, EDUCATION, POVERTY AND CRIME
V. Fuchs, Stanford University

ECONOMICS OF THE HOUSEHOLD AND INDIVIDUAL BEHAVIOR
J. Muellbauer, University of Oxford

ECONOMICS OF TECHNOLOGICAL CHANGE
F. M. Scherer, Swarthmore College

ECONOMICS OF UNCERTAINTY AND INFORMATION
S. Grossman, Princeton University and J. Stiglitz, Princeton University

Continued on inside back cover

Urban Public Finance

David E. Wildasin
Indiana University, USA

A volume in the Regional and Urban Economics section
edited by
Richard Arnott
Queen's University, Canada

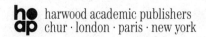
harwood academic publishers
chur · london · paris · new york

©1986 by Harwood Academic Publishers GmbH
Poststrasse 22, 7000 Chur, Switzerland
All rights reserved

Harwood Academic Publishers

P.O. Box 197
London WC2E 9PX
England

58, rue Lhomond
75005 Paris
France

P.O. Box 786
Cooper Station
New York, NY 10276
United States of America

Library of Congress Cataloging-in-Publication Data

Wildasin, David A.
  Urban public finance

  (Fundamentals of pure and applied economics; v. 10.
Regional and urban economics section)
    Bibliography: p.
    Includes index.
    1. Municipal finance. I. Title. II. Series:
Fundamentals of pure and applied economics; v. 10.
III. Series: Fundamentals of pure and applied
economics. Regional and urban economics section.
HJ9105.W55   1986   336'.014   86-14981
ISBN 3-7186-0334-9

Contents

v

Introduction to the Series

Drawing on a personal network, an economist can still relatively easily stay well informed in the narrow field in which he works, but to keep up with the development of economics as a whole is a much more formidable challenge. Economists are confronted with difficulties associated with the rapid development of their discipline. There is a risk of "balkanisation" in economics, which may not be favorable to its development.

Fundamentals of Pure and Applied Economics has been created to meet this problem. The discipline of economics has been subdivided into sections (listed inside). These sections include short books, each surveying the state of the art in a given area.

Each book starts with the basic elements and goes as far as the most advanced results. Each should be useful to professors needing material for lectures, to graduate students looking for a global view of a particular subject, to professional economists wishing to keep up with the development of their science, and to researchers seeking convenient information on questions that incidentally appear in their work.

Each book is thus a presentation of the state of the art in a particular field rather than a step-by-step analysis of the development of the literature. Each is a high-level presentation but accessible to anyone with a solid background in economics, whether engaged in business, government, international organizations, teaching, or research in related fields.

Three aspects of *Fundamentals of Pure and Applied Economics* should be emphasized:

—First, the project covers the whole field of economics, not only theoretical or mathematical economics.

—Second, the project is open-ended and the number of books is not predetermined. If new interesting areas appear, they will generate additional books.

—Last, all the books making up each section will later be grouped to constitute one or several volumes of an Encyclopedia of Economics.

The editors of the sections are outstanding economists who have selected as authors for the series some of the finest specialists in the world.

J. Lesourne   *H. Sonnenschein*

Urban Public Finance

DAVID E. WILDASIN

Indiana University, Bloomington, USA

1. INTRODUCTION

The purpose of this study is to provide a review of current developments in urban public finance. To do so within a limited space requires careful selection of topics. Here I briefly indicate how the survey has been organized, the logical interdependence of the sections, and the kinds of emphasis a reader may expect.

First, in general terms, the survey is relatively analytical rather than descriptive. There is comparatively little discussion, for example, of various applied policy problems. Aside from space constraints, this decision is based on a desire to avoid detailed treatment of country-specific (or, indeed, state, province, or city-specific) issues and institutional structures. Somewhat for the same reason, there is relatively little discussion of empirical results. At the same time, the field of urban public finance derives much of its importance and interest from the many policy issues, and the many opportunities for empirical work, that it offers. Thus, we do refer, at least briefly, to some of the relevant empirical literature, especially where empirical work has prompted extensions and revisions of theoretical models. Similarly, much of the theoretical work that we review has clearly been motivated by a desire to illuminate actual policy issues. It is hoped, therefore, that the survey will at least impart some sense of the interplay between theoretical, empirical, and policy analysis.

The topics to be covered are organized in the following way. First, Sections 2–4 present a discussion of the basic principles of resource allocation in economies with local governments. Section 2

1

focuses on the way that the local public sector influences the locational choices of households, attempting, among other things, to delineate cases in which local government policies do and do not distort the spatial distribution of a mobile population. Sections 3 and 4 discuss the determination of local public expenditure, both from positive and normative perspectives. The problem here is to model how decisions about the provision of local public goods are or might be made, and then to assess the efficiency implications of these decisions. Section 3 (which can be read independently of other sections) focuses on models in which the population in each jurisdiction is regarded as fixed—which includes those models that have been most subject to empirical testing. By contrast, Section 4 examines the implications of household mobility for public expenditure determination. This section relies heavily on the model and notation presented in Section 2.

Section 5 deals with property and land taxation, two major sources of local government financing. The discussion here focuses on tax incidence and possible tax distortions. This section is logically independent of the others.

Finally, Section 6 discusses various types of fiscal interactions, both among local governments and between higher- and lower-level governments. In the first category, we discuss benefit and tax spillovers among local governments, and also the possibility that jurisdictions might use their policies to manipulate the size and composition of the resident population. In the second category, we discuss intergovernmental grants, including both positive issues (how do recipient governments respond to grant policy?) and normative ones (what is an optimal grant design?). Some parts of this section are independent of earlier sections, while others refer back to parts of Sections 2 and 3.

2. EFFICIENT RESOURCE ALLOCATION AND THE LOCAL PUBLIC SECTOR: LOCATIONAL EFFICIENCY

2.1. Introduction

When we study efficient resource allocation in relation to the local public sector, it is evident that all of the basic issues of public economics that arise at the level of the (closed) national economy will be present in the local context as well. Local public expenditures will influence the welfare of many people simultaneously and local taxes will distort resource allocation and affect equilibrium prices. Hence, the familiar problems of characterizing and achieving an efficient level of public expenditure, of tax incidence and the welfare loss from taxation, are sure to arise. What one naturally wants to emphasize, however, are those issues that are unique to the local public sector. Perhaps the most novel feature that needs to be taken into account is the *openness* of local jurisdictions. This has many ramifications.

One aspect of this openness is that people can migrate among localities. To be sure, this involves some cost, and not all households are equally mobile, but mobility is clearly an important fact of life at the local level and analysts who deal with this phenomenon have often assumed that people are costlessly mobile. Household migration is important for several reasons. It helps determine the population served by local public goods or services, and thus must be relevant for both normative and positive public expenditure theory: migration influences the benefit side of the benefit/cost ledger, and it also can influence who will participate in the decisionmaking process that fixes local policy. Migration also raises efficiency issues in its own right. Surely households should not be allocated across jurisdictions arbitrarily. How does one determine, then, how many and what types of households would be efficiently located in each of many localities?

Second, not only households, but commodities, both goods and factors, private and public, can move across jurisdictional boundaries. This raises a number of issues. Mobility of private goods implies that local public policy can affect resource allocation in the private sector. How might localities tax exports and imports, or subsidize certain industries, and what are the efficiency implications of doing so? Conversely, the economic environment provides the backdrop against which the local political process operates. How is the openness of local economy relevant for this process? Finally, publicly-provided commodities can be mobile. One city's water treatment facility may improve water quality for downstream cities, locally-educated individuals may carry their human capital out of their home jurisdiction, and so on. What are the implications of these benefit "spillovers"?

This section begins our discussion of these highly interrelated issues. It is essential, for the sake of analytical and conceptual clarity, to simplify the problem by focusing on just one aspect at a time. To begin with, let us assume away all tax distortions of the traditional type by considering taxes on commodities that are not producible, and/or are inelastically demanded. These will include the cases of land taxes and head taxes. Assuming that no individual faces a labor/leisure tradeoff allows us also to consider wage income taxes. Furthermore, let us ignore the issue of local public good provision by taking the level of public services to be exogenously fixed. Finally, we also suppose there to be no interjurisdictional benefit (or cost) spillovers. All of these assumptions are relaxed in subsequent sections.

In this simplified framework, we can focus on the issue of "group formation" or "locational efficiency." Section 2.2 examines an economy with some exogenously-given jurisdictional structure, where each locality provides certain public services to its residents. With mobile households, we can ask, first, what are the properties of an efficient assignment of households to jurisdictions? Second, under what circumstances, if any, will an equilibrium in a decentralized economy be efficient? A number of conflicting conclusions have emerged in the literature, and we present a general framework in which the role of alternative assumptions in producing different results can clearly be seen.

Section 2.3 takes a somewhat different perspective. Suppose a planner is able to control a jurisdiction's population, as well as resource allocation within the jurisdiction. What would be the optimal population size? In the literature, study of this problem has led to the "Henry George Theorem," which in its simplest form states that local public expenditures should be equated to local land rents. We shall indicate the conditions under which this result obtains, and also the way that it must be modified in some cases. We also discuss the implications of this result for overall social efficiency.

Finally, Section 2.4 considers the issue of "fiscal zoning," that is, restrictions on land use that may be motivated by considerations of fiscally-induced household migration. As will become clear, the main results in the literature on fiscal zoning are closely related to those discussed in Section 2 on locational efficiency.

2.2. Locational efficiency and local taxation

A. The planner's problem. We will consider the problem of locational efficiency in a setting that is not explicitly spatial in the sense that it ignores transportation costs, but that does exploit the spatial fixity of some resources.[1] In some branches of the literature no such structure is imposed, and we shall discuss such cases later. But for the moment, let us observe that cities (and states and provinces) are geographically-defined entities, so that it is not only natural, but is arguably even necessary, to include some spatial considerations in a satisfactory treatment.

We begin with a model akin to those found in Buchanan and Wagner [79], Buchanan and Goetz [78], Flatters *et al.* [127], and Wildasin [371], although it is more general than all of these. It is particularly useful because it yields insights that can help in interpreting many of the results found in the literature. The general approach and main conclusions can be found in Wildasin [371].

Suppose, then, a given set of $M \geq 2$ jurisdictions, which might be individual cities, or larger regional entities such as states or provinces. Each jurisdiction i provides a vector of public goods z_i which benefit resident households but not non-residents. (This is the nonspillover assumption.) Since we are focusing on locational efficiency issues, z_i is taken as exogenously fixed throughout our discussion. One can subsume other exogenous regional attributes in z_i as well, such as environmental/climatic attributes.

Let us assume $N \geq 1$ types of individuals, with all members of type k having identical preferences. The total number N^k of individuals of each type is large enough to be treated as a continuum, and let n_i^k be the number of individuals of type k residing in locality i.[2] We assume that the cost of providing the

---

[1] Many of the results of this subsection are presented, in the context of a monocentric city model, in Kanemoto [196]. Another related work is Wijkander [365], who studies the effect of public good provision on spatial structure in a congested monocentric city.

[2] The assumption of a continuum of agents is common in the literature, and is indeed almost universal whenever spatial problems arise. The reason is that locational decisions introduce fundamental non-convexities in consumer preferences and/or consumption sets. For example, while it may be feasible to consume equivalent housing bundles in either town (or neighborhood) 1 or town (or

(footnote 2 continued next page.)

public goods z_i to the population $n_i \triangleq (n_i^1, \ldots, n_i^N)$ is given by the function $C_i(n_i, z_i)$, expressed in units of a numeraire all-purpose private good.

To avoid any possible confusion, let us elaborate on the specification of the cost of local public goods. Note that we must distinguish the size (and type) of population being served from the level of public services. For example, in the case of education, the quantity z_i provided is *not* to be interpreted as the number of households or pupils served, but as the amount (or "quality") of education received by each. The marginal cost of education, which is given by the partial derivative $\partial C_i / \partial z_i$, is thus the resources required to improve the education received by each student, with the number of students held fixed. The cost of providing a given level of education does depend on the number of residents, however, and this dependence is captured through the partial derivatives $C_{ik} \triangleq \partial C_i / \partial n_i^k$. Sometimes this derivative is also referred to as the marginal cost of the public good (e.g. Hamilton [160]). It reflects the "impurity," "rivalness," (Musgrave [253]) or congestibility of local public goods, and we shall generally refer to C_{ik} as a "marginal congestion cost" or "marginal cost with respect to population." In the case of public goods that are "pure" in the sense of Samuelson [312, 313], one individual's consumption in no way detracts from another person's ability to consume a given level of public good, or, put differently, one person's consumption does not require an increase in inputs to maintain the level of the public good consumed by others. In this special case, we have $C_{ik} = 0$ for all k. For most local public goods, however, including education, highways, public safety, etc., at least some congestion will be the rule.

It may be noted that the cost function $C_i(n_i, z_i)$ is more general

---

(footnote 2 continued)
neighborhood) 2, a convex combination of the two will certainly be less preferred than either taken by itself, thus violating convexity of preferences, and may not even be feasible, thus violating convexity of the consumption set. This introduces discontinuities in demand behavior that may preclude the existence of a competitive equilibrium. See, e.g., Malinvaud [214]. However, Aumann [13], Hildenbrand [173], and many others have shown that when the number of agents is large, these individual-level discontinuities do not result in discontinuities at the market level, and the existence problem resulting from these non-convexities is obviated. For an existence proof in an explicitly spatial setting, see Schweizer *et al.* [322]. Berliant [36], however, has recently questioned the appropriateness of the assumption of a continuum of agents in spatial settings.

than those where costs depend only on the total population $\Sigma_k n_i^k$, since the present specification allows for different types of households to give rise to different congestion effects (e.g., retirees vs. young families). More special still, one might assume that cost is proportional to population, $C_i(n_i, z_i) = (\Sigma_k n_i^k)c_i(z_i)$. This special case, or a local version of it, sometimes plays an important role in the literature. We shall refer to it as *constant per capita costs*.[3]

Now let us describe the remainder of the model. Each jurisdiction has a vector of exogenously fixed resources T_i, which may simply be thought of as homogenous land but could include different types of land or other spatially fixed resources. These resources may be used as direct consumption goods by households (such as residential land), with t_i^k the vector of fixed resources consumed by a type k individual in jurisdiction i, $t_i = (t_i^k)$.[4] They also may be used as inputs in a local production process, along with labor, to produce the all-purpose good. Each household supplies one unit of labor, with different types of individuals possibly supplying different types of labor. Letting t_i^P denote the vector of fixed resources used in local production, we assume a smooth linear homogeneous production function $F_i(n_i, t_i^P)$. The remaining fixed resources in jurisdiction i, $t_i^A = T_i - n_i t_i - t_i^P$, are used as sole inputs in a production process that we refer to as "agriculture," yielding an agricultural output $\phi_i(t_i^A)$, where ϕ_i is concave. (Note that the forms of F_i and ϕ_i are indexed by i. This could reflect environmental amenities that differ across jurisdictions. It could also reflect the role of z_i as a vector of public inputs. Since z_i is held fixed throughout this section, it is suppressed for notational ease.)

Household preferences are represented by smooth, strictly quasi-concave utility functions $u_i^k(x_i^k, t_i^k, q_i^k, n_i, z_i)$, where x_i^k and q_i^k are the consumption of all-purpose good and agricultural output by type k individuals in locality i. Let $x_i = (x_i^k)$, $q_i = (q_i^k)$. Including n_i in the utility function allows for the possibility of crowding phenemona other than those occurring through congestion of public facilities.

---

[3] As one would anticipate, empirical studies such as Bergstrom and Goodman [34] and many others (a long list is cited in Hirsch [174]) find strong empirical evidence of congestion or crowding. In many cases, once a minimum population size on the order of 10–50 thousand is reached costs become approximately proportional to population—i.e., we have constant per capita costs.
[4] It is natural to assume equal treatment of all households of a given type in a given city.

We can now pose the planner's problem. For simplicity, assume that the objective is to obtain a Pareto-efficient allocation of resources by choosing x_i, t_i, q_i, n_i, t_i^P, and, in the case where urban/rural resource use is endogenous, t_i^A, subject to relevant constraints, including

$$\sum_i F_i(n_i, t_i^P) - \sum_i n_i x_i - \sum_i C_i(n_i, z_i) = 0: \quad \mu \qquad (2.1)$$

$$\sum_i \phi_i(t_i^A) - \sum_i n_i q_i = 0: \quad \xi \qquad (2.2)$$

$$T_i - n_i t_i - t_i^P - t_i^A = 0: \quad \rho_i \qquad (2.3)$$

$$N^k - \sum_i n_i^k = 0: \quad \pi^k \qquad (2.4)$$

$$u_i^k(x_i^k, t_i^k, q_i^k, n_i, z_i) - \bar{u}^k = 0: \quad \lambda_i^k, k > 1 \qquad (2.5)$$

$$u_i^1(x_i^1, t_i^1, q_i^1, n_i, z_i) - u_1^1(x_1^1, t_1^1, q_1^1, n_1, z_1): \quad \lambda_i^1, i > 1. \qquad (2.6)$$

Associated with each constraint is a greek letter which will serve as a Lagrange multiplier. Constraints (2.1) and (2.2) are feasibility constraints for the numeraire and agricultural goods. Equation (2.3) is the land constraint when t_i^A is a choice variable. (When t_i^A is exogenous, we need only write $t_i^A = \bar{t}_i^A$ and delete t_i^A from the instrument set. The reader can easily check that subsequent results are the same in this case). By (2.4), all households must reside at some location. Constraint (2.5) fixes the utility of household types $k > 1$ at exogenously-specified levels: characterizing an optimum requires maximizing the utility of the type-1's subject to fixed utilities for all others. Both (2.5) and (2.6) reflect costless mobility of households, by ruling out jurisdictional utility differentials that would be incompatible with free locational choice. In specifying these constraints, and in the first-order conditions to follow, we assume a "classical" optimum: i.e., constraints are written as equalities, non-negativity conditions are ignored, and corner solutions are ruled out. This is done merely for convenience.[5]

---

[5] For example, we could replace (2.5) with the more general condition

$$u_i^k(\cdot) - \bar{u}^k < 0 \Rightarrow n_i^k = 0$$
$$n_i^k > 0 \Rightarrow u_i^k(\cdot) - \bar{u}^k = 0.$$

In characterizing an optimum, we could still obtain conditions like (2.7)–(2.10) for all those i, k such that $n_i^k > 0$ at the optimum, and the results that follow from these first-order conditions would be unaffected.

The planner's objective is to maximize u_1^1 subject to the above constraints. (Any Pareto efficient allocation of resources can be described as a solution to such a planner's problem.) The first-order conditions for this problem are (with instruments being optimized shown in parentheses)

$$(x_i^k): \quad \bar{\lambda}_i^k u_{i1}^k - \mu n_i^k = 0 \qquad \text{all } i, k \tag{2.7}$$

$$(t_i^k): \quad \bar{\lambda}_i^k u_{i2}^k - \rho_i n_i^k = 0 \qquad \text{all } i, k \tag{2.8}$$

$$(q_i^k): \quad \bar{\lambda}_i^k u_{i3}^k - \xi n_i^k = 0 \qquad \text{all } i, k \tag{2.9}$$

$$(n_i^k): \quad \sum_{k'} \bar{\lambda}_i^{k'} u_{i4k}^{k'} + \mu(F_{ik} - x_i^k - C_{ik}) - \xi q_i^k - \rho_i t_i^k - \pi^k = 0$$
$$\text{all } i, k \tag{2.10}$$

$$(t_i^P): \quad \mu F_{it} - \rho_i = 0 \qquad \text{all } i \tag{2.11}$$

$$(t_i^A): \quad \zeta \phi_{it} - \mu_i = 0 \qquad \text{all } i \tag{2.12}$$

where: $\bar{\lambda}_1^1 = (1 - \sum_{i>1} \lambda_i^1)$ and $\bar{\lambda}_i^k = \lambda_i^k$ otherwise, F_{ik} is the marginal product of type k labor in locality i, and subscripts on utility functions denote marginal utilities. Further, ρ_i, u_{i2}^k, F_{it}, and ϕ_{it} are, respectively, vectors of Lagrange multipliers, marginal utilities, and marginal products in all-purpose good production and agriculture, for spatially fixed resources.

The interpretation of most of these conditions is familiar and need not be belabored. Clearly, $\xi/\mu = \mu_{i3}^k/\mu_{i1}^k$ and $\rho_i/\mu = u_{i2}^k/u_{i1}^k = F_{it} = \xi\phi_{it}/\mu$ are the shadow values of agricultural output and fixed resources in terms of numeraire. The crucial condition is (2.10), which describes the optimal location pattern for households. Use (2.7) to eliminate the $\bar{\lambda}_i^k$'s in (2.10), and let $MCC_{ik}^{k'}$ denote $u_{i4k}^{k'}/u_{i1}^{k'}$, i.e., a k'-type household's willingness to pay to reduce the number of k-type households or, in other words, the marginal congestion cost imposed on a k'-type by a k-type. Then (2.10) can be written as

$$F_{ik} - \left(x_i^k + \frac{\xi}{\mu} q_i^k + \frac{\rho_i}{\mu} t_i^k \right) - \left(C_{ik} + \sum_{k'} n_i^{k'} MCC_{ik}^{k'} \right) = \frac{\pi^k}{\mu} \qquad \text{all } i, k.$$
$$\tag{2.13}$$

F_{ik} is a k-type's productive contribution upon locating in jurisdiction i. The first parenthetical expression is the value of private goods consumed by such a household, and the second expression is the congestion cost imposed on public facilities and directly on

other residents. Thus, (2.13) is a social marginal benefit minus
social marginal cost expression. This net marginal benefit from
locating a k-type agent in locality i must be equated to π^k/μ, i.e., it
must be equated across all localities.

At first it may seem surprising that the benefit to a household
from consuming local public goods (or environmental amenities)
does not appear in (2.13). Actually, however, this benefit is
implicitly present because the private good consumption bundle,
together with the local public good and consumer congestion costs,
yields the same level of utility for households of a given type in all
locatities (by constraints (2.5) and (2.6)). The greater the benefit
from local public goods, the less costly the private good consumption bundle that yields a given level of utility, and hence the greater
the net benefit measure on the left of (2.13).

This is easily illustrated when only x_i^k and a single public good z_i
enter the utility function, and indeed the optimality condition itself
is quite easily interpreted in this special case. Figure 1 shows that
the benefit of higher public services in locality 2 is reflected directly
in a lower x_2^k. Figure 2 (following Buchanan and Wagner [79])
portrays the case where $k = 1$ and $M = 2$. The curves MPP_i
represent the marginal product of labor as a function of population
in locality 1. When there is no public good and no congestion, equal
utility implies $x_1^1 = x_2^1$ and the optimality condition (2.13) reduces to

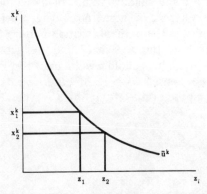

FIGURE 1 Type k households locating in jurisdictions 1 and 2 achieve the same
utility level $\bar{u}^k$. A higher level of public good in 2 corresponds to a lower level of
private good consumption.

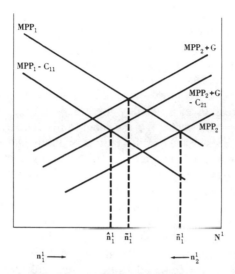

FIGURE 2   An optimal location pattern is characterized by equality of the social marginal net benefit of additional residents in each locality.

$MPP_1 = MPP_2$: with pure private goods, efficiency requires allocating labor in an output-maximizing fashion, and an optimum occurs at $n_1^1 = \bar{n}_1^1$. With uncongestible local public goods, Eq. (2.13) requires that $MPP_1 = MPP_2 + x_1^1 - x_2^1$. Following Figure 1, if we define $G = x_1^1 - x_2^1$ as the differential public good benefit accruing to residents in locality 2, then an optimum occurs at $n_1^1 = \bar{n}_1^1$, where the combined private and public good benefits of adding a household to either locality are equated.[6] Finally, if public facilities are congestible, (2.13) requires that net benefit of an additional resident be adjusted downward in each locality by C_{i1}. In the figure, the optimum now occurs at $\hat{n}_1^1$.

B. Equilibrium locational choice.   Having characterized and interpreted an efficient location pattern in an economy with local public

---

[6] Here, x_1^1 and x_2^1 are evaluated at their *optimal* values. If preferences are linear in the private good, then G, the private-good equivalent of the public service differential, will be invariant to the allocation of resources. In general, however, there is no such fixed equivalent. This limitation is inherent in the diagrammatic approach illustrated in Figure 2.

goods, we now consider the efficiency properties of an equilibrium. We assume competitive conditions throughout the economy and free mobility of households. Taking the all-purpose good as numeraire, let w_i^k denote the wage in locality i for type-k workers, $w_i = (w_i^k)$, r_i the vector of prices for fixed resources in i, $r = (r_i)$, and p the price of agricultural output. For simplicity, also assume that fixed resources in each locality are freely mobile among uses, so that the gross rent vector r_i is the same in residential, industrial, and agricultural uses. (The results extend without change to the case where this mobility is restricted, e.g., by land-use zoning.)

Resource rents and agricultural profits accrue to households according to their resource endowments and ownership shares in agriculture, taken as exogenously fixed. By definition, these are identical for all households of a given type. Local governments finance expenditures through head taxes and taxes on wage income, fixed resources, and agricultural profits. All taxes are initially assumed to be source-based rather than residence-based—that is, taxes on resource rents and agricultural profits are levied by the jurisdictions in which this income originates, not by the jurisdictions in which the recipients reside. The implications of residence-based taxes are considered later.

Thus, let $\bar{t}_i^k$ be a k-type individual's vector of fixed resources in jurisdiction i, $\bar{t}^k = (\bar{t}_i^k)$, σ_i^k a k-type individual's ownership share in the agricultural profits in jurisdiction i, τ_{in}^k the head tax on k-types in locality i, $\tau_{in} = (\tau_{in}^k)$, τ_{iw} the wage income tax rate, τ_{ir} the tax vector on fixed resources in i, $\tau_r = (\tau_{ir})$, and τ_{iA} the agricultural profit tax. It is assumed that

$$\sum_k N^k \bar{t}_i^k = T_i \qquad \text{all } i \qquad (2.14)$$

$$\sum_k N^k \sigma_i^k = 1 \qquad \text{all } i, \qquad (2.15)$$

that is, all fixed resources are initially held by someone and ownership shares in agriculture sum to unity.

We can now specify the budget constraints for individuals and localities, which must hold in equilibrium. For a k-type residing in locality i,[7]

$$x_i^k + r_i t_i^k + p q_i^k = (1 - \tau_{iw}) w_i^k - \tau_{in}^k + (r - \tau_r) \bar{t}^k$$

$$+ \sum_j (1 - \tau_{jA}) \sigma_j^k [p \phi_j(t_j^A) - r_j t_j^A]$$

$$= (1 - \tau_{iw}) w_i^k - \tau_{in}^k + I^k, \qquad (2.16)$$

say, where of course $p \phi_j(t_j^A) - r_j t_j^A$ is agricultural profit in j and I^k is the net income of k-type households that is location-independent. Let v_i^k denote the maximum of $u_i^k(x_i^k, t_i^k, q_i^k, n_i, z_i)$ with respect to (x_i^k, t_i^k, q_i^k) subject to (2.16). The budget balance restriction for jurisdiction i is:

$$C_i(z_i, n_i) = \tau_{iw} w_i n_i + \tau_{in} n_i + \tau_{ir} T_i + \tau_{iA} [p \phi_i(t_i^A) - r_i t_i^A]. \qquad (2.17)$$

In equilibrium, local policies must be consistent with (2.17). Demand and supply must be equal in all markets as described in (2.1), (2.2), and (2.3). Households must make utility-maximizing locational choices, characterized by[8]

$$v_i^k = \bar{v}^k \qquad \text{all } i, k \qquad (2.18)$$

where $\bar{v}^k$ is the equilibrium utility level for k-type households. All households must locate somewhere, as described in (2.4), and firms producing the all-purpose good must earn zero profits. The latter condition of course follows from competitive factor pricing.

Now let us suppose that an equilibrium exists, and examine its efficiency properties. It is most instructive to approach this question

---

[7] We assume that wage and resource taxes are statutorily borne by workers and resource owners, respectively. Thus, w_i and r_i are gross-of-tax prices. As usual, the real equilibrium of the economy is invariant to the statutory assignment of tax liabilities, so the analysis to follow applies as well, e.g., to employment taxes.

[8] This assumes $n_i^k > 0$, all i, k, in equilibrium. More generally, (2.18) could be replaced by

$$v_i^k < \max_{\langle j \rangle} v_j^k \Rightarrow n_i^k = 0$$

$$n_i^k > 0 \Rightarrow v_i^k = \max_{\langle j \rangle} v_j^k.$$

This would not change any essentials.

by checking whether the necessary conditions (2.7)–(2.12), and especially (2.13), are satisfied in equilibrium.

It is obvious that utility- and profit-maximizing behavior implies that, in equilibrium,

$$\frac{u_{i2}^k}{u_{i1}^k} = F_{it} = p\phi_{it}(=r_i) \qquad \text{all } i, k \qquad (2.19)$$

$$\frac{u_{i3}^k}{u_{i1}^k} = p \qquad \text{all } i, k. \qquad (2.20)$$

These conditions are all required by (2.7)–(2.9), (2.11), and (2.12), of course, and simply describe efficient utilization of fixed resources and agricultural output in consumption and production. Note from (2.16) that

$$w_i - (x_i^k + r_i t_i^k + pq_i^k) = \tau_{iw}w_i^k + \tau_{in}^k - I^k. \qquad (2.21)$$

From this it follows that the locational efficiency condition (2.13) can only be satisfied if

$$\tau_{iw}w_i^k + \tau_{in}^k - \left(C_{ik} + \sum_{k'} n_i^{k'} MCC_{ik}^{k'} \right)$$
$$= \tau_{jw}w_j^k + \tau_{jn}^k - \left(C_{jk} + \sum_{k'} n_j^{k'} MCC_{jk}^{k'} \right), \qquad (2.22)$$

for any pair of localities i and j and for any household type k. We now consider whether (2.22) is met in certain special cases.

Case 1. $\tau_{iA} = \tau_{ir} = 0$, $C_{ik} = MCC_{ik}^{k'} = 0$, for all i, k, k'. In this special case, with no congestion effects and only wage or head taxation, it is evident that (2.22) requires $\tau_{iw}w_i^k + \tau_{in}^k = \tau_{jw}w_{jn}^k + \tau_{jn}^k$, that is, wage plus head taxes must be equated across localities for each household type. Such a condition, of course, need not hold in general. The reason why (differential) wage and head taxation results in inefficiency in this case is easily seen intuitively. In an equal-utility equilibrium, moving a household from one jurisdiction to another leaves that household's welfare unchanged. With no congestion effects, the welfare of other households can only be affected if the excess of the value of the household's product less private good consumption, i.e., the expression on the left-hand side of (2.21), differs across jurisdictions. If it does, moving the household where it generates a greater surplus makes it possible to increase the welfare of some other household. In equilibrium, this differential surplus is seen by (2.21) to be equal to the interjurisdictional wage and head tax differential, and it follows that an equilibrium location pattern could be improved upon by moving households from low-tax to high-tax jurisdictions. That is, a jurisdiction with differentially high wage and head taxes inefficiently induces mobile households to relocate elsewhere.

An equivalent way to see this is to note that a household entering community i confers a benefit of $\tau_{iw}w_i^k + \tau_{in}^k$ upon the existing residents by assuming a portion of the tax burden there, but does not take this external benefit into account when making a locational choice. The locational inefficiency induced by head and wage taxation can thus be characterized as a "fiscal externality," the term introduced by Flatters, et al. [127]. (Note that the Pigovian subsidy that would internalize this externality is equal to $\tau_{iw}w_i^k + \tau_{in}^k$, which would result in a net tax of zero.)

It follows from the above discussion that a *local* head tax is not a neutral tax. This is in contrast to the familiar case of a *national* head tax, which does not distort any decisionmaking margin if one ignores (as is customary) the incentives for international migration, fertility, and the like. The reason a local head tax is non-neutral, of course, is that it can be avoided by relocating, thus introducing an economic distortion. This point is sometimes overlooked in the literature.[9]

Case 2. $\tau_{iw} = \tau_{in}^k = 0$, $C_{ik} = MCC_{ik}^{k'} = 0$ for all i, k, k'. In this case, localities rely only on resource or agricultural profit taxation. This insures satisfaction of the necessary condition (2.22).[10] Thus, with

---

[9] See, e.g., Oates [264] and Bewley [37].

[10] It is straightforward to confirm that these necessary conditions are also sufficient, provided that the appropriate convexity conditions are met. In particular $F_{ik} - (C_{ik} + \sum_{k'} n_i^{k'} MCC_{ik}^{k'})$ should be a decreasing function of n_i^k (at least in the neighborhood of the optimum), which will hold if the marginal product of labor is diminishing and congestion costs are increasing. This condition can be problematic if there is a taste for association ($MCC_{ik}^{k'} < 0$), or if there are dominating economies of scale in either private or public production. These conditions are relevant when the problem of community formation arises. Here we have imposed a fixed jurisdictional structure, which essentially assumes away this problem. For many applications—e.g., for household location within metropolitan areas, or within states, provinces, or regions in populous countries—it should be reasonable to assume that economies of scale with respect to population have been exhausted. For some discussion of this issue, see Stiglitz [343] and Atkinson and Stiglitz [12].

pure local public goods and no interpersonal crowding effects,
efficient locational equilibria are certainly feasible.
The rationale behind this optimality result should be evident. In
equilibrium, a household's entry into a jurisdiction creates no
differential surplus and thus no welfare gain for others: the value of
output produced net of private goods consumed is constant across
locations. Equivalently, there is no fiscal externality generated by
migrants. A household's tax contribution to a jurisdiction through
resource and profit taxes is independent of its locational choice (in
particular, it does not depend on whether the household resides in
the taxing jurisdiction(s)), and hence the social net benefit of that
choice is reflected in the private net benefit.

Case 3. $\tau_{iw} = \tau_{in}^k = 0$, $C_{ik} \neq 0$ and/or $MCC_{ik}^{k'} \neq 0$. Here, as in Case
2, we assume resource or agricultural profit taxation, but allow for
congestion effects. Condition (2.22) will hold only if marginal
congestion effects are fortuitously equated at an optimum. While
this is a conceivable outcome (it could certainly emerge in models
with perfect symmetry in community characteristics), one must
conclude that equilibria are generally inefficient in this case.

The reason for the inefficiency here is, of course, that a migrant
imposes an external cost upon entering a jurisdiction, either by
degrading public facilities and thus necessitating an increase in
expenditures to keep public services constant, or by crowding
existing residents in some other way. With the hypothesized tax
structure, these effects are not taken into account by the migrant
and inefficiency naturally results.

Case 4. $\tau_{iA} = \tau_{ir} = 0$, $C_{ik} + MCC_{ik}^{k'} \neq 0$. As in Case 1, head or
wage income taxes are used to finance all local expenditure. Here,
however, we allow for congestion effects. In general there exists no
combination of head and wage income taxes that simultaneously
satisfies (2.17) and (2.22). Consider, however, the following special
case: suppose, at least in the neighborhood of an optimum, that
local public goods are produced with constant per capita cost, so
that $C_{ik} = c_i(z_i) = C_i/\sum_k n_i^k$, and that interpersonal crowding effects
are absent ($MCC_{ik}^{k'} = 0$). Then a *uniform* head tax must, by (2.17),
satisfy $\tau_{in} = c_i(z_i) = C_{ik}$, and, by (2.22), the equilibrium will be
efficient. Somewhat more generally, efficiency is achieved if C_i is
(locally) linear homogeneous in n_i (in the neighborhood of an
optimum), and head taxes are differentiated by household type at

rates $\tau_{in}^k = C_{ik}$. Note that a uniform wage tax is equivalent to a uniform head tax if all households have identical wages. With unequal wages and identical congestion effects, however, a wage tax does not lead to efficiency. Similarly, if congestion effects differ across households, a uniform wage tax would be efficient only by coincidence. Thus, while wage and head taxes may be equivalent instruments in some simple models, personalized head taxes permit more efficient outcomes in the general case.

Case 5. $\tau_{in}^k = C_{ik} + \Sigma_{k'} MCC_{ik}^{k'}$, $\tau_{iw} = 0$, τ_{ir} and τ_{iA} chosen to satisfy (2.17) given τ_{in}. That is, a head tax is set equal to the marginal congestion effect imposed by each household, with resource and/or profit taxes determined residually to balance the local budgets.

This case generalizes Case 2, and shows (see (2.22)) that locational efficiency can always be achieved in the presence of congestion effects by choosing head taxes which internalize them. Note that the head tax must differ by household type if congestion costs are not the same for all types.

Case 6. $\tau_{in} = 0 \neq \tau_{iw}$, $C_{ik} + \Sigma_{k'} MCC_{ik}^{k'} \geq 0$. It is obvious from (2.22) and the above remarks that a uniform wage income tax, coupled possibly with resource and profit taxes, does not result in locational efficiency. Only if $\tau_{iw} w_i^k$ should happen to equal the marginal congestion cost for type k households will efficient locational choices be made. Note that in the special case where $N = 1$, it is always possible to find an efficient wage income tax. This is likewise true if wage income tax rates could be varied across households according to the congestion that they generate.

From the discussion of these cases, it is clear that locational efficiency can, but need not, be achieved in an economy with households freely migrating among jurisdictions. Obviously what is critical in practice is whether the correct mix of taxes is feasible and whether this mix is actually chosen. The efficiency properties of the taxes actually used in urban areas have not yet been carefully assessed from this perspective, so we cannot say anything definite on this empirical question here. On the other hand, it may be useful briefly to consider some implications of major state and local taxes for locational choice.

First, at the local level, the dominant tax in the U.S., Canada, U.K. and other countries has been, and remains, the property tax.

Partly this amounts to a tax on land, i.e., on spatially fixed resources. In larger part, however, the property tax is assessed on structures. While structures are not freely mobile, and indeed may reasonably be treated as spatially fixed for a "sufficiently short" time horizon, the long run supply elasticity of structures is surely greater than zero. This means that if structures (restricting attention now to residential structures) were inelastically demanded by households, either because of consumer preferences or because of institutional constraints such as zoning policy (see Section 2.4 below), the tax on structures would approximate a head tax. In such a case, the property tax would discourage entry into a jurisdiction and could thus play some role in internalizing congestion externalities. More realistically, however, it would perform this function only imperfectly compared with fully optimal congestion charges. In particular, when the demand elasticity for structures is non-zero and the supply is variable, the property tax is a distortionary tax, unlike the idealized taxes discussed above.[11] Thus, the determination of the net effect of the property tax on the efficiency of household locational choices is an important open question.

Let us now turn to other taxes, especially those used by higher level governments such as states or provinces. Income and sales taxes are generally quite important for such governments. Our earlier model incorporates taxation of both wage and non-wage income, but we supposed the latter to be taxed at source (as is true of property taxes). When governments use income taxes, however, they are generally residence-based: households residing in a given state will be taxed at that state's income tax rate on dividends, interest, capital gains, and rental income regardless of the locality in which that income is generated. It is obvious, therefore, that such taxes, like wage and head taxes, are non-neutral with respect to household locational choices. The same is true for sales taxes, provided that they are assessed only on residents. (For large jurisdictions, this may often be a reasonable approximation. The discussion of tax exporting in Section 6 considers more seriously the possibility that sales and other taxes may be paid by non-residents.)

The locational non-neutrality of such taxes is easily seen some-

---

[11] See Sections 5 and 6 for explicit discussions of distortionary local taxes and taxation of mobile commodities.

what more formally by extending our earlier model slightly. Suppose that consumption of all-purpose goods, spatially-fixed resources, and agricultural output are all taxed at a rate τ_{ic} by jurisdiction i. Suppose also that no taxes are imposed directly on the owners of spatially-fixed resources or agricultural enterprises located in the jurisdiction (hence, in the previous notation, $\tau_{ir} = \tau_{iA} = 0$), but that all such income received by residents is taxed at rate τ_{is}. Then the budget constraint changes from (2.16) to

$$(1 + \tau_{ic})(x_i^k + r_i t_i^k + p q_i^k) = (1 - \tau_{iw})w_i^k - \tau_{in}^k$$
$$+ (1 - \tau_{is})\left(r\bar{t}^k + \sum_j \sigma_j^k[p\phi_j(t_j^A) - r_j t_j^A]\right).$$

(2.23)

Given inelastic factor supplies, the uniform sales tax is non-distortionary and is equivalent to an income tax, as can be seen by dividing (2.23) through by $(1 + \tau_{ic})$. Thus, income and sales taxes need not disturb the "consumption quantity" efficiency conditions (2.19) and (2.20). However, in place of (2.21) we now must write

$$w_i^k - (x_i^k + r_i t_i^k + p q_i^k) = \frac{\tau_{ic} + \tau_{iw}}{1 + \tau_{ic}} w_i^k + \frac{\tau_{in}^k}{1 + \tau_{ic}}$$
$$+ \frac{1 - \tau_{is}}{1 + \tau_{ic}}\left(r\bar{t}^k + \sum_j \sigma_j^k[p\phi_j(t_j^A) - r_j t_j^A]\right),$$

(2.24)

and corresponding amendments must be made to (2.22). The upshot is that differential general income taxes or sales taxes will be non-neutral with respect to locational choice in the same fashion as differential wage income or head taxes in the earlier version of the model.

Of course, this discussion has deliberately ignored other possible efficiency effects of sales and income taxation. As is well known, they distort the labor/leisure and consumption/savings margins. Our focus for the moment is on locational issues, however. As in the case of the local property tax, it is not possible to determine *a priori* whether or not these taxes are efficient. Such a determination would require an assessment of the congestion externalities imposed by migrants, and of tax liabilities in relation to them.

While it cannot, by itself, determine the extent to which actual state/local tax systems promote locational efficiency, the general framework presented above helps to clarify the main issues. It can also help in understanding the sometimes apparently conflicting results obtained in the literature. We now turn to a discussion of the relevant studies.

First, note from the above discussion that spatially-fixed commodities play a crucial role in achieving locational efficiency. Thus, for example, Negishi [259] and subsequently Wildasin [368] examine a model with pure local public goods. Although they are concerned with overall efficiency in resource allocation, locational efficiency in particular is possible in their analysis because land taxation is hypothesized (Case 2). In an analogous model, Rufolo [310] allows for congestion effects, and finds that efficiency requires land taxes and congestion fees, as in Case 5.

Similarly, Hochman [177] concludes that land taxation should be used to finance all local expenditure except insofar as revenue is raised from head taxes which are set so as to internalize congestion externalities. This is essentially the result presented in Cases 2 and 5. It is of interest to observe that Hochman's model is explicitly spatial, in that households residing in a city must engage in costly transportation to the city center in order to work. Thus, there is a non-trivial land rent structure in each city, in contrast to the above somewhat simpler model. (see also Helpman, et al. [167] and Hochman [178, 179] for related results.)

Not surprisingly, analyses which do not allow for land (or resource) taxation find that efficiency is not generally attainable in a federal system. For example, Buchanan and Wagner [79], Buchanan and Goetz [78], and Flatters, et al. [127] restrict attention to Cases 1, 4, and 6, and conclude that efficient outcomes are essentially fortuitous. This conclusion is not necessary, however, because these models do incorporate a locationally-fixed commodity (land). In particular, if an optimal mix of head and land taxes were feasible, efficiency could be attained.

In other models, e.g., those of McGuire [221], Wheaton [359], Berglas [28], and Bewley [37], spatially-fixed commodities are not present in the model structure at all. Generally speaking, per capita cost sharing, i.e., uniform head taxes, is the assumed means of financing in these sorts of models. In McGuire's analysis, locally-constant per capita costs are assumed, so that locational efficiency is in fact achieved. Bewley considers the overall problem of efficient resource allocation, including local public expenditures, and finds that efficiency can be sustained in equilibrium only when per capita costs are constant. In particular, Bewley concludes that efficient equilibria are not possible with uncongested local public goods. These results can be easily appreciated in view of Cases 1 and 4 above.

Of course, the existence and taxation of spatially-fixed resources does not by itself insure that locational efficiency will be obtained. Bucovetsky [80], for example, considers an economy where local public goods are produced at constant per capita costs, and financed through a land tax. As expected from the discussion of Case 3, an efficient allocation cannot be sustained in equilibrium under these assumptions. Bucovetsky observes, however, that efficiency can be achieved if head taxes are used (Case 4).

An interesting variation on the cases discussed above is presented by a specification assumed in, e.g., Henderson ([169, Ch. 4]), where all local resource rents accrue to residents. This would arise in practice under a program where all fixed resources are held publicly by localities, or equivalently, all resource rents are completely taxed away, with the proceeds, net of local public spending, distributed to residents on a per capita basis.[12] In this case, we may have $\tau_{in}^k < 0$, and efficiency certainly would not be obtained, as is easily seen from (2.22). Actually, this could be thought of as a restatement of Case 3, where we interpret public expenditure z as including per capita transfers. This type of spending, of course, constitutes a congestible public good, and we have simply a case of resource-tax financing of congestible local public goods, for which locational inefficiency must result. Indeed, this is the conclusion obtained by Henderson.

Finally, we note that the distinction between residence- and source-based taxation figures prominently in Boadway and Flatters [47], who are concerned, in part, with the use of intergovernmental

---

[12] While this institutional arrangement may seem rather odd, it may be approximated in some states and provinces—Alberta comes to mind as a possible example—where a significant amount of resource rents are taxed away and used to provide congestible public services or to reduce location-dependent taxes such as income taxes. See also Stiglitz [345] for some discussion of this case.

grants to offset inefficient fiscally-induced migration. See also Boadway and Wildasin [49, Ch. 15].

By no means does this exhaust the set of studies in which locational efficiency is an important issue, and for which the above general results provide insight. But a number of useful general conclusions have been established. First, locational efficiency is generally attainable if local governments have suitable tax instruments at their disposal. Second, it is not possible to characterize in general "the" efficient local tax structure. In some cases, land taxes may be efficient, in other cases, head or income taxes are efficient, and in other cases a mix may be called for, depending on circumstances. Third, by making different assumptions about the means of financing and congestibility of local public goods, different authors reach varying conclusions about the possibility of efficient resource allocation in federal systems. Evaluation of the relevance of any particular study then turns on the empirical applicability of the assumptions made. This, of course, may vary depending on the problem at hand.

2.3. The Henry George Theorem

A. Statement and demonstration of the result. Section 2.2 has dealt with the problem of locational efficiency from the perspective of the economy as a whole, taking into account the welfare of households in all locations. This is not the only perspective that one might be interested in, however. For example, one can ask how population might be determined in any one jurisdiction so as to achieve maximum welfare there. An analysis of this question is useful not only because it sheds light on a basic normative problem, but also because it illuminates the incentives facing the residents in a jurisdiction when considering policies that affect local population. As will be discussed in Section 6, such incentives can be important when developing behavioral models of local policy determination. Furthermore, as will become clear shortly, an investigation of this problem is important for the determination of optimal jurisdictional structure, that is, for fixing the right number of jursidictions.

Unfortunately (though not surprisingly) the characterization of optimal local population is somewhat problematic when there are heterogeneous individuals in a locality. First, there is the question of defining what is optimal: whose welfare is to count? Second, what sorts of variations in population should be considered feasible—independent changes in the number of each type of household, proportional changes in the numbers of all types of households, or perhaps some other kind of variation? These difficulties are often avoided in the literature by confining attention to the case where all households in a jurisdiction are identical and where all immigrants are treated symmetrically with initial residents. In this case, the welfare criterion is obvious, as is the notion of increases or decreases in population. Some of the results that we shall discuss, however, hold more generally, and it is therefore best to start with a more general framework which includes the single-household type economy as a special case.

Let us consider, then, a single locality, which may be inhabited by several types of households. We can adapt the model presented in Section 2.2, dropping the subscripts i, j that identify a jurisdiction. The utility $u^k(x^k, t^k, q^k, n, z)$ of a type-k household enters a jurisdictional social welfare function $W(u^1, \ldots, u^N)$, which is the maximand for our optimization problem. We suppose the welfare maximizer controls the allocation of the all-purpose private good, land, and the agricultural commodity within the jurisdiction. Moreover, let the population vector n depend on a parameter (or parameter vector) α, controlled by the optimizer, that describes how population may be varied. For instance, one might specify that $n(\alpha) = \alpha n^0$, where n^0 is some initial population vector, in which case an increase in α from $\alpha = 1$ corresponds to a proportional increase in all population groups. As another example, one might have $n(\alpha) = (\alpha n^{10}, n^{20}, \ldots, n^{N0})$, in which case increasing α involves entry of only type 1 households. Thus, $n(\alpha)$ in general describes a wide range of possible variations in population.

The constraints facing the welfare optimizer are

$$F(n, t^P) - nx - C(n, z) + p[\phi(t^A) - nq] = 0 \qquad (2.25)$$

$$T - nt - t^P - t^A = 0. \qquad (2.26)$$

Equation (2.26) is just the fixed resources constraint, while (2.25) is a trade-balance constraint: we suppose that the locality's net exports of agricultural output are traded on a national (or regional) market at a fixed price of p. These constraints imply that consumption in the jurisdiction is constrained by local income, that is, no rents or agricultural profits accrue to non-residents, and no residents, including any entrants, retain property rights in fixed resources or agricultural firms located in other jurisdictions. This assumption must be borne in mind when interpreting the results.

The planner controls x, t, q, t^P, t^A, and α. The maximization exercise is usefully executed in two stages. First, we optimize with α held fixed, choosing x, t, q, t^P and t^A. This yields the necessary conditions

$$W_k u_1^k - \mu n^k = 0 \qquad \text{all } k \qquad (2.27)$$

$$W_k u_2^k - \rho n^k = 0 \qquad \text{all } k \qquad (2.28)$$

$$W_k u_3^k - \mu p n^k = 0 \qquad \text{all } k \qquad (2.29)$$

$$\mu F_t - \rho = 0 \qquad (2.30)$$

$$\mu p \phi_t - \rho = 0, \qquad (2.31)$$

where W_k denotes $\partial W/\partial u^k$ and where μ and ρ are the multipliers for (2.25) and (2.26) respectively. It follows that

$$\frac{u_2^k}{u_1^k} = F_t = p \phi_t \qquad \text{all } k \qquad (2.32)$$

$$\frac{u_3^k}{u_1^k} = p, \qquad \text{all } k. \qquad (2.33)$$

These conditions have the usual interpretation.

Now let $W(\alpha)$ be the value of W, conditional on α, after solution of the first stage. The optimal α is characterized by $W'(\alpha) = 0$. Totally differentiating W, dividing by μ, and using (2.25) and (2.26) yields:

$$\mu^{-1} W'(\alpha) = \sum_k \left[\left(F_k - C_k - \sum_{k'} n^{k'} MCC_k^{k'} \right) \right.$$
$$\left. - (x^k + pq^k + F_t t^k) \right] \frac{dn^k}{d\alpha} = 0 \quad (2.34)$$

where $MCC_k^{k'}$ is the direct interpersonal crowding effect as defined in Section 2.2.

Deferring interpretation of this result for the moment, let us consider its implications in the special case where the population varies proportionally with α, i.e., $n(\alpha) = \alpha n^0$. Then we can apply Euler's theorem, (2.25), and (2.26) to obtain

$$F_t T + (p\phi - F_t t^A) = C - \sum_k \left[C_k + \sum_{k'} n^{k'} MCC_k^{k'} \right] n^k. \quad (2.35)$$

This result takes a particularly simple form when there is no local agriculture, local public goods are purely public and no interpersonal congestion effects arise. We then have $F_t T = C$, that is, (imputed) resource rent is equal to local public expenditure, at the (locally) optimal population. This is known as the "Henry George Theorem," because it indicates that land rents would be entirely taxed away at an optimum.[13] It is discussed in Flatters et al. [127], Stiglitz [343, 344, 345], Arnott [4], Arnott and Stiglitz [9], Atkinson and Stiglitz [12, Lecture 17], Derglas [29], Hartwick [164], and Schweizer [317, 320], among others.

To understand this result, it is instructive first to specialize the model to the case where there is only one consumer type, no agriculture, and consumers only get utility from the all-purpose good and the public good: $u = u(x, z)$. At first we also assume no congestion of public services, so $C_1(n, z) = 0$. Then constraints (2.25) and (2.26) imply $nx = F(n, t^p) - C(z, n) = F(n, T) - C(z, n)$ (since all fixed resources are used in local private good production when $t^A = t = 0$). In this simplified model, maximization of utility is equivalent to maximization of per capita private good consumption. When a new household enters the locality, it consumes x but increases private good production by F_1. Entry will increase per capita consumption until $F_1 = x = (F - C)n^{-1}$, which is equivalent to (2.34). This leads directly to the optimality condition $C = F - F_1 n = F_t T$, i.e., (2.35), the Henry George result. An alternative intuitive justification for this conclusion follows by observing that when a household enters a jurisdiction, it will affect existing residents by sharing in land rents, thus reducing their consumption by $F_t T / n$, and by sharing in the costs of public good provision, thus increasing their consumption by C/n. Population should be increased if $C/n > F_t T/n$, and will maximize utility when $C = F_t T$.

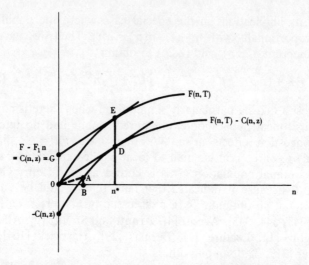

FIGURE 3 With uncongested local public goods, locally-optimal population occurs at n^* where F_1 = slope of F = slope of $F - C = Dn^*/0n^*$ = consumption per capita.

Figure 3 illustrates. The slope of a ray from the origin to the curve $F - C$ measures per capita consumption, e.g., the slope of $0A$ is $AB/0B$ = per capita consumption when $n = B$. The maximum occurs at n^* where $0D$ is tangent to $F - C$. The tangent to F at n^* has the same slope as $0D$, namely F_1, and so the distance $DE = 0G$. But $DE = C(z, n)$ while $0G = F - F_1 n$. Hence land rents are equated to public spending at n^*. This figure also illustrates another interpretation of the Henry George result, that is, that the optimal city size occurs where economies and diseconomies of scale are balanced against one another, such that the rents on decreasing returns activities (here, private production) just equal the cost of increasing return activities (here, provision of a pure local public good). As pointed out in Arnott [4], and Arnott and Stiglitz [9], this principle can be extended to accommodate other types of increasing and decreasing returns activities as well, such as economies of scale in private production and congestion of transportation systems.

The above intuition can be extended to single-household-type cases with agriculture, residential consumption of land, and conges-tion. When there are several consumer goods, the maximization of x is replaced by the goal of maximizing the value of consumption

$x + (u_2/u_1)t + pq$. This is enhanced by entrants because each entrant, as before, bears C/n of the cost of the public good. Now, however, both land rents and agricultural profits are shared with entrants, so that a per capita loss of $(F_t T + p\phi - F_t t^4)/n$ is borne. In addition, when congestion occurs, an added cost of $C_1 + nMCC$ is imposed by the migrant. At an optimum, these costs are balanced against the benefit, utility is maximized and (2.35) holds. Equivalently, we can simply note that the migrant contributes F_1 to local output, adds C_1 to local public expenditure, imposes direct congestion costs of $nMCC$ on existing residents, and consumes private goods worth $x + (u_2/u_1)t + pq = (F - C + p[\phi - nq])n^{-1} + (u_2/u_1)t + pq$. Utililty is maximized when the value of the household's endowment of labor, F_1, is equated to the value of its consumption of private goods and the congestion costs that it imposes, i.e., when (2.34) holds.

When one allows for several household types, matters are somewhat more complicated. Condition (2.34), considered in the general case where $n(\alpha)$ is arbitrary, can essentially be interpreted as before. A feasible population variation $dn/d\alpha$ will bring in households that contribute to local output according to their marginal products, impose congestion costs, and consume a bundle of private goods. It is desirable to increase the number of households of any type for which the benefit of extra product exceeds the costs of private consumption plus congestion. An arbitrary population change is advantageous if the benefits from the entry of households conferring net gains more than offsets the costs from the entry of households imposing net losses.[14]

One can also extend the earlier interpretation of (2.35) to the case of many household types, recalling, however, that (2.35) is only valid for proportionate population changes. Divide (2.35) by $\sum_k n^k$, the total population in the locality, and note that when there

---

[14] This latter interpretation is based on Schweizer [318], who also relates these ideas to the core of a private goods economy under replication. Schweizer shows that the utility of a group of households of one type will be increased by the addition of households of another type to a trading coalition whenever the value of the endowment of the entering household exceeds the value of its consumption, which is essentially the implication of (2.34). In a related paper, Schweizer [319] shows how population-based grants could be used to compensate jurisdictions for accepting "unprofitable" households. This would provide a possible instrument for sustaining efficient outcomes. See also the discussion in Section 6.5.

are no congestion or crowding effects we simply have the previous interpretation that entrants dissipate rents and public good costs, with these effects being balanced at the margin. When there are congestion effects, the last term in (2.35) becomes $\sum_k [(C_k + \sum_{k'} n^{k'} MCC_k^{k'}) n^k (\sum_{k'} n^{k'})^{-1}]$, that is, a weighted average of the congestion costs imposed by each of the household types. As before, these costs reduce the gains from expansion of the population.

While the interpretation of (2.34) and (2.35) thus extends to the general case without difficulty, it is necessary to modify the statement of the Henry George Theorem slightly. Instead of equating resource rents to public expenditure, (2.35) requires that resource rents plus agricultural profits be equated to public expenditure less marginal congestion cost times population (aggregated over household types). If we imagine a locality imposing a head tax at rate $C_k + \sum_{k'} n^{k'} MCC_k^{k'}$ on type k households, the last term in (2.35) would just be total head tax revenue, and the result would state that resource rents plus profits, or simply non-wage income, is to be equated to public expenditures net of head taxes, i.e., public expenditure is less than non-wage income by the amount of head-tax revenue collected. It is interesting to observe that in the special case of constant per capita costs, $C(n, z) = (\sum_k n^k) C(z)$, and no direct personal crowding, $MCC_k^{k'} = 0$, non-wage income should be zero. In this case, adding extra households only dilutes non-wage income, and does not contribute at all to a reduction in per capita public good costs, so the optimal population is $n = 0$. See Figure 4.

B. *The significance of the Henry George Theorem.* Let us now consider the application of the (modified) Henry George Theorem. To begin with, recall the optimization problem which generates it: a planner is able directly to control the number of households residing in a locality, though with several types of households the populations of each type must vary in proportion. The planner is constrained to treat any entrants to the community symmetrically with existing residents. No existing or entering households retain ownership rights in resources located outside the jurisdiction, and any household that leaves the jurisdiction likewise surrenders its ownership of local resources.

These assumptions are open to question. First, planners in an

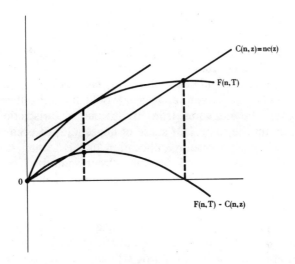

$C(n,z)=nc(z)$

$F(n,T)$

$F(n,T) - C(n,z)$

0

FIGURE 4 With constant per capita costs for the local public good, per capita private good consumption increases as $n \to 0$. Resource rent goes to 0 with n.

economy with a fixed total population cannot independently vary the size or composition of local populations: local decisions must be compatible with overall population constraints. These constraints do not appear in the above problem, however. Second, in practice, jurisdictions do not directly control the size and composition of their populations. Rather, households themselves decide, in a decentralized fashion, whether or not to reside in a particular community. Third, households are generally able to own assets not located in their home jurisdictions. While one could conceivably justify constraint (2.35) by supposing that all jurisdictions are committed to 100 percent taxation of resource rents, this assumption would clearly be restrictive. Thus, the optimization problem underlying the Henry George Theorem may be of doubtful relevance, at least if interpreted literally.

Perhaps a more fruitful interpretation of the Henry George Theorem would be as follows. Imagine a planner, facing an economy with a fixed total population of N^k households of each of N types. This population may be split up into M identical groups, each containing a population $n_i = (n_i^1, \ldots, n_i^N) = (N^1/M, \ldots, N^N/M)$. It is possible to provide each group with the same vector T of

fixed resources, and the same technologies for producing the
all-purpose good, the agricultural commodity, and local public
services. Finally, one could constrain each group to have the same
level of public services.

In this perfectly symmetric situation, each group or jurisdiction
would be like any other, and each would be self-sufficient—i.e.,
there would be no gains from trade among jurisdictions. Each
would contain the same $1/M$ share of households of each type. The
problem of efficient resource allocation in this setting, then, is to
allocate resources efficiently within a "representative" community,
and to find the efficient number of communities, that is, to choose
M such that $Mn = (N^1, \ldots, N^N)$.

If we now set $n^0 = (N^1, \ldots, N^N)$, and $n(\alpha) = \alpha n^0$, it is clear that
the choice of α is equivalent to the choice of M. Of course, this is
just the problem posed above in the special case where all
population variations are proportional across classes.

Evidently, then, the modified Henry George Theorem can be
interpreted as a characterization of the optimal jurisdiction structure in a world of symmetric jurisdictions, where the number of
localities is large enough to be treated as a continuous variable. The
symmetry restriction means that jurisdictions are all alike in terms
of fixed resources (T is the same for all), that technologies are
everywhere the same, etc. This is not a particularly realistic
assumption, but, on the other hand, one cannot expect any simple
results on the optimal number of jurisdictions or optimal population
size when these jurisdictions differ from one another. In this more
general case, the problem is to find the optimal number of each type
of jurisdiction, and the optimal size of each. This problem clearly
cannot be reduced to finding the optimal value of a single variable
such as M or α. Some extensions to the case of heterogeneous
communities are possible, however, although we do not pursue
them here.[15]

The above interpretation gives a clear justification for the
optimization problem leading to the Henry George result. It does,
however, assume that as many identical jurisdictions as desired can

---

[15] See, e.g., Stiglitz [344]. Essentially, the results given here can be applied to
communities of any particular type. Multiple types can be accommodated if
replication of communities of each type is possible.

be set up. As we saw in our discussion of the special case where there is only one household type, no local agriculture, and local public goods are produced subject to constant per capita costs, the optimal population can be zero—i.e., the optimal number of jurisdictions can be infinite. In this special case, of course, the only effect of an increase in the number of jurisdictions is an increase in the resource endowment of the economy. With no economies of scale with respect to population in either the private sector (F is linear homogeneous) or in the public sector (with constant per capita costs), it is clearly optimal to maximize this endowment.

More realistically, however, fixed resources are not available in unlimited supplies. Suppose, instead, that resources have value in some alternative use, and that increasing the number of jurisdictions means foregoing this use. For example, let fixed resources be initially owned by a class of households not otherwise appearing in the model, and assume that they receive a vector of returns r on these resources (denominated in units of all-purpose good). Suppose, for simplicity, that r can be taken as exogenously given (e.g., suppose that fixed resources consist of land used for agricultural production, with land rents determined by exogenously given world prices for agricultural commodities). Now suppose the optimization problem is reformulated as one of maximizing welfare defined over the utilities of mobile urban households subject to a fixed utility level for resource owners. Equivalently, the resource owners can be compensated for resources used in urban development. One then replaces the constraint (2.25) by

$$F(n, t^P) - nx - C(n, z) + p[\phi(t^A) - nq] - rT = 0. \qquad (2.36)$$

The first-order conditions (2.27)—(2.34) are unaffected by this change, but instead of (2.35) we now have

$$(F_t - r)T + (p\phi - F_t t^A) = C - \sum_k \left[C_k + \sum_{k'} n^{k'} MCC_k^{k'} \right] n^k. \qquad (2.37)$$

The difference between (2.35) and (2.37) is easily stated: when communities cannot be formed costlessly, the Henry George rule must be further modified by subtracting the value of fixed resources used in each locality from total resource rents. This can be described, as in Arnott and Stiglitz [9], as "differential land rents."

It is interesting to note that the optimal population is no longer zero in the constant per capita costs case when fixed resources are costly. Instead, the jurisdiction size should be expanded until F_t falls to r—i.e., the value of resources in alternative uses should be equated.

2.4. Fiscal zoning: the locational impact of property taxes

We now return briefly to the problem of locational efficiency with a fixed jurisdiction structure as discussed in Section 2.2. Recall that locational efficiency can be achieved by a combination of head taxes and taxes on resource rents, such that head taxes correctly internalize congestion effects (Case 5). In the special case of constant per capita costs (Case 4), a head tax alone results in efficiency.

Constant per capita costs may in fact characterize the provision of important local public services, including education. In practice, however, head taxes are not used to finance local expenditures. Rather, taxes on property provide the main source of own-revenue, both in the US and elsewhere. Is there any way that property taxes might effectively substitute for head taxes?

To address this question, let us suppose an initial locationally efficient equilibrium in an economy where each jurisdiction is using head taxes. Households in each jurisdiction consume housing, which is supplied in a perfectly competitive market. Suppose that units of housing are perfectly divisible. Figure 5 represents the initial equilibrium for an individual household facing a market price of p^0 and consuming h^0 units of housing.

Now suppose a tax is imposed on property, and the local head tax is eliminated. For simplicity, let us interpret this as a per unit tax at rate τ_h on housing consumed by each household. The effect of this tax on the equilibrium of the individual household depends on supply conditions in the housing market. If housing supply is perfectly inelastic, the after-tax equilibrium price of housing will remain at p^0 and no tax distortion of the housing market results. In addition, if the fixity of the housing stock implies that the local population is fixed, there can be no change in congestion and crowding effects, and locational efficiency is also achieved.

On the other hand, suppose housing supply is perfectly elastic, so

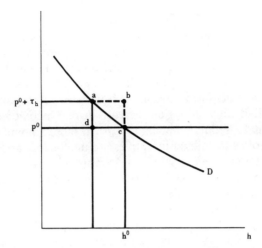

FIGURE 5 Housing equilibrium for an individual consumer, with and without zoning constraint.

that the equilibrium after-tax price of housing rises to $p^0 + \tau_h$. The household shown in Figure 5 would then bear a loss of real income equal to the trapezoid $(p^0 + \tau_h)acp^0$, paying a tax equal to $(p^0 + \tau_h)adp^0$. Clearly the tax wedge between demand and supply prices results in inefficient resource allocation in this case. At the same time, however, the property tax can contribute to locational efficiency. A household entering the jurisdiction will enjoy a real income that is lower by $(p^0 + \tau_h)acp^0$ on account of the property tax, and, to some degree, this can internalize the congestion externality associated with public services. In fact, so long as the housing supply elasticity is non-zero, the property tax will make entry into the jurisdiction more costly and will thus affect locational incentives. The housing market will be distorted in all such cases, however, however, so full efficiency will not be achieved under the property tax regime.

Now suppose that the jurisdiction using the property tax is able to impose effective quantity constraints on consumers of housing. For example, suppose that the consumer in Figure 5 can be forced to consume h^0 units of housing even in the presence of the tax. One way this could be brought about, as discussed by Epple *et al.* [117], Hamilton [156, 157, 160], Mieszkowski [239], Mills [246], Mills and

Oates [247], White [361, 362], and Zodrow and Mieszkowski [394], is through zoning: households may be required to live on lots of a certain minimum size, use construction materials of specified quality, etc.[16] If such constraints worked perfectly, the household in Figure 5 would find itself consuming h^0 units of housing at a price of $(p^0 + \tau_h)$ per unit. In the transition from head to property taxation, the household thus enjoys an increase in real income equal to the head tax, and a reduction equal to $\tau_h h^0$. If these amounts are equal, the household's locational incentives are unaffected, and the zoning constraint implies that its housing consumption is undistorted. If this were the case for every household in the jurisdiction, the fully efficient equilibrium obtaining under head taxation would be unaffected by the transition to property taxation.

It is interesting to relate this outcome to the property tax as usually implemented. Suppose an initial efficient equilibrium with a head tax, in which consumers can buy a flow of housing services at a (rental) price of p^0 per unit. If r is the discount rate and V^0 is the value of a parcel of property providing h^0 units of housing services, we have (ignoring depreciation and intertemporal price fluctuations) $V^0 = p^0 h^0 / r$. Let the head tax borne by an occupant of such a dwelling be τ_n. Suppose the head tax is now eliminated and that zoning constrains the amount of housing to remain at h^0. The equilibrium rental price of the housing unit must rise to p^1 such that $p^1 h^0 = p^0 h^0 + \tau_n$. With a property tax at rate τ_v on the value of the parcel, we have a new equilibrium valuation equation $V^1 = (p^1 h^0 - \tau_v V^1) r^{-1}$, or $V^1 = (p^1 h^0)(r + \tau_v)^{-1}$. If the property tax rate τ_v is set equal to $\tau_v = \tau_n / V^0$, we have $V^0 = V^1$ and no change in the real equilibrium following the tax change.

A notable aspect of this result is that it requires that the property tax rate vary inversely with the value of property. If, instead, property tax rates are constrained to be equal across all properties,

---

[16] Also see Fischel [123], who argues that localities may impose zoning requirements on firms in order to extract compensation, via property taxation, for environmental disamenities that firms impose. Fischel observes that property tax contributions are not necessarily as efficient as direct Pigovian taxes, since they may artificially lower the price of public relative to private goods for the jurisdiction, inducing excess public spending. Fischel explores several possible ways, including differential assessment of residential, commercial, and industrial property, by which the inefficiency of property taxation may be minimized.

the switch from head taxation to property taxation will generate gains for low-value properties and losses for high-value ones, reflected in property values as the capitalized value of the change in tax burdens. (Hamilton [158], discusses this capitalization phenomenon in greater detail.) For this reason, under uniform property taxation, the residents of a jurisdiction will gain from the entry of households with high demands for housing, who will pay more in property taxes than the congestion cost they impose, and, conversely, they will lose from the entry of households who have a smaller demand for housing. Therefore, under uniform property taxation, there is an incentive to impose zoning requirements that will preclude the entry of households with demands for housing lower than the average found in the community.

This sort of zoning practice is referred to as "fiscal zoning" by Hamilton and others because its effect is to impose a certain system of effective taxes (unlike zoning that might be instituted to control environmental externalities and the like). In principle, it would result in fully efficient local taxation. What is required is that the zoning-constrained housing quantity h^0 be the amount that each household would demand at the supply price p^0, and that the increase in the equilibrium tax-inclusive price of housing times the quantity q^0 be equal to the congestion cost imposed by a household. If this should occur, the property tax is effectively converted to an efficient head tax.[17]

Although efficiency is our primary concern in this section, it should be noted that fiscal zoning raises certain equity issues. In particular, it may serve in practice to exclude low-income households from high-income localities. This might be regarded as undesirable in itself. Furthermore, any given level of a public good produced at constant per capita cost could be provided at a lower

---

[17] Authors writing in this area often refer to the property tax as a "benefit tax" when it functions this way, because each household is being charged for the value of the public service that it uses up. We shall resist this terminology, however. As defined by, e.g., Musgrave [252] and other classic sources, a benefit tax is based on a household's willingness to pay for, or marginal benefit from, an additional unit of public service. This is conceptually quite distinct from the cost of providing a given level of public service to one more household, i.e., from the marginal congestion cost imposed by an entrant to a jurisdiction. It seems best to adhere to standard definitions.

property tax rate in a high-income fiscally zoned locality than in a low-income locality, because of the greater per capita tax base in the former. Some US courts have found that this is inadmissible, at least with reference to public education, leading to various proposals for reform of school finance. These issues, including both the legal background and the equity implications of a number of possible reforms, are discussed in Inman [188], Rubinfeld [308], and Inman and Rubinfeld [194].

3. POSITIVE AND NORMATIVE ANALYSIS OF LOCAL PUBLIC EXPENDITURE

3.1. Introduction

In this and the next section, we shall relax the restriction that the level of local public service provision is exogenously determined. Here, the problem is to analyze how local public expenditure levels are or might be determined in existing or alternative institutional settings. We note that the behavioral modeling of local public expenditure determination is a special case of the more general problem of modeling how localities choose a whole range of policies, both fiscal and non-fiscal, including the levels of expenditure on a wide variety of public services, the combination and level of taxes to be used to finance these expenditures, and many other policies as well. The focus in these sections, as in much of the literature, is on the expenditure side, with local tax structure being taken as fixed, and local tax rates varying passively so as to satisfy a government budget constraint. Sections 5 and 6 give more attention to other aspects of local policy.

Our discussion begins in Section 3.2 with a simple but useful model of local behavior, based on the standard theory of the consumer. This model is, however, subject to several limitations, and the thrust of most recent research has been to develop more explicit models of the local political process. Section 3.3 presents perhaps the most popular of these, the median voter model. Section 3.4 presents a variant of the standard model involving self-interested bureaucrats, and also considers the implications of household mobility for the median voter model. In Section 4, the issue of household mobility is pursued at greater length.

3.2. The "community preference" model

The simplest model of local public expenditure determination that appears in the literature is based on the hypothesis that a community can be treated like a single household (or a group of identical households). Examples include Henderson [168], Gramlich [138, 139], Scott [323] and Wilde [379, 380].[18] Oates [264] provides a clear textbook presentation. This model provides a natural starting point for much theoretical work, and has guided many empirical studies as well. In this approach, it is typically assumed that the jurisdiction acts like an individual with a given income I (aggregate community income), who can allocate this income between consumption of private goods x or consumption of a public good z. Usually, units of x and z are chosen to have a price of \$1, so the household's problem is to maximize some utility function $u(x, z)$ subject to a budget constraint $x + z = I$. It is useful to note the normative property that z is chosen efficiently in this model.

The question immediately arises as to the legitimacy of assuming that a community acts in a way that can be described by a utility function interacting with a budget constraint. Whose preferences, for example, are represented by $u(x, z)$? Different interpretations are possible. Perhaps all households in a jurisdiction really do have identical preferences. Then u is the utility function of any one of them. The identical preference assumption, however, is very strong. Even if it is descriptively false, though, the assumption of identical households may not be very troublesome for certain theoretical purposes. For example, the identical-household model often serves as a simple but important special case which can provide a bench-mark to guide deeper investigation into more general and complex models.

To illustrate briefly, consider the implications of the community higher-level governments. Suppose this aid takes the form of lump-sum grants of the amount L, and of matching grants at rate m.[19] Then the local budget constraint becomes

$$x + (1 - m)z = I + L. \tag{3.1}$$

---

[18] See also Barlow [15] and Gramlich [139].

[19] I.e., the higher-level government finances the proportion m of the expenditures of the recipient government. Such grants are commonly used in the U.S., though they are typically applied only to particular categories of expenditure.

It is immediately apparent that a matching grant lowers the relative price of public expenditures, whereas a lump-sum grant simply increases the effective income of the locality. As one might conjecture, and as shown later in Section 6, matching grants induce a larger increase in spending per dollar transferred to the locality than do lump-sum grants. This is because the former has both a substitution effect and an income effect while the latter only has an income effect.

This result is very straightforward in the community preference model. Yet one would intuitively expect it to survive, though perhaps in some qualified form, in more complex settings. Indeed, it has been shown (see Bradford and Oates [58, 59] and further discussion in Section 6) that the basic conclusion does carry over to the case where diverse, self-interested voters determine local public spending through simple majority voting. Here, then, as in many cases, the simple community preference model turns out not to be misleading in any essential way, and actually suggests a conjecture that one can try to verify in more complex and realistic settings. This simple model continues to be exploited in this way in much theoretical work, including the analysis of intergovernmental transfers, tax exporting and competition, and optimal local taxation. These applications are discussed in subsequent chapters.

Despite its usefulness for theoretical purposes though, the identical household assumption is not an appealing one for empirical applications. What alternative justifications can then be given for the community preference model? One possibility is that the utility function $u(x, z)$ represents the preferences of a single agent, such as a city manager, who controls local policy. Casual empiricism, however, suggests that the local political process is too decentralized to be adequately described in this fashion. Another possibility is that this complex political process yields outcomes that can in fact be described "as if" they are the result of a constrained maximization exercise. Two comments are necessary here. First, if this is the interpretation being given to the model, the utility function $u(x, z)$ has no true normative significance since it does not actually represent the preference of any individual. Second, and more fundamentally, one would like to have a demonstration of the assertion that the political process leads to outcomes that can be described in this way. A priori, there seems to be little reason to expect this to be the case in general. This issue cannot be settled, of course, without explicit modeling of the local political process. Efforts along these lines are discussed in subsequent sections.

Even if one is unable to produce a convincing theoretical demonstration that community behavior is likely to be well-described by the community preference model, it is still possible to proceed to empirical applications in a purely empirical spirit: one may simply hypothesize that a community acts "as if" it is a single utility-maximizer, and let the data refute the hypothesis or not. Thus, one may postulate and estimate an equation of the form

$$z_i = f(I_i, m_i, L_i, \alpha_i) + u_i \qquad (3.2)$$

for each city i in some sample, for example where α_i is a vector of other relevant parameters and u_i is a random error term. Equations of this form have been estimated by many authors, with or without explicit appeal to the community preference model. Gramlich [140] provides a useful survey of many of these studies.[20] The estimated coefficients from a regression like (3.2) can be examined for expected sign and significance. Generally, such tests do not refute the model. More rigorously, one can use the theory to impose and test certain restrictions on the equation (3.2). For example, one should expect I_i and L_i to enter with the same sign and magnitude in the determination of z_i. Interestingly, this prediction *is* refuted by the evidence: lump-sum grant funds seem to increase local public expenditures more than income. Gramlich has dubbed this the "flypaper effect," because grant money "sticks where it hits," i.e., it tends not to be rebated to households through local tax cuts, thus enabling them to consume more private goods. The existence of the flypaper effect has stimulated considerable theoretical discussion about the local expenditure response to grant funds, as discussed in detail in Section 6.

Thus, the community preference model continues to be exploited

---

[20] A number of studies run regressions of the form of (3.2) without explicitly appealing to the community preference model, or indeed to any explicit theory. Others run regressions like (3.2) but assert that this represents a sort of reduced form derived from a more complex model incorporating the actual local political process. These studies, in their empirical implementation, can perhaps be thought of as applications of the community preference model. See, e.g., Bishop [41], Bowman [55], Craig and Inman [95], Davis and Haines [98], Feldstein [120], and Sacks and Harris [311].

in empirical work, where the results are somewhat mixed. Clearly, however, its theoretical and empirical limitations invite consideration of alternative models which give more explicit attention to the mechanism of collective choice at the local level.

3.3. The median voter model

A. A review of key ideas. One of the simplest and most popular models of local public expenditure determination is the median voter model, discussed in early studies by, e.g., Bowen [54] and Black [42, 43]. A thorough discussion of the consequences for public choice and normative social choice theory that have flowed from the median voter theory, as treated in, e.g., Arrow [10], Sen [324], Downs [103], and many other works, is beyond the scope of this study. The basic model is by now presented in many texts, such as Boadway and Wildasin [49], Feldman [119], Mueller [250], Musgrave and Musgrave [256] and, for a more thorough and detailed discussion, Enelow and Hinich [111]. It is useful, however, to review a few of the essential features of the model before turning to a discussion of its application in empirical studies.

Suppose a public issue, such as the determination of the level of expenditure on some public service, is to be determined by a series of pairwise votes over a set of alternatives by a fixed electorate. Let us suppose that a simple majority voting procedure is followed and the process continues until an alternative is found that cannot be defeated in a pairwise contest against any other alternative. Let us call this a *majority voting equilibrium*. If the well-known single-peakedness restriction on voter preferences is satisfied, a majority voting equilibrium exists, and this equilibrium will be the preferred outcome of the voter who has the median preferred outcome or "ideal point." If, however, the single-peakedness condition is not met, no majority-voting equilibrium need exist. In this case, the famous paradox of voting can arise, in which an electorate endlessly cycles over a set of alternatives, each in succession being overturned in a majority vote.

For reasons that we shall discuss in the next subsection, it has often been held that voters are likely to have single-peaked preferences over local public expenditure levels, and that the median voter model can therefore be used to describe how these expenditures are determined. This view can be questioned on several grounds, but here we note only that single-peakedness must almost always break down when multi-dimensional issues are to be decided by simultaneous (i.e., non-sequential) majority vote, even when the underlying individual preferences over the issues are perfectly well-behaved. This has been shown, e.g., by Kramer [204], and Plott [282]. The consequence is that cycling can occur, so that the outcome of the voting process depends critically on the precise agenda put before the electorate. In fact, McKelvey [225, 226] has shown that essentially any outcome in the issue space can be contrived as an equilibrium if the agenda is suitably designed. This is in contrast to the single-dimensional case, where the equilibrium is invariant to alternative specifications of the agenda, provided only that the median preferred outcome enters the agenda at some point. One should note, however, that majority voting equilibria can exist when multidimensional issues are uncoupled and voted upon seriatim. (See, e.g., Buchanan [75] for more discussion.) Another way to achieve equilibria with multi-dimensional issues is to restrict the agenda to single-dimensional sets of alternatives (see Slutsky [329]).

Multidimensional issue spaces are important for present purposes because many empirical studies of local public expenditure use the median voter model framework to explain, say, municipal government expenditures, perhaps disaggregated into a few broad functional categories, such as police, education, transportation, etc. Such issues clearly are (or can be) multidimensional. For example, a given sum can be spent on education in a wide variety of ways, among which voters will certainly not be indifferent. It is debatable, therefore, whether the political process that determines aggregate educational expenditure can reasonably be described as majority voting over this single-dimensional issue. If the process operates in such a way that voters perceive the proportions in which (incremental) funds are spent as being invariant across candidates, with each candidate simply taking a position on total expenditures, then the multidimensional issue is essentially reduced to a single dimension and the median voter model would seem to be applicable. Something of this sort undoubtedly does occur in practice, if only because public services are administered in a somewhat decentralized fashion: the details of the design of a new public structure, for example, may be left largely in the hands of architects. It remains to be determined, however, whether this applies up to the level of the aggregates that have been used in empirical research.[21]

B. The median voter model in application. Let us now review the use of the median voter model in empirical studies.[22] The basic framework underlying these studies can be summarized roughly as follows.

Let there be a fixed set of voters in a community. Each voter k has a utility function defined over private good consumption x^k and public good consumption z. For simplicity, choose units of z such that each unit has a price of \$1, z thus representing local public expenditure. The local tax system imposes taxes $\tau^k(z)$ on voter k. Given a fixed before-tax income I^k, the voter will achieve a utility level $u^k(I^k - \tau^k[z], z)$ if z is the level of public expenditure selected by the community. Individual k, as a voter, naturally votes in favor of proposed levels of expenditure that make u^k as high as possible.

This simple model can provide a theory of individual voting behavior. Before the median voter theory can be applied, however, it is necessary to verify the single-peakedness condition. In certain cases, this is easily done. For example, suppose that n is the total

---

[21] For further discussion of voting in multi-dimensional issue spaces, see Shepsle and Weingast [325] and Coughlin and Hinich [89].

[22] Another important approach to empirical demand analysis for local public goods is based on surveys of voter preferences. An obvious potential limitation of such analysis is that respondents to surveys may not corectly report the way that they would respond to alternatives in actual voting situations. Also, surveys seldom provide quantitative data on magnitudes such as desired public spending. However, as shown in work by Bergstrom *et al.* [35] and Gramlich and Rubinfeld [145], qualitative choice techniques can be used to obviate the latter problem. In fact, these authors use the results of a survey of Michigan voters to estimate demand functions for education that depend not only on income and marginal tax price, but on race, age, number of children, and other variables. This highlights one great advantage of survey data: since the individual (rather than the locality) is the unit of observation, it is possible to obtain estimates of the effect of many individual characteristics on public good demand. Another important advantage is that one need not invoke the median voter model or any other theory of collective decisionmaking in order to estimate demand function parameters. Interestingly, analysis of the Michigan data yields price and income elasticities of demand that are similar to those obtained from regressions based on the median voter model. (See Bergstrom *et al.* for a detailed comparison.) This suggests that responses to surveys may indeed be rather consistent with actual voting behavior. See Rubinfeld [309] for additional references and further discussion of this research.

number of households in the locality and that the jurisdiction finances all of its expenditures with a head tax. Then $\tau^k(z) = z/n$, and single-peakedness over z follows directly from the convexity of voter preferences over (x^k, z). (This can easily be verified diagrammatically using either demand curves or indifference curves.) Single-peakedness can also be demonstrated in many other cases. Suppose, for example, that a jurisdiction finances expenditures with a proportional income tax. Then, if each I^k is exogenously fixed, the government budget constraint requires a tax rate $\tau = z/\sum_k I^k$. Hence, $\tau^k(z) = (I^k/\sum_{k'} I^{k'})z$, i.e., each voter bears a share of local costs equal to its fixed share of local income. Clearly, this financing arrangement has the same qualitative properties as the head tax, and single-peakedness obtains. As a final example, one that is important in applications, suppose that localities use a property tax to finance public spending. Assume that household k holds property worth V^k, and that either the value of this property is fixed independently of z, or property is physically homogeneous in the jurisdiction so that all property values change in proportion (if at all) as z changes. Government budget balance requires a property tax at rate $\tau = z/\sum_k V^k$. Hence $\tau^k(z) = (V^k/\sum_{k'} V^{k'})z$, i.e., the voter bears the cost of financing local expenditure in proportion to the share of property owned.

Given well-behaved individual preferences and various plausible cost-sharing systems for local public goods, then, the assumption of single-peakedness may be reasonable. However, it should be noted that a failure of single-peakedness can arise if one takes account of the option of private provision for some local public services. Stiglitz [342] considers education, and the essence of his argument is easily understood. (See also Barzel [21] and Inman [188].) Suppose a household bears a tax $\tau^k(z)$ which is increasing in the level of public education. (z should be interpreted as "quality of education" or "education per pupil.") Each household can choose either public or private education for its children, but must pay the tax $\tau^k(z)$ in either case. Education is available privately at a price p. For z close to zero, say $z = z_0$ in Figure 6, the household chooses to purchase z^* units of education privately despite bearing the tax given by area c. (The marginal tax-price curve is drawn below p because the marginal cost of public education is shared among all taxpayers whereas the marginal cost of private education falls entirely on the

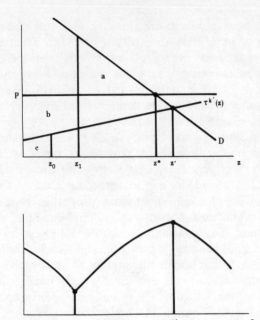

FIGURE 6   The availability of private education can produce non-singlepeaked preferences for public education.

purchaser. It approaches p because the number of students in the public system increases with z.) A marginal increase in z from z_0 adds to the household's tax burden but does not induce it to switch to public education, and hence only makes the household worse off. On the other hand, for some z, say $z = z_1$, the household is indifferent between public and private education.[23] A move from z^* purchased privately to z_1 obtained publicly results in a loss of consumer's surplus of a, but a cost savings of $b = a$, leaving the household equally well-off with either public or private education. Once having moved to public schools, however, further increases in z increase utility, up to point z'. The upshot is a preference curve such as that shown in the lower panel of Figure 6.

---

[23] We ignore income effects on the demand curve for education, D. This affects nothing essential. If one follows Stiglitz and models education as investment in human capital which only increases future income, rather than as a consumption good, income effects will be absent in any case.

Thus, preferences for public education may not be single-peaked because of the existence of a private option. On the other hand, single peakedness may still hold for small variations around a given level of education, and hence at least local majority voting equilibria may exist. Presumably, this argument can be used to justify application of the median voter model even when single peakedness is not assured. Let us therefore examine how the median voter model has been used in practice.

One possibility is to run a regression of the form

$$C_i = f(\tau_i^{m'}, I_i^m, n_i, \alpha_i) + u_i, \qquad (3.3)$$

where C_i is the level of expenditure in locality i, $\tau_i^{m'}$ is the marginal tax-price for the median voter m (that is, the derivative of $\tau_i^m(z_i)$, e.g., $V^m/\sum_k V^k$ in the proportional property tax case), I_i^m is the income of the median voter, n_i is local population, α_i is a vector of other relevant parameters, and u_i is a random error. For example, in a pioneering study, Barr and Davis [18] estimate a model like (3.3). Their left-hand variable is per-capita expenditure, either in total or by functional category, for a cross-section of Pennsylvania counties. Implicit in this specification is the assumption that local public services are produced under constant per capita costs. To identify the median voter, Barr and Davis assume that all households have identical utility functions and incomes, but that they differ in their ownership of property. They assume that all local expenditures are financed by a proportional tax on property, and (implicitly) that property value shares are invariant to changes in expenditure. The median voter will then be the household with the median property value share $V^k/\sum_{k'} V^{k'}$, and this share will be that voter's tax-price. Unfortunately, data limitations prevent the authors from determining this share directly so they resort to proxy variables. Their version of the relationship (3.3) is linear in these variables. Regression estimates find the coefficients to be generally significant and of the expected sign. This is taken as evidence compatible with the median voter hypothesis.

Subsequent studies have improved on Barr and Davis by using better data, by allowing for more complexities such as variations across jurisdictions in the cost of supplying public services, and by using a more general specification of the effect of population on the cost of public services. They have also used a log-linear specification for the demand equation (3.3) that permits identification of price and income elasticities. Examples of such studies include Barlow [16], Edelson [108], Borcherding and Deacon [51], Bergstrom and Goodman [34], and Inman [187]. Inman [189] and Rubinfeld [309] provide critical reviews of much of the literature. It is convenient to summarize the Bergstrom–Goodman model here, since it generalizes those used in preceding studies.

To begin with, the model allows for several different types of households in each jurisdiction. Let n_i^k denote the number of k-types in jurisdiction i, let $G_i^k(I)$ be the *cdf* for income among k-types in locality i, and let $\tau_i^k(I)$ be a function relating income to the share of taxes paid by a k-type in i. Let the total cost of providing a level z_i of public service to a population of $\sum_k n_i^k$ in i be given by $C(n_i, z_i) \triangleq (\sum_k n_i^k)^\gamma c z_i$, where γ is a fixed parameter and c is the price per unit of z_i. γ describes the degree of congestion in public good provision. The special case $\gamma = 0$ implies no congestion at all, $\gamma = 1$ implies constant per capita costs, and other values of γ allow for intermediate (or more extreme) cases. This generalizes Barr–Davis, Barlow, and other models which implicitly assume $\gamma = 1$.

Hence, if z_i is provided in i, the tax bill of a k-type household with income I will be $\tau_i^k(I)C(n_i, z_i) = \tau_i^k(I)c(\sum_{k'} n_i^{k'})^\gamma z_i$. This determines the effective price $t_i^k(I) = \tau_i^k(I)c(\sum_{k'} n_i^{k'})^\gamma$ of the public service to the household. The demand function for a k-type household in i with income of I is assumed to be of the form

$$z_i^k(I) = b^k f(\alpha_i) t_i^k(I)^\delta I^\varepsilon, \qquad (3.4)$$

where b^k is a class-specific multiplicative taste parameter, $f(\alpha_i)$ is a class- and jurisdiction-invariant function of a vector α_i of jurisdiction characteristics, and δ and ε are price and income elasticity parameters which are the same for all types and localities. This gives a desired expenditure level of

$$E_i^k(I) = c\left(\sum_{k'} n_i^{k'}\right)^\gamma z_i^k = b^k f(\alpha_i) c^{(1+\delta)} \left(\sum_{k'} n_i^{k'}\right)^{\gamma(1+\delta)} \tau_i^k(I)^\delta I^\varepsilon$$

$$(3.5)$$

for a k-type household in i with income I.

Equation (3.5) now shows the desired expenditure of each

household in the jurisdiction. Under simple majority voting, the median $E_i^k(I)$ will equal $E_i \triangleq C(n_i, z_i)$, the level of expenditure actually selected. How can we use this fact and the structure embodied in (3.5) to determine which voter is at the median, and/or to estimate the parameters δ, ε, and γ?

This is relatively straightforward in the special case, considered by Borcherding and Deacon, where there is only one household type $k = 1$ and where each household bears a fixed, per capita share of the local tax burden, $\tau_i^1(I) = (n_i^1)^{-1}$. $E_i^1(I)$ is then monotonically increasing in I, and it follows that the median amount of expenditure demanded will be the amount demanded by the household in jurisdiction i with median income, I_{im}. Borcherding and Deacon depart from Bergstrom and Goodman by using data on jurisdiction-specific costs of producing public goods, c_i. Now, setting $E_i = E_i^1(I_{im})$ in (3.5) and taking logarithms, we can regress[24]

$$\log E_i = \beta_0 + \beta_1 \log c_i + \beta_2 \log n_i^1 + \beta_3 \log I_{im} + \log f(\alpha_i) + u_i$$
(3.6)
where

$$\beta_0 = \log b^1$$
$$\beta_1 = (1 + \delta)$$
$$\beta_2 = \gamma(1 + \delta) - \delta$$
$$\beta_3 = \varepsilon.$$

By including the cost data, c_i, this regression allows one to identify not only the income elasticity of demand, ε, but the price elasticity δ and the crowding parameter γ.

In the general case of several types of households, however, this procedure does not work. To see this, suppose that there are $N \geq 2$ classes of households, with income distributions $G_i^k(I)$, such that a particular k-type household with income I_{im} has the median income. Suppose also that for some initial parameterization of tastes (b^k) this voter has the median desired level of public expenditure so that $E_i = E_i^k(I_{im})$. Would this median income household continue to be the median voter for alternative taste parameters? Suppose that for some class k', there exist income levels such that some households in this class desire more than $E_i^k(I_m)$ and some desire less—a weak restriction essentially requiring that some k' households have "sufficiently high" and "sufficiently low" income. Then a change in the parameter $b^{k'}$, say an increase, with other parameters held fixed, will increase the demands of all k' households. For a large enough change in $b^{k'}$—if $G_i^{k'}$ is continuous and strictly increasing, any finite change will do—some (non-null set of) k' voters will move from the left of $E_i^k(I_m)$ to the right. The median income household will no longer be the median voter.

This shows that the median income household is not, in general, the median voter. One cannot therefore presume that a regression like (3.6) is always justified. Bergstrom and Goodman show, nonetheless, that there are circumstances under which a regression of this sort can be used to estimate the demand and crowding parameters. To do this requires additional assumptions, however. First, the tax share $\tau_i^k(I)$ is assumed to depend on income with an elasticity ξ, and to vary with class and jurisdiction only by multiplicative constants: $\tau_i^k(I) = \tau_i \tau_k I^\xi$. Second, it is assumed that $\varepsilon + \delta\xi \neq 0$. This insures that the demand for the public good is strictly monotonically increasing or decreasing in income I, taking into account the effect of income on tax-price as well as the direct effect of income on demand.[25] Third, a restriction is imposed on the interjurisdictional variation in income distribution. For each class k there exists a function G^k, and for each jurisdiction i there exists a constant h_i, such that

$$G_i^k(I) = G^k(h_i I) \qquad \text{all } k, i. \qquad (3.7)$$

That is, the income distributions for all classes in jurisdiction i are the same as those in any other jurisdiction j, up to jurisdiction-

---

[25] Buchanan [74] discusses the fact that under a progressive tax structure, tax shares and hence effective tax-prices for public goods increase with income. He observes that if tax shares rise sufficiently quickly, and if the price-elasticity of demand for public goods is sufficiently great, the desired level of public expenditure on public goods could be inversely related to income. In the present notation, this would occur if $\varepsilon + \delta\xi < 0$. In applications to local public expenditures, as discussed below, it is reasonable to assume that $\varepsilon + \delta\xi > 0$, i.e., desired expenditures vary positively with income. See also Beck [23].

specific multiplicative factors h_i and h_j (the same for all classes). If, for instance, $h_j = 1$ and $h_i = 1.1$, the income distributions for all classes in i are identical to those in j except that incomes in i are 10% lower than in j.

Under these assumptions, it is possible to establish that the level of public expenditures demanded by the median voter will equal

$$E_i = \phi(s_i^1, \ldots, s_i^N) b^k f(\alpha_i) c^{(1+\delta)} \left(\sum_{k'} n_i^{k'} \right)^{\gamma(1+\delta)} \tau_i^k (I_{im})^\delta (I_{im})^\varepsilon$$

(3.8)

where k refers to some arbitrary class of households, s_i^k is the proportion of type-k voters in the population of city i, and $\phi(\cdot)$ is a function common to all jurisdictions. (The form of ϕ will depend on the class k that is selected.) If one has data on the tax-price for some class of households, the median income in the jurisdiction, the population shares of different classes, and relevant other variables, and if one knows the form of the ϕ function, one can regress (3.8) in its log-linear form and identify the parameters γ, δ, and ε. Though the function ϕ may in general depend on the population shares in a rather complicated way, Bergstrom and Goodman assume that it can be approximated by a simple linear or log-linear relationship. Using expenditure data for several functional categories and local governments in several states, they estimate coefficients that are generally of the anticipated sign and that often pass standard significance tests. This is seen as evidence compatible with the median voter model. It is interesting to note that coefficients vary in magnitude by category of expenditure and by state.

A somewhat curious feature of the model (3.8) is that it does not necessarily represent the demand function for the median voter, nor does it permit a determination of the identity (i.e., class and income level) of the median voter. It also does not generally determine the taste parameters for all classes (the $b_s^{k'}$), although it depends on them, directly through the b^k appearing in the equation and indirectly through the ϕ function. A subsequent contribution by Inman [187] addresses this issue among others. Inman observes that since the demand for public expenditures by a member of group k

with income equal to the community median, I_{im}, is

$$E_i^k(I_{im}) = b^k f(\alpha_i) c^{(1+\delta)} \left(\sum_{k'} n^{k'} \right)^{\gamma(1+\delta)} \tau_i^k(I_{im})^\delta (I_{im})^\varepsilon, \quad (3.9)$$

we have by (3.8) that

$$E_i = \phi(s_i^1, \ldots, s_i^N) E_i^k(I_{im}). \quad (3.10)$$

Hence, the level of expenditures chosen by the median voter in jurisdiction i is the same as that demanded by the household of type k with median income if $\phi = 1$. Inman studies a sample of school districts on Long Island, and subdivides the population into 10 groups, by voter-nonvoter, homeowner-renter, age, income class, and religion. More than half of the voting population are young, nonpoor, noncatholic homeowners, so Inman selects them as a reference group (group k in Eqs. (3.8)–(3.10)), and tests whether $\phi = 1$. He finds that for about 75% of school districts, the hypothesis that $\phi = 1$ cannot be rejected. Moreover, in the remaining cases, ϕ averages at least 0.8, and thus does not differ from 1 by a very large amount. Hence, Inman concludes that it is reasonable to model the community public expenditure decision "as if" it is made in accordance with the wishes of a median income voter from some reference group.

This is an interesting result. Note, however, that there is no way to specify a priori what the reference group in the population should be, and there is no assurance that different specifications of this group would lead to similar conclusions. For instance, in the Inman analysis, the results might have been different had a disaggregation by housing tenure or religion not been feasible. Thus, one cannot conclude that a regression equation derived from (3.8) necessarily portrays the actual demand function for any population subgroup.

On the other hand, even if $\phi = 1$, one can identify the preference parameter b^k of the reference population subgroup in Eq. (3.8). This is shown in an unpublished appendix to Sonstelie [332]. First, note that one can write $\phi(s_i^1, \ldots, s_i^N)$ as $\phi'(s_i^1, \ldots, s_i^{k-1}, s_i^{k+1}, \ldots, s_i^N)$ since $\sum_k s_i^k = 1$. The essential observation to make is that $\phi'(0, \ldots, 0) = 1$, since the right side of (3.8) must reduce to the demand function for group k when no other groups are present.

Hence, one can approximate $\log \phi = \log \phi'$ by

$$\text{Log } \phi'(s_i^1, \ldots, s_i^{k-1}, s_i^{k+1}, \ldots, s_i^N) = \log \phi'(0, \ldots, 0)$$
$$+ \sum_{k' \neq k} s_i^{k'} \frac{\partial \log \phi'(0, \ldots, 0)}{\partial s_i^{k'}}$$
$$+ \text{ terms of higher order}$$

$$\simeq \sum_{k' \neq k} \theta^{k'} s_i^{k'}, \tag{3.11}$$

say. In a regression of the log form of (3.8), then, the ϕ' function is captured by the $\theta^{k'}$ parameters, and the constant term is just $\log b^k$ if units of public good are chosen so that $c = 1$. Sonstelie applies this result in a model which also incorporates a private school/public school choice and is able to determine, for the reference subgroup of homeowners in California school districts, the welfare cost of free public provision of education. In Sonstelie's analysis, this loss is substantial, and arises partly from allocative inefficiency due to the fact that all households using the public school system are constrained to consume the collectively-determined quantity rather than the quantity that would be utility-maximizing for each. Mainly, however, the loss arises from an inferred public/private cost differential.

Despite this useful result, the fact remains that the class-specific demand parameters, the b^k's, can be identified for at most one class of households in a regression like (3.8). For many purposes, this need not be a matter of serious concern. For example, if one wishes to explain or predict the response of local public expenditure to certain parametric changes, such as a change in median income or grant policy, the fact that one cannot determine the public expenditure demands of individual population subgroups is irrelevant. On the other hand, if one wishes to use information on local demand for public goods for normative purposes, this limitation is a fundamental one. As is well-known (see, e.g., Stiglitz [342]), the level of expenditure chosen by a median voter does not in general satisfy the Samuelsonian conditions for (first-best) efficiency. It would therefore be of considerable interest to know whether and by how much an observed level of expenditure differs from the efficient one. Notably, in the special case where there is only one "type" of household—i.e., if all of the taste parameters b^k are identical, then inverse demand functions for households in every income class can be computed from regressions like (3.8), allowing a determination of the marginal benefit of local public spending for all households. This information could be used, then, to ascertain the extent to which the local political process operates efficiently, and to suggest policies (e.g., matching grants) to improve efficiency. Such was the approach taken in Barlow [16], who concluded that school districts in Michigan tend to provide less than efficient levels of expenditures.[26] Unfortunately, the assumption of homogeneity of preferences in this sense is not supported by the evidence (e.g., Inman [187]) Thus, simple regressions like (3.8) do not provide enough information to make normative judgments about local public expenditures.

C. Limitations of median voter models. We now discuss several possible criticisms or limitations of median voter studies such as those discussed above.

First, as in all applied consumption analysis, an assumption is generally made that all households within a given socio-economic class have identical preferences, differing only in their incomes and tax-prices. Moreover, it is assumed that such preferences can be described in terms of some specific functional form, such as the constant elasticity demand function.

One might be skeptical of either the assumption of identical preferences, or the assumption that the functional form of these preferences is known. One can try to weaken the assumptions by allowing more observable household characteristics (race, number of children, etc.) to enter the demand function, or by using ever more general functional forms for preferences. Some maintained hypotheses must inevitably be introduced, however, with attendant risks of misspecification. Issues of this sort can never be completely settled, and researchers will continue to experiment with alternative specifications along the lines already noted above. It is worth

---

[26] See also Martinez-Vazquez [217] for a study which assumes identical preferences in estimating a Bergstrom–Goodman type model. For further discussion of the Barlow analysis, see Barlow [17], Bergstrom [33], Edelson [108], and Hogan and Shelton [181].

observing, however, that with every change in specification it becomes important to show how to identify the median voter, as Bergstrom and Goodman do for the constant-elasticity demand function. There is no *a priori* reason why, in the general case, the median voter should be the household with median income or median house value, and the Bergstrom–Goodman argument justifying Eq. (3.8) certainly does not apply for other functional forms. Second, as discussed by Romer and Rosenthal [296], it is not clear from regressions like Eq. (3.3) or (3.8) that the z_i chosen by a locality is actually *equal* to the level of public expenditure preferred by the median voter. How can one be certain that z_i is not simply positively related to the median voter's preferred outcome? Suppose, for example, that there is some aspect of the local political process that causes the level of public expenditure to be some fixed proportion, say 80% or 200%, of that desired by the median voter. A regression such as (3.3) or (3.8) does not allow one to identify this phenomenon, which Romer and Rosenthal call the "multiple fallacy."

Romer and Rosenthal also discuss another problem with the median voter model, the "fractile fallacy." If local expenditures are determined by some decisive voter, how does one know that this voter is actually the one with the median preferred outcome? Suppose, for example, that preferred points are monotonically related to income, and that the political process operates in such a way as to satisfy the voter in the 60th percentile rather than the median. This might occur because voter participation rates vary with income, or because higher income voters are more influential. Then the appropriate regression to run is not (3.3) or (3.8), but one in which the characteristics of the 60th percentile voter appears.

One possible defense of the median voter model against the multiple and fractile fallacy criticisms is that for some purposes these criticisms are irrelevant. For example, if one's objective is to develop a behavioral model with good predictive power, and if one could be sure that the level of expenditure selected by a community were always equal to a given multiple of that preferred by the median voter, then a specification like (3.3) or (3.8) would remain quite appropriate. In this view, the real problem is to determine what level of expenditure will be chosen, not what the median voter prefers *per se*. Similarly, if it happens that the 40th percentile voter is controlling, this may not make much difference if the median voter's preferred outcome bears some definite relationship to that of the 40th-percentile voter. (Indeed, in this case, the fractile and multiple problems are the same thing.)

A more compelling defense of the median voter model, of course, would be to show that it is in fact superior to proposed alternatives. One difficulty in doing so, however, is defining alternative models and formulating appropriate tests. For example, suppose we vary the Bergstrom–Goodman model by experimenting with income levels ranging from the 10th to 90th percentiles as alternatives to the median income. Applied economics being what it is, there would probably be some income level other than the median which would fit the data better. What would we conclude from such a result? In a statistical sense, we have imbedded the Bergstrom–Goodman model in a class of models, and we may reject it in favor of some other member of this class—perhaps one using the 60th percentile of the income distribution. But what is the *economic* significance of this 60th percentile model? Indeed, is it even an economic model in any meaningful sense?

To provide a more satisfactory test of the median voter model, one might wish to avoid essentially *ad hoc* alternatives. It might be better to start with differing economic *theories* of local public expenditure determination, to derive the testable implications of such theories, and contrast them with those of the median voter model. Perhaps empirical tests could then be devised that would allow one to judge among these models. An early attempt at such an approach is reported in Pommerehne [288]. In this study, a sample of Swiss municipalities is broken down into subsamples according to the institutional mechanism through which expenditures are determined (direct referenda, representative governments, with or without referenda on petition), and the median voter model with a single class of households (as in Borcherding–Deacon) is estimated for each. Pommerehne finds that the institutional structure makes a difference: the median voter model does not do as well under representative governments without recourse to referenda. Pommerehne also tries to take into account the effect of local bureaucracies and the ideology of political parties in each of these subsamples. Unfortunately, there is no fully articulated theoretical model to explain how these factors might enter, so the approach is exploratory in nature. The finding that institutional structure influences the explanatory power of the median voter model is highly suggestive, however, indicating the need for explicit analysis of the political process.

In the remainder of this and the next section, we review a number of alternative behavioral models of local policy determination which could provide useful alternatives to the standard median voter model. Some of these have been the subject of empirical estimation. As yet, however, there have been few attempts at direct comparisons with the median voter model. At least in part this is because it is not immediately apparent how these models can best be empirically distinguished.

3.4. Variations on and extensions of the median voter model

Let us now examine some alternatives to the median voter model based on richer institutional structures. First, we consider the role of interested government officials in the determination of local public spending. Second, we explore some implications of household mobility for voting behavior.

A. Voters vs. bureaucrats. The median voter model emphasizes the preferences of voters in determining outcomes. It also makes an important implicit assumption about the agenda to be voted upon: alternatives are somehow brought before the electorate, such that one of these alternatives is (at least approximately) the median preferred outcome. This might result from candidates for office attempting to position themselves as near to this median point as they can in order to get elected. Since some agents might have strong incentives, and the opportunity, to restrict the alternatives to be voted upon, however, one might find this assumption unsatisfactory. In a series of papers, Romer and Rosenthal [294, 295, 297, 298, 299], Filimon, *et al.* [122] and Romer, *et al.* [300] have advanced and tested a theory based on the role that bureaucrats might play in determining the agenda in a majority-voting decision process. Romer and Rosenthal assume that local bureaucrats, e.g., a school board, can propose a budget to voters which is either approved or disapproved in a referendum. If the bureaucrats' proposal is rejected, then the budget is set at an alternative level, called the *reversion* level, which is determined according to some procedural rule. For example, the level of expenditure could be set equal to zero, or equal to the previous year's budget, or the previous year's budget plus a given percentage increase, etc. Following Niskanen [260], bureaucrats are assumed to seek the maximum attainable budget.[27]

The general properties of this model are easily seen. Let z be a single public service provided to the residents in a locality, and suppose that the units of z are chosen such that each unit costs \$1.[28] Let z_R denote the reversion level of z, and let z_m denote the median preferred outcome. If $z_R = z_m$, it is clear that z_m will be the outcome actually selected: no higher level of z could be proposed by the bureaucracy and achieve majority approval. If $z_R > z_m$, the outcome selected will be z_R: the bureaucrats will offer a level of z at least equal to z_R and a majority of voters will support z_R against any higher alternative. (The median voter, and all voters with ideal outcomes less than z_m, constitute such a majority.) Finally, and most interestingly, if $z_R < z_m$, the outcome will be strictly greater than z_m, and the lower is z_R, the further above z_m will be the level of z finally selected.

This last case is illustrated in Figure 7, where the preferences of the voter with the median ideal point are portrayed: x is of course the household's consumption of all-purpose private good, and the budget line reflects this household's tax-price for local public expenditures, as determined by the given financing system. If the reversion level is z_R, this household would support any proposed level of z up to z_0. It is therefore possible to find a level of $z > z_m$ that would be supported by a majority, namely, the median voter together with all those whose ideal points lie above z_m. Indeed, if the preferences of households are similar in the sense that each above-median voter is indifferent between z_R and some level of z above z_0, the bureaucracy can push the level of z up to z_0. Furthermore, if the reversion level of z is $z_R' < z_R$, the median voter

[27] Epple and Zelenitz [115, 116] model local governments as maximizers of revenue less expenditure. Perhaps this could be interpreted as optimal bureaucratic behavior, where the local "profit" flows to officials who spend it on items of value only to themselves. Also, see Inman [193].

[28] See Mackay and Weaver [213] for an extension to multi-attribute public services.

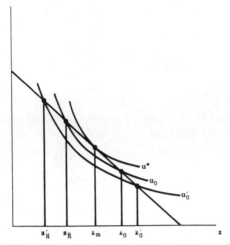

FIGURE 7   The median voter will accept higher levels of $z(z_0, z'_0)$ as the reversion
level of z falls below $z_m(z_R, z'_R)$.

will be willing to accept levels of z even higher than z_0, up to z'_0,
and other voters, too, will accept higher levels of z. It follows that
the maximum level of z that secures majority support rises as the
reversion level falls. This is an intuitive result: voters might accept a
very high level of public services if the alternative is, say, to do
without them altogether.[29]

Romer, Rosenthal, and their coauthors have extended this simple
model in various ways. For example, they allow for uncertain voter
turnout, the impact of intergovernmental grants, and a sequence of
referenda in which bureaucrats obtain information about voter
preferences in successive votes. A main testable implication of the
model is that a reversion level variable should be significant in
explaining local spending. Empirical tests on Oregon school districts
indicate that this in fact is the case. Simple median voter models are
not compatible with such a finding.[30]

---

[29] Public employee unions are presumably well aware of this fact, as are electorates
that deny them the right to strike.

[30] One might ask whether this model is open to a form of the fractile fallacy. How
can one be sure that the bureaucracy is playing against the median voter, rather than
a voter in some other percentile? Romer and Rosenthal [281] discuss this issue, and
indicate that other percentiles have explanatory power, in their empirical analysis,
comparable to the median.

While these empirical tests support the Romer–Rosenthal model, they more generally suggest the importance of the precise institutional structure through which expenditure decisions are made. In this spirit, one can raise a number of questions regarding the model that deserve further exploration. One obvious question is why voters are not able to replace the bureaucrats that seek to maximize expenditures. If incumbent school board members, mayors, etc. are "captured" by the public service systems that they govern, challengers who propose reduced spending levels should be able to secure majority support and take their places. Perhaps these new officals end up being captured also, which is to say that challengers cannot make credible promises to the electorate. Some modeling of this breakdown of electoral competition might be revealing. Moreover, explicit modeling of rent-seeking through control of local public spending might suggest additional implications of the budget-maximizing model. For example, there might be a bias in favor of labor-intensive expenditures, one in favor of local construction, etc.

A study by Ott [272] can be mentioned in this regard. Ott does not adopt the Romer–Rosenthal reversion concept, but does assume a budget maximizing bureaucracy. The bureaucrats are assumed to have better information about the costs of producing local public services than elected officials, which they exploit to increase budget size above the amount preferred by the median voter. Electoral competition obviously cannot eliminate this problem, as long as an informational asymmetry persists.

It would also be worthwhile to examine the effect of household mobility on the ability of bureaucrats to increase the level of expenditure above the majority voting equilibrium level. For example, if the median voter in Figure 7 could leave the jurisdiction and obtain a utility level of at least u_0 elsewhere, and other households are similarly mobile, z_0 might present bureaucrats with an upper limit on spending, even if the reversion level were below z_R. Results of this type are obtained in Courant et al. [93], who study a voting model in which part of the electorate consists of public employees, and in which the private-sector employees who make up the remainder of the electorate are able to migrate to other jurisdictions.[31] As bureaucrats (i.e., the public employees) try to expand public employment and wages, they drive away private employees, shrinking the local tax base. Thus, even if public employees are able to manipulate political outcomes in their favor, private sector mobility constrains the opportunities for public employees to overtax and overspend. While Courant *et al.* use a framework with certain special features that distinguish it from the Romer–Rosenthal model, the general conclusion that it suggests seems likely to reappear in other contexts. It would be useful, however, to modify one of these budget-maximizing bureaucrat models to incorporate mobility in a world with locationally-fixed resources. It is possible that capitalization effects (see Section 4 for discussion) might work to weaken the constraints that household mobility would otherwise impose on a local bureaucracy.

B. The median voter model and mobile households. The median voter studies reviewed so far have all assumed that voter-households are immobile. We now consider the implications of relaxing that assumption.

To begin with, the Bergstrom–Goodman model may not apply in the mobile-voter case. To see why, suppose, following Goldstein and Pauly [136], that there is a very wide variety of levels of provision of a single public good being provided by a large number of otherwise identical communities. (We shall henceforth refer to this condition by saying that there is a *continuum* of jurisdictions.) Suppose that some system of financing local expenditures is in place, and is common to all jurisidictions. Conditional on this system, assume that each household has a demand for the public good given by

$$z = f(I) + \varepsilon \qquad (3.12)$$

where I is income, f is an increasing function, and ε is a variate with symmetric (e.g., normal) distribution reflecting taste variations within each given income class. Finally, suppose that the income distribution is not uniform and that each household always locates

---

[31] See also Bush and Denzau [83], Borcherding, *et al.* [50], Gramlich [142], and Gramlich and Rubinfeld [146] for further discussion and some empirical evidence. In particular, Gramlich and Rubinfeld use the survey of Michigan voters cited above (see n. 22) and find that public employees have higher voting participtation rates, and tend to support more public spending, than the general public.

in a jurisdiction which provides the level of public good that it demands.

Consider, then, a level of income I_0 such that the density of income is increasing around I_0. Households with income I_0 and $\varepsilon = 0$ will locate in a jurisdiction providing $z_0 = f(I_0)$ of the public good, as will households with income above I_0 and $\varepsilon < 0$, and households with incomes below I_0 and $\varepsilon > 0$, such that $I = f^{-1}(z_0 - \varepsilon)$. This determines the equilibrium income distribution in the jurisdiction providing z_0, and similarly for other jurisdictions.

Now, depending on the distribution of ε and the form of f, it may well be the case that the distribution of income in the city providing z_0 contains a relatively high proportion of households with incomes above I_0, since we have assumed that, near I_0, there are more households with incomes above I_0 than below. Then I_0 will be below-median in the jurisdiction, which will have an income distribution skewed to the left. A symmetric argument shows that for a level of income I_1 such that the density of income is declining around I_1, there will be a jurisdiction providing a level of public good $z_1 = f(I_1)$ in which the income distribution is skewed right and I_1 is above-median.

Because the income distributions in different jurisdictions are of different skew, the Bergstrom–Goodman condition (3.7) will fail to hold. Moreover, it is easy to see that a regression of z on median income in each jurisdiction can result in an upward-biased estimate of the effect of income on demand for the local public good. Thus, household mobility can create serious difficulties for the median voter model as it is regularly applied.

Actually, household mobility can raise even more fundamental problems for the median voter model. For instance, how can we be certain of the existence of an equilibrium in which no community's voters wish to change the level of public expenditures and no household wishes to move to another jurisdiction? Westhoff [357, 358] and Brueckner [65] show that such equilbria need not in fact exist in general. We briefly review the Westhoff model.

Westhoff assumes a continuum of households with exogenously given wealth. Households consume only a pure local public good z and a single private good x. An exogenously-given number M of communities are constrained to finance their expenditures with a proportional wealth tax. For households of type k residing in jurisdiction i, the level of utility attained will be $u_i^k(x_i^k, z_i) = u_i^k([1 - \tau_{iw}]w^k, z_i)$ where w^k is the wealth of a k-type household and τ_{iw} is the tax rate in i. Each locality has the same costs of production for z, and the level of z is chosen according to majority voting. Communities differ only in their policy characteristics (τ_{iw}, z_i) and there are no locationally-fixed commodities in the model.

Westhoff uses a fixed point argument to prove the existence of a majority voting equilibrium with free mobility. The proof requires continuity of a mapping which is insured by some innocuous restrictions on preferences and technology, and by one restriction that is not innocuous. If k indexes a household's position on the unit interval, the assumption is

(W) $MRS_i^k(w^k)^{-1}|_{\tau_{iw}, z_i}$ is continuously increasing in k for all τ_{iw}, z_i.

One way to interpret this condition is to note that household k in locality i will have above (below) median preferences for local spending if $MRS_i^k|_{\tau_{iw}, z_i} > (<)w^k/W_i$, where W_i is total wealth in the jurisdiction and the price of z is set at unity. Thus, by (W), we know that for households k and k' located in the same locality i, with $k' > k$, household k' has a higher demand for local public spending than k irrespective of the existing tax and expenditure policy. Moreover, by continuity, we know that there exists a household k'' whose demand would occupy an intermediate position between k and k', if it were also located in locality i. Westhoff shows the necessity of this continuity assumption by presenting an example with $M = 2$ in which an equilibrium fails to exist. The essence of the example is that the discontinuity occurs around the location (in the unit interval) of the median voter in one jurisdiction, so that there are discontinuous changes in the level of public good selected as the identity of the median voter changes slightly.

The Westhoff analysis prompts several questions. First, the combination of proportional wealth taxation and uncongested local public goods insures that any equilibria which do exist are locationally inefficient, as discussed in Section 2.[32] This fact points to the

---

[32] In n. 3, Westhoff indicates that some extensions of his existence result to congestible publilc goods are possible. Interestingly, however, the widest class of cases for which this is claimed is one characterized by decreasing costs with respect to population size. By the results of Section 2, we know that exclusive reliance on a proportional wealth tax will still preclude locational efficiency in all such cases.

observation that a proportional wealth tax is not the only sort of financing mechanism one might wish to consider, and, indeed, casual empiricism would recommend others, including taxes on locationally-fixed commodities.

Second, the restriction to a given number M of jurisdictions may be questioned. It should be noted that in Westhoff's terminology, an equilibrium with M communities means that each of the M localities contains a set of households of non-negligible size: no locality can be empty. This is significant because it is obvious that an equilibrium always exists with one occupied locality, and any number of potential but inactive localities, even without (W). Indeed, in Westhoff's two-community examples, existence and, in [340], stability of equilibrium is precluded precisely because of a knife-edge problem: starting from an equilibrium or "near-equilibrium," a perturbation that starts households migrating in one direction is never offset, and all households end up in one community or the other (and it makes no difference which one, in terms of the resulting equilibrium). One suspects that the in-divisibility resulting from the pure publicness of local public goods, together with the absence of sufficiently scarce locationally-fixed commodities, accounts for this problem.

The above remarks suggest that it might be useful to investigate a voting model with mobile households in a setting with locationally-fixed commodities. Such an approach would give land or property prices a role in equilibrating locational choices: migration would raise or lower the value of the fixed resource. But then the owners of the fixed resources will be concerned with local public policy through its induced effect on their wealth. Should the interests of these individuals be included when modeling voting behavior? If they are absentee landlords, perhaps not, though a more sophisti-cated model of the political process would presumably allow them to exert influence other than by voting. But suppose the fixed commodity is residential property, or the land on which it is built, and voters are homeowners, a case that is important in empirical applications of the median voter model discussed previously. Here the question becomes how the household will weigh the benefits of a local public good against its tax-price, should it remain in the locality, as against the wealth effect of local policy operating through the value of property, should it decide to sell its property and relocate. Clearly, locational fixity does more than just offset indivisibilities associated with local public goods. It changes the structure of the utility-maximizing voter's decision problem in a way that is relevant both for the existence of voting equilibrium with mobile households and for the application of the Bergstrom–Goodman type models. Indeed, the Goldstein–Pauly critique of the standard median voter model should perhaps be pushed further: once we open up the issue of household mobility in voting models, it seems necessary to provide a more explicit analysis of the precise mechanism through which locational choices are effected, and its implications for the voting process. These issues are examined in the next section.

4. HOUSEHOLD MOBILITY AND PUBLIC EXPENDITURE DETERMINATION: TIEBOUT MODELS

4.1. Introduction

Much of the recent research on the implications of household mobility for the determination of public expenditures by local governments has been motivated by a provocative paper by Tiebout [350]. Tiebout, writing in response to Samuelson's famous papers [312, 313] on public expenditure theory, sought to rebut the Samuelsonian conclusion that no market-like mechanism exists to determine efficient levels of public good provision, at least for local public goods. Tiebout claimed that, at the local level, mobile households would make locational choices according to the expenditure levels chosen by various cities. In particular, Tiebout asserted that the choice of a community of residence would reveal a household's preferences for local public goods, solving the informational obstacle to efficient public expenditure repeatedly emphasized by Samuelson. If true, this would be a remarkable result.

Tiebout presented a series of assumptions meant to be sufficient to establish this claim. Even a casual perusal of the paper, however, indicates that Tiebout does not in fact prove any such result.[33]

---

[33] For instance, nowhere in the paper do the Samuelsonian conditions for efficient public expenditure appear. It should be noted here, incidentally, that there are many (footnote 33 continued next page.)

Nonetheless, the Tiebout claim remained unchallenged for a long period, receiving favorable notice from Musgrave [254, 255], among others. Recently, however, there have been many studies that have attempted to formalize models in which "the" Tiebout hypothesis can be examined. It should be noted that this recent literature deals with a wide range of issues in addition to expenditure efficiency, e.g., locational efficiency, which we have already discussed in Section 2. In this section, our focus will be narrower: only the problems of preference revelation and expenditure efficiency will be discussed. We begin with a review of a number of intriguing empirical studies which have attempted to test "the" Tiebout hypothesis. This leads naturally to a consideration of more basic theoretical issues.

4.2. Tax and expenditure capitalization

A standard argument in public finance asserts that a stream of taxes levied on an asset over time will reduce its market value by an amount equal to the present value of the tax stream. The essence of the argument is obvious: an asset's value is given by the present value of the stream of *net* returns it offers, and these net returns are reduced by taxes. Accordingly, it is often held that property tax increases (cet.par.) reduce house values. A number of empirical studies (e.g., Church [87], Dusansky *et al.* [104], Orr [270], Heinberg and Oates [166], Rosen [305], Smith [330], Wicks *et al.* [363], and, for a review, Bloom *et al.* [44]) have sought to ascertain whether this is so, and have generally found at least partial evidence of tax capitalization.

Testing for capitalization is complicated, of course, by the fact that other things often vary when local taxes change. Notably, when local taxes increase in order to finance more local public services, one important attribute of a house—the local public services which its occupant is able to consume—changes as well. One would expect

---

(footnote 33 continued)
different possible interpretations of "what Tiebout really meant." One is simply that people with similar "tastes" for local public goods, by which is usually meant similar quantities demanded, will tend to congregate. If utility functions are identical, this proposition reduces to stratification of the population by income level. This issue is discussed, e.g., by Burstein [82], Eberts and Gronberg [105], and Hamilton, *et al.* [162]. For other interpretations and surveys of the Tiebout literature, see Mills and Oates [247], Henderson [170], Rose-Ackerman [302], Zodrow [393], and especially Pestieau [276] and Rubinfeld [309].

that the net effect on house value would be ambiguous—higher taxes would depress its value, and higher public services would increase it. Of course, if people are ignorant of or uninterested in these local policies, neither effect would operate: property values would reflect neither tax nor "expenditure" capitalization.

In a well-known empirical study that examines these questions, Oates [263] estimates regressions of the form

$$r_i = f(z_i, \tau_{ir}, \alpha_i) + u_i \qquad (4.1)$$

where r_i is the price of housing in jurisdiction i (in Oates' case, median house value), z_i is a measure of local public services (education), τ_{ir} is an effective property tax rate, α_i is a vector of other variables, and u_i is an error term. The coefficients on z_i and τ_{ir} are significant and of expected sign. The finding that house values are influenced by local tax and expenditure policy provides evidence in favor of a minimal requirement for Tiebout's conjecture to be correct: people are not oblivious to local policy, which is obviously essential if their locational choices are somehow to insure that these policies are efficient. By itself, however, findings of non-zero coefficients on the z_i and τ_{ir} variables would seem to indicate nothing about whether efficiency is actually achieved. However, Oates at least hints that regressions like (4.1) could be used to *test* for efficiency. He suggests that $\partial f / \partial z_i + (\partial f / \partial \tau_{ir})(\partial \tau_{ir} / \partial z_i)$ can be used as a measure of the net benefits of local public services. Oates' finding that this expression is close to zero would thus indicate that the level of education expenditure is close to optimal.

Following Oates, there has been a host of theoretical and empirical discussions of these issues.[34,35] Here, we shall focus on the

[34] Among the more or less direct descendants of Oates, we may note Cowing [94], Cushing [96], Edel and Sclar [107], Gustely [154] (who reviews several earlier studies), Hamilton [159], Hyman and Pasour [183, 184], King [200, 201], McDougall [220], Meadows [236], Oates [265], Pollakowski [287], and Rosen and Fullerton [304]. See also Sonstelie and Portney [334].

[35] The parallel with the literature on air pollution and property values is striking. A noted early empirical study by Ridker and Henning [292] found that property values tend to be depressed by higher pollution levels, and the coefficients of the regression equation were used to provide an estimate of the benefits of air pollution abatement. This spawned a substantial literature, a main goal of which was to determine under what conditions, if any, such an interpretation of regression coefficients is legitimate. See, *inter alia*, Anderson and Crocker [2, 3] Lind [210, 211], Freeman [129, 130, 131, 132, 133], Pines [278], Pines and Weiss [280, 281], Polinsky and Shavell [285, 286], and Polinsky and Rubinfeld [284]. There are many similarities between the Tiebout literature on tax and expenditure capitalization and the air pollution and property value debate. For a discussion relating the two, see Wildasin [369].

underlying theory of capitalization, which has been the subject of considerable debate. For example, it has been argued, in contrast to Oates, that non-zero coefficients on policy variables in a cross-section regression indicate that certain policy combinations are commanding a premium relative to others. Some "supply adjustment" mechanism should operate to reduce such premia in the long run, resulting in a fully efficient "Tiebout equilibrium" with zero capitalization effects (Edel and Sclar [107], Hamilton [159], and others). Other authors argue that capitalization can occur, but need not, depending, among other things, on the structure of preferences (Starrett [339]), or that zero-capitalization equilibria are possible but not necessary, but in any case may not carry information about efficiency (Pauly [275]).

To illuminate these issues, we shall examine three models in which property values reveal information about household preferences for local public goods and/or expenditure efficiency. Then we discuss the special features of these models that allow such results to emerge. Finally, we examine the question of capitalization and underfunding of municipal pensions. This is a particularly interesting aspect of the capitalization issue because it involves changes in the intertemporal structure of local taxation. Before starting, however, it is useful to note a possible ambiguity in the concept of capitalization. This term could refer to the change in equilibrium land or property values in a locality that results from some change in local policy. We shall refer to this as *comparative static* capitalization. Alternatively, capitalization could refer to the variation in property across jurisdictions that is observed in a given equilibrium. We call this *cross-sectional* capitalization. Both types of capitalization are widely discussed in the literature, though they are often not clearly distinguished.

Model I. The first model to be discussed is based on Brueckner [68], although the presentation here is different.[36] The basic structure and notation are borrowed from Section 2, but in somewhat specialized form. In contrast to the general model, a special assignment of property rights is assumed here: all non-wage income accrues to households who only consume an all-purpose

---

[36] See also Brueckner [66, 69]. Brueckner and Wingler [71] provide an extension to the case of public inputs.

good, and who are immobile. All mobile households receive only wage income. Variations on these assumptions are possible, but their main purpose is to simplify the discussion by ignoring the effects of local policy on the value of the endowment of mobile households. The subsequent discussion suppresses all further consideration of the immobile households.

Thus, let the utility of a (mobile) household of type k in locality i be given by $u_i^k(x_i^k, t_i^k, q_i^k, n_i, z_i)$, where x_i^k, t_i^k, and q_i^k are consumption of all-purpose good, "property," and an agricultural good, n_i is the vector of local population, and z_i is the vector of local public goods. Following Brueckner, and in contrast to Section 2, let us interpret t_i^k as housing rather than as land. However, suppose also that the time frame of analysis is sufficiently short that t_i^k can be regarded as an exogenously fixed parcel of property which can only be occupied by one household. Alternatively, one could suppose that each t_i^k is fixed by zoning controls (recall Section 2.4). By this assumption, the total population of the locality is fixed at $\sum_k n_i^k$.

The budget constraint of a household of type k in locality i is

$$x_i^k + r_i^k(1 + \tau_{ir}^k)t_i^k + pq_i^k = w_i^k \qquad (4.2)$$

where r_i^k is the price of the parcel t_i^k, τ_{ir}^k is the ad valorem property tax rate on this property, p is the price of the agricultural good, and w_i^k is the household's wage income. Note that the tax rate is allowed to vary by household type, although it need not.

We now assume that while structures are fixed, households are costlessly mobile. Also assume that preferences and endowments of different household types are such that only households of type k compete for the parcels t_i^k, at least for sufficiently small parametric changes around an initial equilibrium. This assumption is of course vacuous in the special case where there is only one household type in each locality, and it should generally be satisfied if the preferences, incomes, and parcels of the different household types are discretely distinct. A consequence of this assumption is that the local population vector n_i can be taken as exogenously fixed. Finally, assume that no resident household's equilibrium utility level depends on policies taken in jurisdiction i alone. That is to say, jurisdiction i is a small utility-taking locality. Let $\bar{v}^k$ be the parametrically given utility level for class k. Then, recalling that t_i^k is taken as given to the consumer, equilibrium in the local property market requires that

$$v_i^k(p, z_i^k, w_i^k - r_i^k[1 + \tau_{ir}^k]t_i^k) = \bar{v}^k. \qquad (4.3)$$

For simplicity, let the production side of the model remain identical to that in Section 2. We assume that z_i does not affect the local production process, and we abstract from taxation of business property (see Brueckner for this extension). With only a tax on residential property, the local government's budget constraint is

$$\sum_k n_i^k \tau_{ir}^k r_i^k t_i^k = C_i(n_i, z_i). \qquad (4.4)$$

This completes the specification of the model. Let us now explore the capitalization issue, first considering the comparative statics of a change in local public good provision z_i, financed by a change in local taxes. Assume that the price of the agricultural commodity is taken as given by an individual jurisdiction. The population vector n_i is unaffected by z_i because of previous assumptions. Thus, the markets for labor and property in the local production sector are unaffected by the policy change.[37] With p and w_i^k fixed, the utility constraint (4.3) can be solved for $r_i^k(1 + \tau_{ir}^k)$ implicitly in terms of z_i to yield

$$-t_i^k \frac{\partial(r_i^k[1 + \tau_{ir}^k])}{\partial z_i} + MRS_i^k = 0 \qquad (4.5)$$

where $MRS_i^k = u_{i5}^k/u_{i1}^k$ is the household's marginal rate of substitution of public for private good.[38] Hence,

$$\sum_k n_i^k MRS_i^k = \sum_k n_i^k t_i^k \frac{\partial r_i^k}{\partial z_i} + \sum_k n_i^k t_i^k \frac{\partial(r_i^k \tau_{ir}^k)}{\partial z_i}. \qquad (4.6)$$

But by (4.4), this becomes

$$\sum_k n_i^k MRS_i^k - C_{iz} = \sum_k n_i^k t_i^k \frac{\partial r_i^k}{\partial z_i}, \qquad (4.7)$$

where $C_{iz} \triangleq \partial C_i/\partial z_i$. Note that (4.7) has been derived without specifying exactly how local tax rates change with z_i. In particular, they need not change uniformly.

---

[37] A convenient alternative specification is to assume, as discussed below, that the decisions about location of employment and location of residence can be made independently. Under this assumption it will again be true that a household's income will be independent of its residential locational choice.

[38] Here we treat z_i as a scalar for notational simplicity only. Equations (4.5), (4.6) etc. can be interpreted as holding coordinatewise for z_i a vector.

Equations (4.5) and (4.7), which imply perfect comparative static capitalization, are of substantial interest. Suppose it were possible to predict or observe how property values would respond to changes in local public good provision and tax rates. If this information were known at the level of individual properties, then, by (4.5), it would be possible to deduce the MRS_i^k for an individual household. Thus, while the individual household's MRS is not directly observable, a knowledge of equilibrium house value variations in response to policy changes, which can in principle be observed or predicted, can be used to infer the MRS. In this sense, at least, household mobility results in revelation of preferences for local public goods.

Even if property value changes could not be predicted at a micro level, it might be possible to estimate or observe the response of aggregate property values to a change in z_i. By (4.7), this is equal to the "social marginal net benefit" of the local public good. A test for public expenditure efficiency could be developed on the basis of this information: efficiency would obtain only if aggregate property value is locally invariant to the level of public good provision.

Before discussing further the design of such tests, let us briefly consider a specialization of the model. Suppose that all parcels in a locality are identical (perhaps because of zoning constraints) and are taxed at equal effective rates, and that all localities have an equal number, N, of such parcels. Suppose also that all congestion/crowding effects depend only on the total population in a jurisdiction and not on its composition. Finally, suppose the incomes of households are independent of their location.[39] This is essentially the model presented in Wildasin [369].

All properties in a given jurisdiction must trade at a common price, r_i, and hence the local government budget constraint (4.4) becomes $\tau_i r_i = C_i/N$, where the quantity of housing in each parcel is normalized at one unit. Substituting into (4.5) we have[40]

$$MRS_i^k = \frac{C_{iz}}{N} + \frac{\partial r_i}{\partial z_i}. \tag{4.8}$$

---

[39] See n. 37 above.

[40] It is best to think of (4.8) as derived from the condition for utility-maximizing locational choice rather than as showing the hypothetical response of property values to a variation in local public good provision by a utility-taking jurisdiction. The reason is that with identical parcels, there is no reason to expect the composition of the population to remain unchanged.

The condition (4.8) has an interesting interpretation in the special case where $\partial r_i / \partial z_i = 0$. Recall the median voter model discussed in Section 3.3 above, where a household's marginal tax-price for a local public good under property taxation was defined as the household's share of property value times the marginal cost of the public good. In the present special case, this is precisely the right-hand side of (4.8). But then (4.8) just reduces to the condition for a Lindahl [212] equilibrium, such that each household's MRS is equated to its marginal tax-price. Attaining the conditions for Lindahl equilibrium is of interest because, while it underlies the benefit principle of taxation (Musgrave [252]), it cannot be implemented directly due to strategic misrepresentation of preferences (Samuelson [312, 313, 314]). Given the special structure that we have imposed (identical parcels), (4.8) also implies that all households in a jurisdiction have identical MRS's and, in that sense, identical "preferences" for the local public good. (Households need not be alike in other respects, however, such as incomes or the underlying structure of preferences.) The fact that a Lindahl equilibrium emerges in this special case is somewhat of a curiosum, of course, since the concept of marginal tax-price as used in Section 3 only makes sense when households are immobile, whereas it is essential to the present model that they be freely mobile.

Returning now to the more general case where properties need not be identical, there remains the question of how one is to determine the response of property values, at either the micro or aggregate levels, to changes in local public good provision. One possibility is by using time-series observations on a given jurisdiction. The difficulty here is that, in practice, there are too few observations, too little variation in z_i and/or too many other changes occurring to make estimation feasible. An alternative is to use a cross-section regression of property values on public goods levels, which is the approach taken in most empirical work. For this to succeed, however, one must verify the conditions for cross-sectional capitalization in this model. To see how this might be done, assume that jurisdictions are alike in all respects except the level of public good provision, so that wage income, the public good cost function, the housing stock size and composition, etc. do not vary across jurisdictions. Suppose also that the number of jurisdictions is sufficiently large and that the variation of public goods levels among them is sufficiently fine that households can continuously vary their consumption of public goods through locational choice. Finally, suppose that effective tax rates vary smoothly across jurisdictions.[41] Under these assumptions, (4.5) could be interpreted as a condition characterizing utility-maximizing locational choice for a type-k household. Such a household, by choosing a jurisdiction in which to reside, can vary its consumption of the local public good, and would choose a level such that the total derivative of its utility function with respect to the public good is zero. (Though the assumptions imposed do not strictly insure that this derivative exists, they at least imply continuity of the utility function in z.) By differentiating (4.4), and using (4.5), one again obtains (4.7). Now, however, the interpretation of (4.7) is different: $\partial r_i^k / \partial z_i$ reflects the observed *interjurisdictional* variation in the price of a specific kind of property, not the predicted or observed comparative statics variation in the price of a parcel of property in a particular locality.

The cross-sectional capitalization of net benefits can thus be verified in this model, under certain assumptions. Equation (4.7) can be used to justify a cross-section regression of property value on public good provision, where the coefficient of the public good variable is used to test for efficiency: a positive coefficient implies under-provision of the public good, and a negative coefficient over-provision. Constancy of property values with respect to public expenditure would imply efficiency.[42] Brueckner estimates a relation of this type for a sample of Massachusetts cities, using education and other public expenditures as two measures of public good provision. He finds no evidence of systematic over- or under-provision of local public goods.

Upon what main assumptions do the foregoing capitalization results depend? In deriving the comparative statics capitalization result, the utility-taking assumption (4.3) is obviously crucial. So is

[41] This will obtain if tax rates are uniform, $\tau_{ir}^k = \tau_{ir}$ for all k, i, or if they bear a given relationship to one another, e.g., $\tau_{ir}^k = 0.9\tau_{ir}^{k'}$, all i, for classes k and k'. One could, for example, capture systematically different assessment of owner-occupied and rental housing in this fashion.

[42] As Brueckner notes however, it may not be easy to ascertain whether property values are actually invariant to public goods levels in a given sample. A non-monotonic variation of property values with z_i might produce a zero coefficient if the functional dependence is assumed to be linear. Pauly [275] also makes this observation.

the assumption that no utility-determining parameters other than the tax-inclusive price of land can change in response to local policy. For cross-sectional capitalization, one would ideally require communities to be identical in all respects except public expenditures and taxes, in order to insure that the only differences among communities that are reflected in property values are variations in public good provision and taxes. It is instructive to see what sorts of problems might arise if these assumptions are relaxed.

For brevity, let us focus on the cross-sectional capitalization case. Suppose first that the burden of equilibrating household migration were to fall on the labor market rather than the property market. (Note that this cannot happen in the above model because the size and composition of the population in each jurisdiction is exogenously fixed.) One could imagine a situation where entry to comparatively attractive jurisdictions would depress wages, rather than, or in addition to, increasing property values. Clearly, results like (4.5) and (4.7) must be modified in such cases. Most writers in local public finance, however, would argue that Tiebout-type arguments are valid only in the context of household migration among jurisdictions *within* a given metropolitan area, and that in this context is is reasonable to assume that the employment and residence decisions can be made independently. If a household is able to work in a given location and reside elsewhere, it is appropriate to assume that income does not vary with the residential locational choice.[43]

Now consider what happens when jurisdictions differ in other respects than local public goods. In a typical metropolitan area, for example, localities will have differing air quality, access to grant aid from higher level governments, technology for producing local public goods, types of houses, racial mix, etc. If these are all unaffected by changes in local public good provision, they are irrelevant for the comparative statics capitalization results. From the cross-sectional perspective, however, these variations are im-

---

[43] In the analysis of household migration among metropolitan areas, by contrast, the opportunity to change jobs and obtain a higher wage may be of paramount importance, and variations in property values may be less significant. See, e.g., Rosen [307] for a discussion of inter-city wage differentials as a measure of the monetized value of amenities.

portant. They will be reflected in property values along with local public service differentials, thus invalidating the simple derivations of (4.5) and (4.7). On the other hand, it may be possible to control statistically for these other interjurisdictional variations, which amounts conceptually to inferring how property values would vary with public services conditional on all other attributes. This method is in fact used in all cross-section regressions. In effect, cross-section studies attempt to construct hedonic price indexes through observations drawn from implicit markets. The derivatives in (4.5) and (4.7) are then interpreted as partial derivatives, with respect to the level of local public good provision, of the hedonic price index. One difficulty with such an approach is determining an appropriate functional form for estimation, especially since the implicit value of different attributes, including public services, will generally vary over the data points in the attribute space. In addition, public services and other attributes may be highly correlated, precluding reliable estimation of the implicit values of individual attributes.[44]

Before concluding this discussion of our first model with capitalization effects, it is instructive to note the role of certain crucial assumptions in this model *vis-à-vis* private sector efficiency. First, the housing stock is fixed. As a consequence, the property tax does not distort the housing market, and hence it does not produce any deadweight losses. The absence of tax distortions is significant in itself, but it is especially important here because the Samuelsonian condition does *not* characterize (second-best) optimal public expenditures when such distortions are present.[45] By way of contrast to

---

[44] See Rosen [306] on implicit markets. There are many applications of this type of analysis in urban economics. The air pollution and property value debate has already been mentioned above. In addition, see, e.g., Mieszkowski and Saper [240], the studies in Diamond and Tolley [102], Roback [293], and the literature on race and property values, including Bailey [14], and, for a review and further references, Yinger [387]. The standard monocentric urban model in which transportation costs include travel time, the value of which is not directly observable, provides another example. In such models, land or house values must vary with distance from the CBD in such a way as to compensate households for the cost of commuting. By observation of the former, the latter can be inferred. See, e.g., Mohring [249] for an early example of such an approach. Below, we provide an example of this type of model. See also Kanemoto [198] for a review of such techniques.

[45] Among numerous studies in the optimal tax literature dealing with this point, see Atkinson and Stern [11], Atkinson and Stiglitz [12], Diamond and Mirrlees [100, 101], Topham [351, 352], Usher [354], and Wildasin [370, 374].

the Brueckner assumption, consider a model such as that of Sonstelie and Portney [333]. Here, property taxes are assumed to finance local spending, housing is a produced good with non-zero supply elasticity, and the Samuelsonian condition is shown to hold when property values have been maximized in all jurisdictions. This is a striking result. But because the property tax is distortionary, it is incorrect to infer that expenditure efficiency is achieved in this situation.

A further consequence of the fixity of the housing stock is the fixity of population. If assumptions are made to fix the composition of the population as well (as in the above discussion), or if all congestion and crowding effects depend only on the total population and not on its composition, the property tax will ensure attainment of locational efficiency.

Model II. Let us now consider a second model, from Wildasin [366, 367, 375], in which capitalization can be studied. This model, which differs from the foregoing in several respects, is designed to shed light on cross-sectional capitalization. Suppose first that the total amount of land available for residential consumption in each jurisdiction, T', is exogenously fixed, say because of fixity of jurisdictional boundaries and/or zoning constraints, and is the same for all jurisdictions. In contrast to the preceding model, residential land is perfectly divisible and homogenous. Given competitive markets, all land in locality i must therefore trade at the same gross-of-tax price. Because we assume a local property tax at a uniform effective rate τ_{ir} for all land, the net-of-tax price of land, r_i, must also be uniform within community i. Preferences are as in Section 2 and the Brueckner model, except that there are no interpersonal crowding effects. For reasons suggested above, incomes are given independently of locational choice, say w^k for a household of type k. Thus, the budget constraint for a k-type household residing in locality i is

$$x_i^k + r_i(1 + \tau_{ir})t_i^k + pq_i^k = w^k. \tag{4.9}$$

Assume that localities have identical technologies for producing local public goods, given by a common cost function $C(n_i, z_i)$, and we assume no congestion of public services, i.e., $C_{ik} = 0$ all i, k. Thus, local public goods are purely public. Localities use only land taxes to finance their expenditures, which, by Section 2 (Case 2), guarantees locational efficiency. The local government budget constraint

$$\tau_{ir}r_i T^r = C(n_i, z_i) \qquad (4.10)$$

allows one to eliminate $\tau_{ir}r_i = C/T^r$ and to suppose, in effect, that the local tax is simply a per-unit land tax.

Communities differ in no respect other than their levels of public good provision and taxes. Let $v^k(r_i + C(n_i, z_i)/T^r, p, w^k, z_i)$ denote the indirect utility function for type-k households. In equilibrium, all households will be located in jurisdictions in which their utilities are maximized. Let us suppose there are many communities, providing levels of public good that vary only marginally so that households face a continuous spectrum of choice. As a condition of equilibrium, the price of land must vary continuously with the level of public good. If we also assume differentiability, the condition for utility-maximizing locational choice is that, for a household of type k locating in jurisdiction i,

$$MRS_i^k = t_i^k\left(\frac{C_{iz}}{T^r} + \frac{\partial r_i}{\partial z_i}\right) \qquad (4.11)$$

This follows, like (4.5), from standard properties of the indirect utility function. Aggregating across households in community i,

$$\sum_k n_i^k MRS_i^k = C_{iz} + T^r \frac{\partial r_i}{\partial z_i}, \qquad (4.12)$$

using the land market equilibrium condition $\sum_k n_i^k t_i^k = T^r$.

These results imply cross-sectional capitalization of the net benefits of local public goods. As in Eqs (4.5) and (4.7), one can use (4.11) and (4.12) to infer individual household MRS's, and to judge whether the Samuelsonian condition for (first-best) public expenditure efficiency is achieved. In the special case where land values are equal in all jurisdictions ($r_i = \bar{r}$ all i), (4.12) implies that public goods are optimally supplied. Moreover, with equal land prices (4.11) shows that each household's marginal benefit from public good provision is equated to its marginal tax-price, $(t_i^k/T^r)C_{iz}$. Thus, as in the version of the preceding model with homogenous but indivisible parcels, here the conditions for Lindahl equilibrium are satisfied with homogenous divisible parcels. Unlike the previous case, however, not all households in a jurisdiction need have identical MRS's in a Lindahl–Tiebout equilibrium. However, if one defines a household's "preference" for the local public good as the amount at which its marginal benefit and tax-price are equated, it is still true that households have identical preferences in the Lindahl equilibrium.

Under certain assumptions, this model can be extended to accommodate impure local public goods also. Suppose we allow the cost of local public good provision to depend on total local population, i.e., we have a cost function $C(n_i, z_i)$ such that $C_{ik} = C_{ik'} = C_{in}$, say, for all k, k'. Let each jurisdiction provide a given amount of public good, and suppose ideal head taxes are imposed such that all congestion costs are internalized. Thus, the head tax in jurisdiction i satisfies $\tau_{in} = C_{in}$. The local government budget constraint becomes

$$C(n_i, z_i) = \sum_k n_i^k \tau_{in} + \tau_{ir} r_i T^r. \qquad (4.13)$$

We assume that the total population of each jurisdiction, and the corresponding head tax, vary smoothly with respect to the level of public good. Then the value of z_i that maximizes the indirect utility function $v^k(r_i[1 + \tau_{ir}], p, w^k - \tau_{in}, z_i)$ is characterized by

$$MRS_i^k - t_i^k \frac{d(r_i\tau_{ir})}{dz_i} - \frac{d\tau_{in}}{dz_i} = \frac{dr_i}{dz_i} t_i^k. \qquad (4.14)$$

Aggregating and using (4.13) yields (4.12), which re-establishes the capitalization result in the presence of congestion. If head taxes are not optimally set, however, the resulting expression differs from (4.12) by a term reflecting uninternalized congestion effects.

Model III. As a third and final example, consider the case of public good provision in a monocentric city. (For examples of such models, see Polinsky and Shavell [286] and Kanemoto [196].) Suppose that households of type k living at distance ξ from a central business district (CBD) incur pecuniary travel expense of $\gamma^k(\xi)$, and earn a wage of w^k in the CBD. For simplicity, this is their only source of income. Let $(x^k(\xi), t^k(\xi), q^k(\xi))$ be the private good consumption of a k-type at location ξ, and let $z(\xi)$ be the amount of public good available to households at ξ. We abstract from all crowding and congestion effects. Let all land within the city be homogeneous and let $r(\xi)$ denote the price of land at location ξ. Suppose that households located at ξ must pay a property tax at rate $\tau_r(\xi)$. A k-type living at ξ thus faces a budget constraint

$$x^k(\xi) + r(\xi)[1 + \tau_r(\xi)]t^k(\xi) + pq^k(\xi) = w^k - \gamma^k(\xi). \quad (4.15)$$

The indirect utility function $v^k(r(\xi)[1 + \tau_r(\xi)], p, w^k - \gamma^k(\xi), z(\xi))$ shows the maximum utility attainable at point ξ.

For simplicity, suppose that all k-types live in an interval $[\underline{\xi}^k, \bar{\xi}^k]$. (The analysis extends trivially for the case of many such intervals.) In equilibrium, free locational choice implies

$$v^k(r(\xi)[1 + \tau_r(\xi)], p, w^k - \gamma^k(\xi), z(\xi)) = \bar{v}^k \quad \text{for all } \xi\varepsilon[\underline{\xi}^k, \bar{\xi}^k]$$
$$(4.16)$$

where $\bar{v}^k$ is the equilibrium utility for k-types. If $\tau_r(\xi)$, $\gamma^k(\xi)$, and $z(\xi)$ are differentiable in ξ, (4.16) implies, via Roy's identity,

$$t^k(\xi)r'(\xi) = MRS^k(\xi)z'(\xi) - \gamma^{k\prime}(\xi) - t^k(\xi)r(\xi)\tau_r'(\xi), \quad (4.17)$$

which shows that cross-sectional net benefit capitalization obtains within the urban area, but that allowance must be made for the effect of transportation costs on the spatial variation of land values.

A comparative static capitalization result can also be established if one assumes that the urban area is small and open, i.e., if $\bar{u}^k$ can be taken as parametrically given when considering variations in public good provision. Let $\eta(\xi)$ be some smooth function, and define $z(\xi, \varepsilon) = z(\xi) + \varepsilon\eta(\xi)$. Suppose there is a cost functional for local public good provision given by $C(z(\xi, \varepsilon))$. (Recall that congestion effects have been assumed absent.) Total tax revenues are given by

$$T = \int_{\underline{\xi}}^{\bar{\xi}} \tau_r(\xi)r(\xi)n^k(\xi)t^k(\xi) = \int_{\underline{\xi}}^{\bar{\xi}} \tau_r(\xi)r(\xi)\theta(\xi) \quad (4.18)$$

where $\underline{\xi}$, $\bar{\xi}$ are the inner and outer boundaries of the residential area of the city (taken as exogenously given, for simplicity), $n^k(\xi)$ is the density of type-k households at ξ, and $\theta(\xi)$ is the density of residential land at ξ. (Strictly speaking, the first integral in (4.18) is the sum of integrals over the intervals $[\underline{\xi}^k, \bar{\xi}^k]$.) Equation (4.18) reflects the equilibrium condition in the land market, $n^k(\xi)t^k(\xi) = \theta(\xi)$.

We now consider a marginal increase in ε, with the tax function $\tau(\xi)$ varying to insure that $dC/d\varepsilon = dT/d\varepsilon$. By (4.16) and Roy's identity,

$$MRS^k(\xi)\eta(\xi) - t^k(\xi)\frac{d[r(\xi)\tau_r(\xi)]}{d\varepsilon} = t^k(\xi)\frac{dr(\xi)}{d\varepsilon}. \qquad (4.19)$$

Multiplying (4.19) by $n^k(\xi)$, using market-clearing in the land market, and using the government budget-balance constraint, we have

$$\int_{\underline{\xi}}^{\bar{\xi}} n^k(\xi)MRS^k(\xi)\eta(\xi) - \frac{dC}{d\varepsilon} = \int_{\underline{\xi}}^{\bar{\xi}} \theta(\xi)\frac{dr(\xi)}{d\varepsilon}. \qquad (4.20)$$

The term on the right is the change in aggregate land value, while the terms on the left show the aggregate marginal net benefit of the policy change. This establishes comparative static capitalization for this model.

From the analysis of the above models, certain results seem evident. For comparative static capitalization to occur, each jurisdiction should be a utility-taker. The results of Starrett [339], who considers comparative static capitalization at length, show that it requires stringent assumptions on preferences in the absence of this condition. This also is confirmed by the analyses of Polinsky and Shavell [286], Kanemoto [196], Pines [279], and others. For cross-sectional capitalization, we need continuous spatial variation in the policy variables, with other jurisdictional attributes held fixed. In the absence of these assumptions, the result naturally breaks down. Pauly [275], among others, presents a model in which the number of jurisdictions is sufficiently small that almost all households would suffer discrete utility losses by moving to other jurisdictions. Only fortuitously are property values equalized across jurisdictions in the Pauly model, and, whether zero capitalization occurs or not, one cannot draw inferences about efficiency of public spending from cross-sectional regression estimates.

The above remarks identify a common attribute of the comparative static and cross-sectional capitalization results, namely, that the welfare of the residents of a jurisdiction are unaffected by policy changes. In the utility-taking case that we have already discussed, this is explicit. It is implicit in the case of the cross-sectional capitalization results, where the stationarity of utility with respect to local policy (implied by utility-maximizing locational choice), derived within a framework where households face a continuous spectrum of policies, insures that the next best location for each household is just as good as the initial equilibrium. A change in local policy by a single jurisdiction can be offset by moves to neighboring (in policy space) jurisdictions such that no resident suffers a utility loss. It is intriguing that benefits can be measured through capitalization when local policies appear to be irrelevant for welfare. This raises a question about the true welfare significance of capitalization effects, which we clarify in Section 4.3.

Despite their limitations, the positive results on capitalization that are available are of considerable interest. The conditions under which they hold, though non-trivial, might nevertheless be approximately satisfied under existing or conceivable alternative institutional structures. Above all, these results, however limited, present cases where the fundamental problem of obtaining information on preferences for publicly-provided goods can be resolved. The next subsection discusses how this information might be exploited.

Two important issues involving capitalization and allocative efficiency seem to require further study. First, what sorts of capitalization results obtain in second-best situations? If less than perfect head taxes are used to deal with congestion effects, and, especially, if distortionary local taxes are used, what information is imparted by cross-section or time-series regressions of property values on policy variables? Second, to what extent does the variation in public good levels observed in actual urban economies adequately approximate the continuum assumed in derivations of cross-sectional capitalization results? (Alternatively, how adequately satisfied is the utility-taking assumption that underlies the comparative statics capitalization results?) Intuitively, it might seem that large metropolitan areas containing scores of suburbs offer a sufficient number of choices that the models should apply. At what point, then, does the number of jurisdictions become too small? Some approximation theory needs to be developed before one can interpret the results of empirical studies with complete confidence.

Capitalization and pension funding. The capitalization models discussed above are really static models of equilibrium price determination. Like other static models, they can be interpreted as dynamic models of an economy in a stationary state. They are quite useful despite (or because of) this simplifying characteristic, since they still contain adequate structure for the primary question at hand, namely the effect of local government policy on property values. They cannot, however, shed much light on explicitly intertemporal questions. For one example of such a question, consider the compensation package offered to municipal employees. This generally consists of a mix of current wage payments and deferred compensation in the form of pensions. Suppose that a locality is not legally bound to fund fully its pension obligations, that is, it can employ workers now, thus obligating itself to future pension payments, without setting aside current resources to accumulate in a fund sufficient to finance those future payments. Then the degree of funding chosen by the locality in effect determines the intertemporal structure of taxation required to finance current public services, that is, how much will be paid by current vs. future taxpayers. In a world of mobile households, one could imagine that current residents would opt for underfunding of pensions, hoping to leave the jurisdiction before pension obligations fall due. In this way they might be able to shift the cost of public services to future residents.

The obvious obstacle to successful operation of such a scheme is that future residents may not be so easily tricked. If they anticipate having to pay for previously unfunded pensions, they will offer less for property in the jurisdiction. If unfunded pension liabilities are fully capitalized, the initial residents will not be able to shift the burden of provision of public services to future residents and the incentive to underfund disappears. In contrast to the essentially static models discussed previously, the key question here is whether a change in intertemporal tax structure—in this case, tax deferral through underfunding of pensions—results in offsetting changes in property values through capitalization effects.

Municipal pension funding has been discussed by Mumy [251], Epple and Schipper [114], Inman [190, 191, 192] and Ochs and Merz [269]. The analysis in these papers shows that the incentive to fund or underfund pensions depends not only on undercapitalization of future pension obligations, but on tax arbitrage possibilities arising from differential federal government tax treatment of income accruing to individual resident-taxpayers and the return to pension funds. Epple and Schipper do find evidence of substantial capitalization of pension obligations, and attribute pension underfunding largely to intertemporal smoothing of tax liabilities so as to minimize excess burden, along the lines of Barro [20]. Inman [191], however, does not find the excess burden argument persuasive, at least for plausible values of relevant parameters. Rather, he finds [192] evidence of undercapitalization of pension liabilities, and suggests that pension underfunding is nonetheless limited because of the fear of public employees that unfunded pension obligations may not be honored. As Epple and Schipper point out, however, capitalization of unfunded benefits would also be less than complete if local taxpayers anticipate higher-level government assistance in the event of a failure to meet pension payments. This provides an alternative explanation for Inman's undercapitalization findings that does not rely on informational asymmetries. Thus, the empirical fundings on capitalization and pension underfunding are somewhat mixed. Perhaps additional theoretical and empirical work will help resolve this issue.

4.3. Fiscal profitability and local policy

It is quite clear that the theory of tax and expenditure capitalization, which deals with exogenously given cross-section or comparative-statics variation in public good provision, does not provide a positive theory of public expenditure determination. When capitalization results are valid, however, it is easy to envisage models in which the agents responsible for controlling public expenditure find their welfare linked to property values. Such agents could be entrepreneurs owning land and developing a new town, powerful landlord interests in an established jurisdiction, or voters who are owner-occupiers. A number of studies in recent years have developed one or another of these approaches. They have in common the feature that profit opportunities are exploited in equilibrium, so that (because capitalization results hold) an equilibrium is efficient. Such results vindicate the Tiebout intuition, since they portray a decentralized equilibrium system in which Samuelson's fundamental preference revelation problem is solved. There are several ways one can classify the literature in this area. One way is in terms of the underlying capitalization results, i.e., cross-sectional vs. comparative static. Another way is in terms of the agent(s) making local public policy, mainly either profit-maximizing entrepreneurs, with no political decisionmaking process *per se,* or voters. We shall begin with entrepreneurial models of utility-taking localities.

Profit-maximizing localities. The notion that local government policies are chosen in such a way as to maximize land or property values, or at least that this is an important element in the policy process, has been discussed by Margolis [215], Negishi [259], and others. Our main interest here is in the normative properties of equilibria: Does profit-maximizing behavior lead to efficient outcomes?

The Brueckner model discussed earlier provides a convenient starting point. Though the previous analysis was directed toward the capitalization problem, it is easily adapted to our present purpose. Suppose that each locality is controlled by a developer who owns all properties. Since all parcels contain an amount of property (land or housing) that is regarded as fixed for the time period under consideration, property taxes become a redundant instrument that may as well be ignored. The developer in community i receives a net return of

$$\sum_k n_i^k r_i^k t_i^k - C_i(n_i, z_i), \qquad (4.21)$$

which is to be maximized by choice of z_i and (r_i^k) subject to

$$v_i^k(r_i^k, p, w_i^k, z_i) = \bar{v}^k, \qquad (4.22)$$

which takes the place of (4.3) when $\tau_{ir}^k = 0$. Recalling that p and w_i^k are taken as exogenously fixed, one can use (4.22) to solve implicitly for each r_i^k as a function of z_i. Hence

$$MRS_i^k = t_i^k \frac{\partial r_i^k}{\partial z_i} \qquad (4.23)$$

as in (4.5), and the first-order condition for maximization of (4.21) becomes

$$\sum_k n_i^k MRS_i^k - C_{iz} = 0, \qquad (4.24)$$

recalling that the vector n_i is exogenously fixed. Thus, profit-maximizing developers will act so as to achieve expenditure efficiency. Notice that these developers do not actually know or care about the preferences of the residents in their jurisdictions. They merely are assumed to be able to discover or infer how the demand for property responds to the instruments (public services) under their control.

As a second illustration of an entrepreneurial model, let us adapt the model of Section 2. A developer in locality i owns T_i, now interpreted as a given amount of homogeneous land, which can be sold to households for consumption at a price r_i. The developer can also levy a head tax τ_{in}^k on type k households and can determine the level of public good provision z_i (which may be regarded as a vector if desired). Assume that no households initially hold any land, and ignore the possibility of agricultural land use.

Since local private good production is characterized by constant returns to scale (the production function F is assumed linear homogenous), the demand for workers and land is a correspondence, not a function. To deal with this problem, it is technically convenient to suppose that the developer controls the local production process as well. Later we show how private production could be decentralized without changing the results.

Thus, dropping the head tax for the moment as a separate instrument, suppose that the developer in i offers a net income I_i^k to workers of type k. This net income, the price charged for land, and the level of public services must ensure that the exogenously-given level of utility is achieved. If

$$v_i^k(r_i, p, I_i^k, n_i, z_i) = \bar{v}^k, \qquad (4.25)$$

then I_i^k must be identically equal to the expenditure function

$$I_i^k = e_i^k(r_i, p, n_i, z_i, \bar{v}^k). \qquad (4.26)$$

The developer's profit will be

$$r_i \sum_k n_i^k t_i^k + F_i(n_i, t_i^P) - \sum_k n_i^k e_i^k - C_i(n_i, z_i), \qquad (4.27)$$

which is to be maximized with respect to (r_i, n_i, z_i, t_i^P) subject to an overall land constraint of the form (2.3) (with $t_i^A = 0$), where $t_i^k = t_i^k(r_i, p, n_i, z_i, \bar{v}^k)$ is the compensated demand for land. Using the land constraint to eliminate t_i^P, we have the first-order conditions for a maximum of (4.27):

$$r_i: \sum_k n_i^k t_i^k + r_i \sum_k n_i^k \frac{\partial t_i^k}{\partial r_i} - F_{it} \sum_k n_i^k \frac{\partial t_i^k}{\partial r_i} - \sum_k n_i^k t_i^k = 0$$

(4.28)

$$n_i^k: r_i t_i^k + r_i \sum_{k'} n_i^{k'} \frac{\partial t_i^{k'}}{\partial n_i^k} + F_{ik} - F_{it} t_i^k - F_{it} \sum_{k'} n_i^{k'} \frac{\partial t_i^{k'}}{\partial n_i^k}$$

$$- e_i^k - \sum_{k'} n_i^{k'} \frac{\partial e_i^{k'}}{\partial n_i^k} - C_{ik} = 0 \quad (4.29)$$

$$z_i: r_i \sum_k n_i^k \frac{\partial t_i^k}{\partial z_i} - F_{it} \sum_k n_i^k \frac{\partial t_i^k}{\partial z_i} - \sum_k n_i^k \frac{\partial e_i^k}{\partial z_i} - C_{iz} = 0. \quad (4.30)$$

By (4.28), $r_i = F_{it}$ in equilibrium. Using this in (4.29) and (4.30) and letting $MCC_{ik}^{k'} = \partial e_i^{k'}/\partial n_i^k$ and $MRS_i^k = -\partial e_i^k/\partial z_i$, one has

$$e_i^k = F_{ik} - C_{ik} - \sum_{k'} n_i^{k'} MCC_{ik}^{k'}$$

(4.31)

$$\sum_k n_i^k MRS_i^k = C_{iz}.$$

(4.32)

Now it is clear that the developer's profit-maximizing solution can be sustained as an equilibrium with profit-maximizing private producers, where land is bought from producers at price r_i, workers are hired at wages $w_i^k = F_{ik}$, and head taxes are imposed at rates

$$\tau_{in}^k = C_{ik} + \sum_{k'} n_i^{k'} MCC_{ik}^{k'}.$$

(4.33)

In such a case, a developer's profits,

$$r_i \left(\sum_k n_i^k t_i^k + t_i^P \right) + \sum_k n_i^k \tau_{in}^k - C_i(n_i, z_i),$$

(4.34)

would be equal to the expression in (4.27), and all markets would clear.

It is evident that this developer's equilibrium is characterized by both public expenditure efficiency (4.32) and locational efficiency (4.33). Thus, given the utility-taking assumption, profit-maximizing entrepreneurs price congestion externalities efficiently, so that jurisdictions contain the correct numbers and types of households, and they solve the Tiebout–Samuelson problem of efficient public good provision.

One can now see the precise welfare implications of the comparative static capitalization results discussed in Section 4.2. When policy in one locality changes, no mobile household's utility can change, by hypothesis. However, developers experience a real income change precisely equal to the change in land values. Thus, if any one locality improves its policies, this will make the developer better off.

While the above presentation is new, aspects of the results obtained have appeared in a number of studies, including Henderson [172], Kanemoto [196], Schweizer [317], Sonstelie and Portney [333], Stiglitz [344, 345], and Wildasin [373].[46] We need only 'add that developers' profits in (4.34) will be driven to zero if "entry" into this industry is free. In this case, the (modified) Henry George theorem will hold. If entry is not free, however—e.g., if all land is already attached to some jurisdiction, and jurisdictional boundaries are fixed—then developers' profits will not vanish in equilibrium, and the Henry George result will not hold.

The theory of clubs. At this point we digress briefly to discuss the theory of clubs. In this theory, initiated by Buchanan [75], households are assembled into groups which jointly consume some public good or service, possibly with individually-determined rates of utilization.[47] Questions examined in the literature include char-

---

[46] The Henderson model is particularly interesting because it incorporates a distortionary local tax on produced housing, and explains how the level of public good provided by entrepreneurs will be second-best optimal, conditional on this distortion.

[47] Our discussion is most closely related to Berglas and Pines [31], although for simplicity we ignore the possibility of variable use of the club good. See Berglas [30] for discussion of variable use with two or more public services. Starrett [341] also provides a thorough analytical discussion of clubs models. For additional references and a survey, see Sandler and Tschirhart [315]. Since there is some debate about the point in the literature (Sandler and Tschirhart [316], Berglas and Pines [32]), it may be noted that the following analysis does not impose any constraint on financing mechanisms in the characterization of the optimal composition and number of clubs. Indeed, in our first-best approach, any concept of financing is quite irrelevant. We do show, however, that a zero-profit condition obtains in the equilibrium system that sustains the optimum if "continuous" replicability of clubs is assumed to be feasible. (See Eqs. (4.41), (4.42), (4.45) below.)

acterization of optima, existence of (and definition of) equilibria, and equivalence of equilibria and optima. The structure of the clubs models obviously bears a close resemblance to local governments. Perhaps the major characteristic differentiating the club models from those of the type discussed above is the absence of spatial structure or locational fixity. This is significant because optimal club size is not achieved until economies of scale (with respect to population) in public good provision are exhausted. Hence a club optimum is generally characterized by minimum average cost = marginal congestion cost, i.e., locally constant per capita costs.

To illustrate this fact and its implications, it is convenient to adapt the model of Section 2. Drop t_i^k as a consumption good, and suppose that there is a fixed stock of productive resources T available to the economy as a whole which is used in economy-wide production processes yielding $F(\{N^k\}, t^P)$ of all-purpose private good and $\phi(t^A)$ of agricultural output.

To begin with, hold the level of z_i, a single public good, arbitrarily fixed. Then the remaining problem of finding an efficient allocation of households to a fixed number of clubs can basically be formulated using constraints (2.1)–(2.6), except that (2.1) and (2.2) involve the aggregate production functions F and ϕ instead of F_i and ϕ_i, and (2.3) becomes an economy-wide constraint $T - t^P - t^A = 0$. First-order conditions like (2.7)–(2.12) follow, yielding a modified version of (2.13):

$$-\left(x_i^k + \frac{\xi}{\mu} q_i^k\right) - \left(C_{ik} + \sum_{k'} n_i^{k'} MCC_{ik}^{k'}\right) = \frac{\pi^k}{\mu} \qquad (4.35)$$

for all i, k with $n_i^k > 0$.

If one wishes to allow for a variable number of clubs, there is a possible problem with discreteness of club size. To obviate this problem, suppose that any number β_i of clubs of type i can be formed, where β_i is a continuous variable. Then we must rewrite the constraints as

$$F(\{N^k\}, t^P) - \sum_i \beta_i n_i x_i - \sum \beta_i C_i(n_i, z_i) = 0 \qquad (4.36)$$

$$\phi(t^A) - \sum_i \beta_i n_i q_i = 0 \qquad (4.37)$$

$$T = t^P + t^A \qquad (4.38)$$

$$N^k - \sum_i \beta_i n_i^k = 0, \qquad (4.39)$$

while (2.5) and (2.6) are essentially the same. We still obtain (4.35) as a first-order condition, but we also have the first-order condition for β_i, which, after division by μ, is

$$-\left(n_i x_i + \frac{\xi}{\mu} n_i q_i + C_i\right) = \sum_k \frac{\pi^k}{\mu} n_i^k, \qquad \text{all } i. \qquad (4.40)$$

By (4.35), this yields

$$C_i = \sum_k \left(C_{ik} + \sum_{k'} n_i^{k'} MCC_{ik}^{k'}\right) n_{ik}, \qquad \text{all } i. \qquad (4.41)$$

Thus, total cost is equal to the sum of many marginal costs times quantities. In the special case where there is only one household type and no interpersonal crowding effect, this reduces to costs per capita equal to marginal cost, or minimum average cost with respect to population.

Now it should be clear how an optimal location pattern, with or without a fixed number of clubs, can be sustained as an equilibrium. Let club i impose a head tax $\tau_{in}^k = C_{ik} + \sum_{k'} n_i^{k'} MCC_{ik}^{k'}$ on households of type k, making up extra revenue requirements (or disposing of surplus revenues) in the fixed-club case by some locationally-neutral tax: a uniform (economy-wide) wage tax, or taxes on agricultural profits or rents to fixed resources. If the number of clubs is variable, (4.41) implies that this head tax provides all necessary revenue. This is the locally-constant per capita cost outcome mentioned above.

So far, we have not discussed how z_i is determined by each club, nor indeed how the number of clubs is determined in equilibrium. Suppose, following Berglas and Pines [31], that each club is run by an entrepreneur whose profit is equal to

$$\tau_{in} n_i - C_i(n_i z_i), \qquad (4.42)$$

which is maximized by choice of (n_i, z_i) subject to a utility-taking constraint. That is, households facing budget constraints

$$x_i^k + r q_i^k + \tau_{in}^k = I^k, \qquad (4.43)$$

where I^k is wages and profits (not location-dependent) of type-k individuals, must achieve the level of utility obtainable elsewhere, i.e.,

$$v_i^k(p, I^k - \tau_{in}^k, n_i, z_i) = \tilde{v}^k. \qquad (4.44)$$

Equation (4.44) can be solved for τ_{in}^k as a function of (n_i, z_i), the derivatives of τ_{in}^k being the marginal congestion costs from interpersonal crowding effects and the marginal willingness to pay for public services. The first-order conditions for maximization of (4.42) with respect to (n_i, z_i) then become

$$\tau_{in}^k = C_{ik} + \sum_{k'} n_i^{k'} MCC_{ik}^{k'} \qquad (4.45)$$

$$\sum_k n_i^k MRS_i^k = C_{iz}. \qquad (4.46)$$

Conditions (4.35), (4.43), and (4.45) yield locational efficiency, i.e., the correct assignment of households to clubs is sustained in equilibrium. Equation (4.46) of course implies expenditure efficiency. If the number of clubs is fixed, the analysis is complete. With a variable number of clubs, if an optimum is characterized by a large number of each type of club so that discreteness of club size can be ignored, free entry will drive (4.42) to zero, insuring satisfaction of the efficiency condition (4.41).

The above model is closely related to the local public goods model of land-value-maximizing entrepreneurs discussed earlier. But note that the absence of spatially fixed goods in the clubs model means that a minimum average cost condition (4.41) obtains at an optimum. For club goods that are purely public, therefore, the optimal club size is indefinitely large, and the utility-taking entrepreneurial model, with its competitive flavor, must break down in this case. Indeed, this is true whenever optimal club size is "large." By contrast, this problem need not arise in models with locationally-fixed commodities, for which optimal population size may be small even in the absence of congestibility or crowding effects.

The absence of locationally-fixed resources is also significant for the positive theory of clubs. As we have seen, an equilibrium theory can be based on entrepreneurial profit-maximizing both with and without spatial fixity. On the other hand, many voting models exploit the existence of land or property in a central way. As an example, the standard median-voter models typically use property ownership to determine tax-prices for voters. Moreover, in voting models (to be discussed shortly) which incorporate household mobility, the property market is a crucial feature of the environment in which voting takes place, giving rise to results qualitatively quite different from those of, say, the spaceless voting model of Westhoff [357] discussed earlier.

Finally, note that property taxation, which is the historically predominant financing mechanism at the local level in many countries, has no counterpart in a spaceless club. These observations by no means obviate the usefulness of clubs theory for problems in urban public finance. They do, however, suggest reasons why clubs models may not be directly applicable for either normative or positive analysis of certain issues.

Profit-maximizing entrepreneurs: further considerations. We conclude our discussion of entrepreneurial models with a mention of some extensions and limitations.

Henderson [171, 172] has studied the developer's problem in a two-period setting. There is assumed to be a set of initial residents in a locality, to whom the developer sells lots in the first period which they continue to inhabit in the second period. The developer provides public services in both periods, financed by a land tax. In the second period, additional lots may be sold to new entrants to the community, who must achieve an exogenously-given level of utility. The new entrants also pay taxes and consume local public services. Henderson shows that when developers must offer a given level of lifetime utility to initial residents, which involves making a credible commitment in period 1 to period 2 policies, a Pareto-efficient outcome is achieved. This indeed is like the static utility-taking model discussed above.[48]

However, Henderson also points out that developers would find it

---

[48] One question that might be raised about the Henderson model is why initial residents are constrained to accept the second-period decisions of developers. In particular, the possibility that initial residents must be guaranteed a specified minimum level of *second-period* utility could be explored.

profitable to renege in period 2 on commitments made earlier. In this specific model, the reason is that allowing second-period entrants to buy smaller than planned lots results in shifting more of the second-period tax burden to existing residents, which the developer captures as a higher sale price on lots sold to new entrants. Fiscal zoning and other possible institutional arrangements might arise to prevent developers from engaging in this behavior.

More generally, one would expect similar issues to arise in other intertemporal models of community development, with perhaps different implications depending on the assumptions about financing of local expenditures, congestibility, etc. This issue clearly seems to warrant further investigation.

Another issue that has not yet been investigated in the literature is what happens when the utility-taking assumption breaks down. Entrepreneurs might then find that their decisions affect the market environment (required utility levels) of other entrepreneurs. It would be interesting to explore the strategic interactions that would result.

Finally, we must note the obvious fact that entrepreneurial models of local government behavior are, for the most part, descriptively false in a conspicuous way: most local government policies are not chosen by profit-maximizers, they are the outcome of a *political* process. One should not be so naive as to suppose that profit opportunities are not felt, one way or another, by political decisionmakers. However, it would be useful to present a more explicit treatment of the public choice mechanism, which would either incorporate other possible interests than land value maximization, or explain why this is the only interest that matters. Eventually, some empirical testing of entrepreneurial vs. competing models of local government behavior should force this issue.

Voting models. We now explore voting models which, in contrast to the median voter models of Section 3, explicitly incorporate a market for property. This is an important difference because if a homeowner is to vote on, say, some incremental public expenditures, this can result in a change in the value of property. If this capital gain or loss is correctly anticipated, how will it affect the household's voting behavior? Will concern about wealth changes supplant, wholly or partly, the marginal benefit/tax-price considerations underlying the standard median voter model? This issue has been studied, theoretically and empirically, by Epple, *et al.* [112, 113], Martinez-Vazquez [217], Rose-Ackerman [301], Sonstelie and Portney [333, 335], Stiglitz [345], Wildasin [368, 369, 375], and Yinger [388, 389, 390], *inter alia.*

The most clear-cut results emerge in the case where cross-section capitalization obtains. Recall the model of the preceding subsection, in which each one of many localities contains the same amount T^r of homogeneous land and provides a single pure public good using identical technology. In place of the budget constraint (4.9), however, suppose now that households have initial endowments of land. In particular, let us focus on the simple special case where each household initially owns land in only one locality. Since household types are defined in terms of both preferences and endowments, this means that households initially holding land in different localities must be regarded as different types. Thus, letting $\bar{t}_i^k$ be the initial endowment of land by a type-k household in locality i, we have

$$\sum_k N^k \bar{t}_i^k = T^r, \qquad (4.47)$$

for all localities. Those households for whom $\bar{t}_i^k > 0$ are referred to as *initial residents* of locality i.

Now suppose the following sequence of events. Each locality determines a level of public good provision z_i through a referendum in which only initial residents can vote. Conditional on the outcome of these choices, a market equilibrium is established in which all households make utility-maximizing consumption and locational choices. This results in the determination of equilibrium land prices such that the price r_i in each locality i depends only on the level of public good provision selected by the voters there (given the decisions made by other localities): $r_i = r(z_i)$, where we call $r(z_i)$ the *equilibrium price function*. The voters in each locality are assumed to have known this equilibrium price function in advance of voting, and to have voted in the belief that the function itself is exogenously given by the market and does not depend on their political decision.

This last assumption, of course, reflects a perfect foresight, perfect competition view of the local public sector.[49]

Provided that there are (in equilibrium) many jurisdictions providing a wide range of levels of public good, the voters in a particular jurisdiction will all vote unanimously for a level of public good provision that maximizes the net value of land. The reason is evident from the budget constraint of a household initially holding land in jurisdiction i, contemplating entry into jurisdiction j:

$$x_j^k + \left[r(z_j) + \frac{c(z_j)}{L} \right] t_j^k + pq_j^k = w^k + r(z_i)\bar{t}_i^k, \qquad (4.48)$$

to be contrasted with (4.9). Once voting has occurred and an equilibrium land price function $r(z)$ has been established, the household will choose that locality j for which utility is maximized, subject to (4.48). It is obvious that at the voting stage, the choice of z_i can influence the budget constraint, and thus the final realized utility, only through its effect on $r(z_i)$, the price at which the household's land endowment is valued. Hence the household will vote for a level of z_i which maximizes $r(z_i)$. Since all land is homogenous, all voters in jurisdiction i will have the same maximand. The only equilibrium land price function which is compatible with equilibrium is one for which $r(z) = $ constant for all values of z, since no locality's voters would select a z yielding less than a maximum value of land. Recalling (4.11) and (4.12), it is evident that this politico-economic equilibrium is characterized by public expenditure efficiency, and the "pseudo-Lindahl equilibrium" condition will be satisfied as well.

---

[49] By contrast, Epple et al. [112, 113] and Rose-Ackerman [301] study voter behavior with less than perfect foresight. Epple et al., for example, suppose that households start in an initial equilibrium in the housing market, but that variations in local policy leave the net-of-tax price of housing unchanged, so that the gross-of-tax price rises by the marginal cost of public expenditure times the household's share of the property tax base. This, of course, would not be a correct perception of the change in equilibrium gross rents. In addition, households in this model do not actually own property, i.e., they experience no capital gains or losses from local policy changes. Thus, unlike the model presented above, there is no prospect for wealth-maximizing motives to drive voting behavior.

This voting model obviously has much in common with the entrepreneurial models. In fact, the voters in this model can be seen as entrepreneurs, in the sense that a Fisherian separation theorem holds such that their only objective, in the political decisionmaking part of their choice problem, is to maximize the value of their land holdings. The allocative efficiency property of the equilibrium would be unaffected if some voters were actually absentee landlords, or if local public expenditure decisions were made by city managers on incentive contracts with payoffs (bribes?) tied to land values. In this sense, voting by residents *per se* is not a crucial aspect of the public expenditure determination process in the model. What differentiates it most from the entrepreneurial model is that it permits any or all mobile households to own land. Land ownership sets up an inherent asymmetry between resident and non resident households that invalidates the utility-taking assumption underlying the entrepreneurial model.

Of course, in exchange for this added generality, the voting model requires stronger assumptions. In particular, cross-sectional capitalization requires that jurisdictions be numerous and diversified with respect to public expenditures, while not varying with respect to land endowments, etc. Let us briefly consider what happens when these assumptions break down. It is sufficient to suppose that some jurisdiction i provides a level of public good z_i that is discretely different from any other locality. Suppose that residents in i take the policies of other jurisdictions, and equilibrium prices elsewhere, as given. How then does a voter evaluate a marginal change in public spending? If z_i changes, the equilibrium price of property will change in i. The household will then either relocate or remain in the locality. If it relocates, it will wish to increase the value of its property, as we have already seen. But if the household is not on the margin of relocating—and this may characterize some or all households when no communities provide neighboring levels of the public good—it will actually consume the new level of z_i, and actually pay the new level of property taxes. It will not realize the capital gain or losses resulting from a change in equilibrium property values. Such a voter will, in short, act like those in the standard median voter models with immobile households, comparing marginal benefits and tax-prices of public expenditures and ignoring the wealth effects resulting from property value changes.

4.4. Alternative models of local government decision making

While we have reviewed a number of important approaches to the analysis of household mobility, community formation, and tax and expenditure policy determination, there are others which are not conveniently accommodated within the framework developed so far. This section focuses on alternative ways of modeling how groups of individuals may form and make collective decisions.

One alternative equilibrium concept that has been exploited in the local public good context is based on the idea of a public competitive equilibrium, introduced in the non-local context by Foley [128]. Foley argues that, while the detailed workings of a collective choice mechanism need not be specified, it is reasonable to suppose that any such mechanism will not produce an outcome such that there exists some unanimously-preferred alternative. At first, this appears to be a weak requirement. However, Foley allows the set of alternatives, which an equilibrium must Pareto-dominate, to be very large. In particular, for an allocation to be a public competitive equilibrium, Foley requires that there be no alternative level of public good provision and set of personalized lump-sum taxes that is (weakly) unanimously preferred. Foley proves that public competitive equilibria are Pareto-efficient, and that Pareto-efficient allocations are public competitive equilibria. In addition, Foley proves the existence of a public competitive equilibrium such that all individuals pay taxes that are a given proportion of their wealth.

To illustrate this idea, Figure 8 shows how such an equilibrium can be achieved in the special case where there is only one private good, x, and one public good, z, where the utility function for each household k is linear in the private good and concave in the public good, say $u^k(x^k, z) = x^k + \phi^k(z)$, each household has an endowment w^k of the private good, and the public good is produced at a constant per unit cost of c. Because of linearity of u^k in x^k, there is a unique efficient level of z such that $\sum_k d\phi^k/dz = c$, say z^*, that is independent of the distribution of private good consumption among households. Clearly, for any vector x such that $\sum_k (w^k - x^k) = cz^*$, (x, z^*), constitutes a public competitive equilibrium. If one sets $\tau = cz^*/(\sum_k w^k)$, the allocation $((1 - \tau)w^k), z^*)$ is a public competitive equilibrium with a proportional wealth tax. In Figure 8,

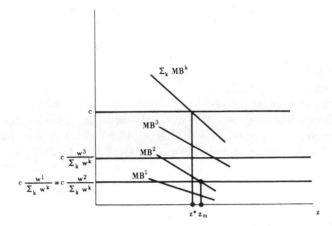

FIGURE 8 z^* is a proportional wealth tax competitive equilibrium that is not a majority voting equilibrium.

household 3 is assumed to have twice as much wealth as households 1 and 2. From the diagram, it is clear that the public competitive equilibrium concept rules out the possibility of achieving z_m in equilibrium, where z_m would be the majority voting equilibrium under a proportional wealth tax. In some sense, then, this is a rather restrictive equilibrium concept. Moreover, the public competitive equilibrium literature does not offer a mechanism with desirable incentive properties to explain how the efficient level of public good provision z^* would be achieved. Of course, once z^* is achieved, an insistence on unanimous approval will insure that it is maintained. But, on the one hand, unanimity is rarely required in observed forms of collective decision-making, and, on the other hand, it seems possible that strategic interplay might preclude unanimous approval of a move to the efficient public competitive equilibrium allocation z^*.

Foley's results have been extended to the local context by Greenberg [147, 148] and Richter [289, 290, 291]. In Richter [291] and Greenberg [148], free mobility is added as an equilibrium condition. Richter imposes proportional wealth taxation as a constraint on financing in equilibrium, while Greenberg allows for an arbitrarily-constrained lump-sum financing arrangement. Since local public goods are purely public, the results of Section 2 indicate that locational efficiency, and hence overall allocative efficiency, will not generally be attainable under wealth taxation. Thus, these authors demonstrate that their public competitive equilibria are optimal in the limited sense that private and public goods are allocated efficiently, conditional on the equilibrium assignment of households to jurisdictions. As in the public competitive equilibrium analysis in the non-local context, the problem of preference revelation for public goods is not addressed. In particular, mobility of households is not exploited to shed light on the preference revelation problem. Perhaps the public competitive equilibrium research could be extended in this direction, so as to overcome the preference-revelation difficulties noted above.

In related work, Ellickson [109, 110] considers the concept of a *global Lindahl equilibrium.* Such an equilibrium occurs when households are grouped into jurisdictions and face personalized prices for local public goods such that any consumption bundle that is preferred by any household to the equilibrium one, including consumption bundles in other jurisdictions, lies outside the household's budget set. The public goods technology in each jurisdiction can reflect congestion phenomena. Ellickson shows that a global Lindahl equilibrium is Pareto efficient and in fact is in the core. A global Lindahl equilibrium is also a public competitive equilibrium. However, it is possible for Lindahl equilibria not to exist, even when the core is non-empty, and it is also possible for the core to be empty. Of course, for very well-known reasons concerning preference revelation, there can be some question as to the interest in Lindahl "equilibria" as an equilibrium concept. Indeed, a similar question might be raised concerning the core as a solution concept for cooperative games with public goods: for example, it is not entirely obvious how the members of a blocking coalition can ascertain their common interest in overturning an allocation outside the core. In any event, we note further that the Ellickson model is non-spatial. This implies, for instance, that it is efficient to have only one jurisdiction when local public goods are pure.

Finally, we mention studies by Guesnerie and Oddou [152, 153], Greenberg and Weber [149], and Stahl and Varaiya [336]. These authors present models in which localities are constrained to use proportional wealth taxes to finance local public goods. Guesnerie and Oddou observe that the local public good game with this tax constraint is not necessarily superadditive. In particular, they show that the payoffs to households in the grand coalition may be dominated by the payoffs obtained in smaller coalitions, even if there is no crowding in the local public good technology. The reason (at least in part) is that households with very diverse preferences for local public goods, and with no ability to tailor cost sharing to preferences, may sacrifice more in compromising on public good provision in a larger group than they gain from spreading the cost of the public good over a larger population. This is, of course, a second best problem, because of the assumed tax structure. Guesnerie and Oddou find necessary and sufficient conditions for superadditivity of the game, which also ensures that the game has a non-empty core, where the core corresponds to unblocked levels of public good provision for the grand coalition. When superadditivity is not guaranteed, the core may be empty and the grand coalition may break apart. Guesnerie and Oddou also obtain some partial results on *stable structures*, that is, a partition of the population into groups, with levels of public good provision for each, such that no subset of the population can split away to form a new group that improves upon the initial situation. For example, there is a stable structure if the number of households is less than 4. It remains an open question whether their results generalize.

Greenberg and Weber [149] use a somewhat similar approach. They assume additively separable preferences between public and private goods, with the public good component of the utility function identical across consumers. When the private good component of the utility function also allows an ordering of households by their marginal utilities of income, Greenberg and Weber establish the existence of a stable structure. Moreover, each coalition will consist of similar households, that is, households with consecutive positions in the ordering.

Stahl and Varaiya [336] also impose a proportional wealth tax, but suppose a continuum of agents of two types. They consider whether efficient outcomes will be sustained when households are fully mobile. For example, in the case where local public goods are pure, they show, for particular utility functions, that only one locality should exist. They also show, however, that this outcome is not an equilibrium if households can move to a new jurisdiction, and if localities act to maximize the sum of utilities of their residents. (This result seems related to the subadditivity of the game condidered by Guesnerie and Oddou.) They establish a similar result when each locality follows majority rule decision-making. In conclusion, note that the Guesnerie–Oddou, Greenberg–Weber, and Stahl–Varaiya models have no spatial dimension—e.g., there are no locationally-fixed factors in these models. Previous sections have indicated the important role such factors can play in determining equilibrium locations and in influencing local government decisionmaking. It might therefore be of interest to extend these models to a spatial setting.

5. PROPERTY AND LAND TAXATION

5.1. Introduction

The property tax has historically been, and remains, the major source of revenue from own sources for local governments in the U.S. It also plays a major role in many other countries. This section evaluates the distributive and efficiency effects of property taxation, and examines the closely related question of land value taxation.

5.2. Property taxation

A. Tax incidence. In a well-known survey of the problem of property tax incidence, Aaron [1] contrasts the "old" and "new" views of property tax incidence. According to the old view, a tax on property is levied in part on land and in part on the structures that together determine the assessed value of a parcel of property. Since land is regarded as fixed in supply, landowners bear the tax in proportion to land's share in the value of the property. Structures, i.e., capital, are however regarded as perfectly mobile in the long run, and the net return to capital is taken as given. In the case of residential property, this means that the tax on structures is borne by consumers of housing. Owner-occupiers, of course, both own and consume the services of their land and structure, so there is no question of burden shifting in this case. For rental property, however, the perfectly elastic supply of capital means that renters bear the property tax through higher rents and that landlords do not bear the burden of the tax on structures at all. In the case of commercial/industrial property, perfect mobility of capital means that the gross cost of capital rises with the property tax. The resulting rise in production costs means that the tax burden is shifted to consumers in higher prices. In summary, then, the part of the property tax falling on structures—that is, the bulk of the tax—is borne by housing consumers and consumers of produced goods. If housing and other consumption expenditure is a declining proportion of income as income rises, the tax burden is distributed regressively.

There are several reasons why this "old view" might be incomplete or incorrect, as Aaron discusses. One is that housing and other consumption expenditures may have permanent income elasticities not too far from unity. Another is that assessment practices, which are widely variable across jurisdictions and classes of property, could mitigate (or perhaps exacerbate) the alleged regressivity of the tax. Third, the partial equilibrium nature of the traditional analysis makes it difficult to incorporate other possible incidence effects. For example, a tax on commercial structures could not be passed on to consumers if the taxed firms face perfectly elastic demand curves, as would be the case if one considers firms in a small, open jurisdiction. In this and also in less extreme cases, there might be tax-induced substitution in production that would lower the equilibrium prices of other factors, including labor and land. The extent to which it occurs would depend, however, on the elasticity of supply, and thus the mobility, of labor. To sort out these issues, a more explicit general equilibrium analysis is called for.

The major challenge to the old view, however, is a new view which takes an entirely different perspective on the property tax. Mieszkowski [238] argues that "the" property tax can be viewed as a tax simultaneously imposed in thousands of jurisdictions throughout the entire economy. (See also McLure [233].) While the effective tax rate varies by jurisdiction and type of property, there is in some sense an "average" tax rate on all property, which determines the incidence of the property tax system as a whole. The tax in any one jurisdiction is then seen as the average plus some differentials, the effects of which can be analyzed separately.

It is the examination of the incidence of the property tax

throughout the entire economy that most markedly distinguishes the
new from the old view. The tax becomes, in effect, a general tax on
land and capital. If capital is inelastically supplied (as is assumed,
typically, in standard general equilibrium tax incidence models[50]),
then the tax will simply lower the net return to capital and land,
with no shifting of the tax burden. Since capital income is
distributed progressively with respect to total income, the tax will
be *progressive* in its incidence.[51]

This view, which is obviously dramatically different from the
traditional view, seems essentially unassailable given its (explicit
and implicit) assumptions. It should be observed, however, that the
conclusion that the property tax is progressive rather than regressive
stems largely from two features of the new view analysis. First, the
new view and the old view actually attempt to answer different
questions. The old view, by assuming the net return to capital to be
fixed, clearly can only be applied to the analysis of a property tax in
a "small" jurisdiction—e.g., an individual locality. The new view
explicitly looks at the effect of an entire economy-wide *system* of
property taxation and does not necessarily support the conclusion
that the property tax in any one locality or small group of localities
is progressive in its incidence. Second, the new view requires the
supply of capital to the economy as a whole to be fixed. This
empirical assumption is open to question. In the context of "small"
countries, it may be more appropriate to assume that the net rate of
return is taken as fixed, with capital flowing freely across national
boundaries. Even in the US context, the assumption of a closed
economy with respect to capital flows can be challenged. In

---

[50] See Harberger [163] and Mieszkowski [237]. The Harberger model is thoroughly
evaluated in McLure [232]. See also Atkinson and Stiglitz [12], Boadway and
Wildasin [49], and Tresch [353] for textbook expositions.

[51] This result depends on the usual assumptions underlying tax incidence analysis.
Essentially, the demand side of the model must be sufficiently well-behaved that the
disposition of tax revenues can be ignored. One might assume that the property tax
is rebated to the private sector in the form of an income tax cut, or that it is spent by
the public sector. In either case, it is assumed that there is no change in the
composition of demand that would cause any intersectoral reallocation of resources
and that the benefits of the property tax revenue, however disposed of, are
proportional to income so that their distributional impact may be ignored. These
assumptions are made for analytical purposes, and one would wish to relax them if
one knew in what respects they are invalid.

addition, the assumption of a fixed supply of capital may even be unsupportable in the setting of a closed economy. A major issue in the public finance literature of the past decade has been precisely how and to what extent tax policy, including especially capital taxation, influences capital formation. While the issue remains contentious, there are numerous theoretical and empirical studies that at least cast doubt on the assumption that the supply of capital is insensitive to its net rate of return. The importance of a variable capital supply for the new view of the property tax should be apparent: if property taxation reduces the supply of capital, it will lower capital/land and capital/labor ratios, reducing equilibrium land rents and wage rates. Some of the burden of the tax would then be shifted to other factors of production, perhaps reducing significantly the supposed progressivity of the tax. Thus, there is still considerable scope for debate about the incidence of the property tax, even if one accepts the new view perspective that it is the incidence of the property tax system as a whole that should be evaluated.[52]

Consider now the implications of property tax differentials across jurisdictions or industries.[53] The first point to note is the ambiguity of the concept of a nationwide "average" tax rate. One precise definition of such an average rate is that it is a uniform rate that (i) produces the same revenue as a given non-uniform system of taxes and (ii) results in the same equilibrium net rate of return on capital. If K_i is the amount of capital and t_i is the property tax rate in jurisdiction i, a simple average tax rate $\bar{t} = \sum_i t_i K_i / \bar{K}$ can be computed, where $\bar{K} = \sum_i K_i$ is the aggregate stock of capital, taken as fixed. It is possible to show, however, that neither $\bar{t}$ nor any other uniform rate will, in general, satisfy the two above-specified conditions, as demonstrated by Courant [90].

---

[52] We cannot discuss the effects of capital taxation on the supply of capital here. See, e.g., Atkinson and Stiglitz [12], Boadway and Wildasin [49], Bosworth [53], Kotlikoff [203], and references therein to the extensive literature on this subject.

[53] Mieszkowski and Zodrow [242, 243] note that fiscal zoning requirements of the type analyzed in Section 2.4 can prevent the interjurisdictional capital flows that property tax differentials would otherwise create. They argue, however, that zoning constraints will not be strictly binding for most households, and that they can therefore be ignored in property tax analysis. Following the literature, the discussion in this section will abstract from zoning constraints.

To see this in a simple way, suppose that there are two jurisdictions initially imposing a uniform tax rate t. Each jurisdiction has a production function $f_i(K_i)$ which is strictly concave in capital, thus subsuming other (immobile) factors of production. In equilibrium, capital must be allocated so that net rates of return, $f_i'(K_i) - t_i$, are equalized. Hence, with initially uniform taxation, we have

$$f_1'(K_1) - t = f_2'(K_2) - t. \tag{5.1}$$

Now suppose that t_1 changes incrementally by dt_1, while t_2 changes to keep total tax revenue constant. Since the total capital stock is fixed,

$$dK_1 + dK_2 = 0, \tag{5.2}$$

and the constant-revenue requirement thus implies

$$K_1 \, dt_1 + K_2 \, dt_2 = 0. \tag{5.3}$$

If the new, differentiated tax system is to leave the net return to capital unchanged, we must have, from (5.1),

$$f_1'' \, dK_1 - dt_1 = f_2'' \, dK_2 - dt_2 = 0. \tag{5.4}$$

Defining $\eta_i = d \log K_i / d \log f_i'$, (5.4) implies

$$\frac{dK_i}{dt_i} = \frac{K_i}{f_i'} \, \eta_i \qquad i = 1, 2. \tag{5.5}$$

But (5.2), (5.3), and (5.5) are mutually consistent only if

$$\frac{K_1}{f_1'} \eta_1 = \frac{dK_1}{dt_1} = \frac{-dK_2}{dt_2} \frac{dt_2}{dt_1} = \frac{K_1}{f_2'} \eta_2, \tag{5.6}$$

which, because $f_1' = f_2' = r + t$ initially, reduces to $\eta_1 = \eta_2$.

It follows that any move to a differentiated system that keeps tax revenue constant cannot simultaneously leave the net return on capital unchanged, unless the demand elasticities for capital are equal in both jurisdictions. In general, of course, this condition will not be satisfied. Thus, equal-yield uniform and differentiated tax regimes have different net returns to capital, and thus different distributions of tax burden. Courant [90] presents numerical simulations which show that the burden on capital can be either greater or smaller under uniform taxation as compared with equal-yield differentiated taxes.

The concept of the "average" property tax rate is thus somewhat problematic. This is not to suggest that the essential new view insight—that the net rate of return on capital can be depressed by a system of property taxation, uniform or differentiated—is invalid. But it is clear that a precise estimate of the property tax burden on capital, as measured by the reduction in the net rate of return, depends on the underlying production technology in the various jurisdictions and not just on the total tax revenue collected.

Turning now to a more detailed analysis of the incidence and other effects of property tax differentials *per se,* we note that a number of studies, including Carlton [85], Grieson [151], Haurin [165], LeRoy [208], Polinsky and Rubinfeld [284], and Sonstelie [331] (in addition to Aaron [1] and Mieszkowski [238]), have analyzed tax rate changes in only one jurisdiction, taking the net cost of capital as exogenously given.[54] To review these results, it is useful to distinguish several special cases. Suppose first that locality *i* exports a particular commodity, that property used in that industry is differentially taxed, and that capital, land, and labor are all available to the locality at fixed prices. (This would result from capital and labor mobility, and from the assumption of a variable urban boundary with an agricultural hinterland.) Then a higher property tax raises the cost of production, affects no equilibrium net factor price, and therefore must be borne by consumers of the exported good.[55] Similarly, a differentially higher tax on residential property in community *i* would result in higher housing costs.

These conclusions must be modified if land and/or labor are not perfectly mobile. Consider, for example, a differentially higher tax on industrial property. This would induce a substitution away from capital and toward labor and land, but would also cause a reduction in demand for labor and land as higher costs cause the industry's

---

[54] See also Coen and Powell [88], Heinberg and Oates [166], and Orr [270, 271] for earlier studies of property tax differentials. Brueckner [67] presents an analysis in which households are freely mobile, and examines the effect of tax increases by one jurisdiction alone and by all jurisdictions simultaneously. This model relies on somewhat special assumptions about the structure of production, however. Wheaton [360] presents an empirical analysis of property tax and rent differentials for commercial property.

[55] This assumes that local producers, in the aggregate, have some market power in the output market. Otherwise the tax increase simply causes the local firms to shut down.

output to contract. The effect of the tax on other factor prices is therefore ambiguous. To illustrate some of the possibilities in the popular special case with only one immobile factor, suppose output Q is produced using only mobile capital K and fixed land T, with p_K the net price of capital and r the gross price of land. This output might be residential housing, or it might be some exported good. In either case, if the output price is p, gross land rents are given by

$$rT = pQ - (p_K + t)K$$
$$= pD(p) - (p_K + t)K, \tag{5.7}$$

where $D(p)$ is the demand for Q, with elasticity $\varepsilon = pD'/D < 0$, and where t is a tax applied at a uniform percentage rate to land and capital. Assume constant returns to scale production, and let f_K and f_T denote the (gross) factor shares of capital and land. In equilibrium, the output price must be equal to the unit cost of production,

$$p = c(p_K + t, r). \tag{5.8}$$

Letting an asterisk denote proportionate changes, differentiation of (5.7) and (5.8) yields (using $T^* = 0$)

$$r^* f_T = (1 + \varepsilon)p^* - f_K[K^* + (p_K + t)^*] \tag{5.9}$$
$$p^* = f_K(p_K + t)^* + f_T r^*. \tag{5.10}$$

Using the elasticity of substitution $\sigma = K^*/[r^* - (p_K + 1)^*]$ to eliminate K^* and substituting from (5.10), (5.9) yields

$$r^*\left[\frac{f_K \sigma}{\varepsilon} - f_T\right] = f_K\left[\frac{\sigma}{\varepsilon} + 1\right](p_K + t)^*. \tag{5.11}$$

This equation shows what happens to gross rents when the property tax rate t increases. Net rents must fall further below the gross rent by the amount of the tax change, so a constant gross rent means that net rents fall by just the amount of the tax increase. Alternatively, this model can be interpreted as one in which land and structures are taxed separately, with t being just the tax on structures. In this case, $r^* = 0$ means that the tax on structures is not shifted to land.

It is clear from (5.11) that the effect of t on land rents depends on certain parameters, especially ε and σ. LeRoy [208] focuses on the case where $\varepsilon = -1$.[56] In this special case, if production is also Cobb–Douglas so that $\sigma = 1$, we have $r^* = 0$. Here, the output price increases just enough to absorb the higher cost of capital (see (5.10)). If instead $\sigma > 1$, the right-hand side of (5.11) is negative, while the bracketed expression on the left is always negative, so that an increase in t increases r. The intuition is that the increased substitution of land for capital more than offsets the reduction in demand for land brought about by contraction of the industry. Conversely, $\sigma < 1$ and $\varepsilon = -1$ implies that r decreases with t. $\sigma < 1$ is the empirically more relevant case.

The role of the demand elasticity ε is easily understood from (5.11). In particular, if $|\varepsilon| > \sigma$, the output reduction effect outweighs the substitution effect and gross land rents are therefore reduced by the property tax (or improvement tax). In the limit, as $\varepsilon \to -\infty$, we have

$$-r^* f_T = f_K (p_K + t)^*, \tag{5.12}$$

and the entire burden of the tax increase falls on land values.

This model can be seen as a generalization of Grieson [151], Haurin [165] and others who do not separately model taxes on land and taxes on improvements. While (5.11) shows that the effect on *gross* rents of the improvements part of a general property tax is ambiguous, and while it is clear that the land part of a property tax depresses net land rents, what can one say about the total effect on net land rents of a general property tax increase? To answer this, we must suppose equal percentage increases in the tax on rents and capital returns, say a 1% increase. Then $(p_K + t)^* = 1$, and the percentage change in net land rents is given by

$$r^* - 1 = \frac{f_K\left[\dfrac{\sigma}{\varepsilon} + 1\right]}{f_K \dfrac{\sigma}{\varepsilon} - f_T} - 1 = \frac{f_K + f_T}{f_K \dfrac{\sigma}{\varepsilon} - f_T} = \frac{1}{f_K \dfrac{\sigma}{\varepsilon} - f_T} < 0, \tag{5.13}$$

which confirms the conclusion of Grieson (non-spatial model) and

---

[56] LeRoy actually uses a monocentric city model, but the results of that analysis parallel those of our non-spatial model. See also Carlton [85] for a spatial analysis which shows how land or housing taxation differentially affects land rents at different distances from the city center.

Haurin (spatial model assuming Cobb–Douglas preferences and technology) that a uniform tax on structures and land must depress land rents. (Hobson [175] presents a similar but somewhat more general model than the above, in which land is elastically supplied. In this model, the basic qualitative conclusion is unaffected: a general property tax lowers net land rents. However, the higher the elasticity of supply of land, the smaller is the *magnitude* of the reduction in land rents.)

In the general case where there are two or more immobile factors, it is naturally more difficult to get specific results (see, e.g., Mieszkowski [238] for more details). Basically, the same general considerations apply, but substitute/complement relations among factors need to be taken into account.

The analysis of property tax differentials can be extended to allow for within-jurisdiction tax rate variation as well as variations across jurisdictions. Sonstelie [331] considers the effect of differentially higher taxation of (say) commercial property within a locality. Provided that land is mobile between sectors, Sonstelie finds that a tax on commercial property drives land into the residential sector, depressing land values in both uses. This effect is cushioned if there are high elasticities of substitution between capital and land in each sector. Also, a low elasticity of demand for commercial real estate will allow the property tax differential to be passed forward to firms and, of course, ultimately to the consumers of the output of the commercial sector, which again cushions the drop in land rents. The elasticity of demand for residential real estate, on the other hand, works in the opposite direction. If this elasticity is high, relatively small decreases in land values will suffice to increase the demand for housing and thus the demand for land, allowing this sector to absorb land released from the commercial sector more easily. A related analysis appears in Lin [209], who supposes that residential housing is taxed in one locality while the "other goods" production sector is untaxed. Lin assumes housing is produced with land and capital while other goods are produced with land and labor. Both labor and capital are mobile across jurisdictions, while land is mobile across uses within jurisdictions. The housing tax shrinks the housing sector, causing an outflow of capital to other jurisdictions and a reallocation of land to the other goods sector, which in turn results in an inflow of labor. The upshot is that wages rise, so workers are better off, capital returns fall, so capital owners are worse off, and the effect on land rents and landowners is uncertain. As noted earlier, studies that focus on the incidence of property tax differentials in particular jurisdictions often impose the "small, open" assumption that the net return to capital is exogenously given for any one locality. Bradford [57] and Mieszkowski and Zodrow [243] argue that this may be misleading, however. Suppose there are $n + 1$ jurisdictions, none of which initially imposes a property tax, and suppose jurisdiction 1 now introduces a small tax at rate t_1. In order to equalize net returns, capital, which is used to produce a numeraire private good, must be allocated across jurisdictions such that

$$f_1'(K_1) - t_1 = f_2'(K_2) = f_2'([\bar{K} - K_1]/n) \tag{5.14}$$

where K_1 is the amount of capital in locality 1 and K_2 is the amount of capital in each of the remaining jurisdictions, assumed identical for simplicity. It is straightforward to solve (5.14) for K_1 as a function of t_1, and thus to show that the change in the net return to capital resulting from a small increase in t_1 is

$$\frac{df_2'}{dt_1} = -\frac{f_2''}{n}\frac{dK_1}{dt_1} = -\frac{f_2''/n}{f_1'' + f_2''/n} = -\frac{1}{1 + nf_1''/f_2''}. \tag{5.15}$$

If the number of jurisdictions is large, and each has roughly the same amount of capital and roughly the same technology, (5.15) shows that the net return to capital will only fall by a small amount. In fact, if all localities have identical technologies and endowments, $f_1'' = f_2''$ and the right-hand side just reduces to $-1/(1 + n)$, which is small if n is large. However, since $\bar{K} = (n + 1)K_1$ under these assumptions, the reduction in the net return to capital in the economy as a whole is $\bar{K}(df_2'/dt_1) = -(n + 1)K_1(n + 1)^{-1} = -K_1$, which is the incremental tax revenue raised in locality 1. This means that capital bears the full burden of a differential tax in one jurisdication, no matter how small that jurisdiction is.

As Mieszkowski and Zodrow explain, this result does not contradict the conclusion that part of the tax burden falls on owners of fixed factors in the taxing locality. Rather, the capital flow that lowers returns to fixed factors in community 1 also raises the returns to fixed factors in the rest of the economy. The increase in their returns, like the reduction in the net return to capital, may be very small on a per unit basis, but it is very widespread. In the aggregate, the increased return to fixed factors outside the taxing jurisdiction just offsets the loss to fixed factors within it.

Thus the assumption of a fixed net return to capital may obscure certain important general equilibrium interactions. If one is interested in the purely local effects of a local tax change, it may be quite appropriate to ignore the very small impact of local policy on the net return to capital. If one wishes to evaluate the economy-wide effect of a local tax change, however, this small change is not truly a negligible change. Only if the marginal product of capital in the rest of the economy were literally constant, corresponding to an infinite elasticity of substitution between capital and other inputs ($f_2'' = 0$), could one safely assume a constant net return to capital.

In the studies cited so far, capital mobility naturally plays a crucial role in the analysis of property tax differentials. To the extent that they allow for household mobility, they generally assume that migration occurs in such a way as to equalize net wage rates.[57] Suppose, however, that we are examining the effect of tax differentials on property that is used to produce some locally-consumed good, such as residential housing. Even if wage rates are equalized between jurisdications, it would not necessarily follow that no household has an incentive to relocate. According to the usual arguments, a property tax differential on housing will be reflected in housing prices. Hence, with equal wages, real income or utility would be higher in low-tax jurisdictions, and migration might ensue.

The implications of property tax differentials are analyzed from this perspective in Wilson [382]. Wilson postulates an initial equilibrium where all jurisdictions have uniform property taxes, and where there is a continuum of mobile households who have equal labor endowments and varying demands for a non-traded good. (In the model, households have unequal non-wage incomes and this results in demand variations.) In this initial equilibrium, it is further assumed that factor and non-traded goods prices are equal in all localities, and that each jurisdiction contains a mix of high-

---

[57] An exception is Brueckner [67], who imposes an equal-utility equilibrium condition for mobile households, and, more recently, Hobson [175] who does the same.

and low-income households. (Given symmetry of jurisdictions, such an equilibrium exists.) All households are in utility-maximizing locations.

Now consider a small increase in the property tax rate in one locality, with revenues paid out as per capita transfers to households. Suppose that the price of the locally-produced good were to increase slightly as a result. Then all households with a high demand for the non-traded good would seek to relocate to another jurisdiction. They would be replaced by an inflow of a nearly equal number of low-demand households. (An approximately equal number of residents is required to maintain labor market equilibrium.) But then, as a result of the change in the composition of the population, there is a discrete reduction in demand for the non-traded good. In short, the elasticity of demand for this good, starting from an equal-tax equilibrium, is infinite. It follows that a small property tax differential need *not* give rise to a corresponding price differential. This analysis prompts the observation, which should be generally relevant to analyzing the effects of local policy changes in an economy with mobile households, that market demands and supplies may be (multivalued) correspondences, even if individual demands and supplies are single-valued. Though this occurs in Wilson's model (by construction) at an equal tax symmetric equilibrium, it could occur in many other situations as well.

B. *Property taxation and resource allocation.* The preceding discussion has focused on the incidence of the property tax, i.e., its effect on factor and output prices. Another important question concerns the effect of the property tax on the efficiency of resource allocation. There are several dimensions to this problem.

Section 2 has already discussed the possibility that the property tax can serve as an entry fee for access to public services in a jurisdiction, especially when coupled with optimal zoning. Such a tax/regulatory policy can result in fully efficient resource allocation in the private sector, conditional on whatever level of public expenditure might be chosen by local governments. If perfect zoning is not possible, however, the property tax may drive a wedge between the gross and net price of housing. A similar wedge is created for other kinds of property. As is well known, this may result in resource misallocation. This is the efficiency issue on which we focus in the present subsection. To keep matters simple, let us abstract completely from household mobility, since it plays no essential role in the issues that we now wish to discuss. Thus, suppose each jurisdication has a fixed population, and that land and capital combine to form residential or non-residential property, which yield, resp., a flow a housing services or other goods. As in the discussion of property tax incidence, we may distinguish between the effects of a system of property taxation in the economy as a whole, and the effect of a property tax differential in one jurisdication.

For the economy as a whole, property taxes drive a wedge between gross and net returns to capital, much like a tax on capital income. In the simplest case of a project yielding an infinite stream of returns of R, where the net return to capital is r, and t is the property tax rate, the value of the project is

$$V = \frac{R - tV}{r} = \frac{R}{r+t}, \qquad (5.16)$$

so that the property tax effectively raises the discount rate. This is equivalent in its effects to a tax on capital income of τ such that

$$\frac{R}{r+t} = \frac{(1-\tau)R}{r}, \qquad (5.17)$$

or,

$$\tau = \frac{t}{r+t}. \qquad (5.18)$$

Thus, if the property tax rate is 3 percent and the gross return to capital is 6 percent, a general property tax is economically equivalent to a capital income tax at rate $\tau = 50$ percent. Rates as high as this sometimes occur in the US and no doubt other countries as well.

If the aggregate supply of capital is fixed, a uniform property tax or capital income tax causes no misallocation of resources. More generally, however, these taxes disturb the efficiency of resource allocation by driving apart intertemporal marginal rates of substitution and transformation. The size of this efficiency loss depends crucially, of course, on the response of consumption/savings decisions to changes in the net return to savings. This topic has been extensively analyzed in recent years but since it does not have a specifically urban focus, a review of the literature in the area lies beyond the scope of the present survey. Suffice it to say that the conventional assumption of fixed capital supply has been strongly challenged on the basis of theoretical and empirical research, and that there is substantial controversy about the size of the elasticity of capital supply.[58]

In addition to their effects on intertemporal resource allocation, property and capital income taxes can have important effects on intersectoral resource allocation. For example, capital income taxes generally are not levied on the return to owner-occupied housing, a quantitatively important part of the capital stock. Property taxes, by contrast, may fall particularly on just this form of capital. Indeed, Devarajan et al. [99] and Hamilton and Whalley [155] find that a property tax actually improves the efficiency of resource allocation when imposed in an economy in which housing capital would otherwise be differentially undertaxed. This result, which is quite intuitive from the perspective of second-best welfare economics, illustrates the importance of studying the property tax within the context of a general structure of capital taxation. Of course, this requires the simultaneous analysis of taxes that, in practice, are levied by different levels of government. See Hobson [176] and Thirsk [347] for more discussion.

Let us now turn to the efficiency analysis of property taxation from the viewpoint of an individual jurisdiction or sector. For this purpose, it is reasonable to regard the supply of capital as perfectly elastic in the long run. Differentially higher or lower property taxation would thus affect the allocation of capital across jurisdictions or sectors and the consumption of goods produced in different jurisdictions or sectors. Note, however, that it is the size of the property tax *differential* that is important here, at least if the supply of capital in the aggregate is fixed. Figure 9 illustrates a one-consumption-good, two-region economy with a fixed supply K of capital and marginal product of capital schedules MP_1 and MP_2. With equal effective tax rates $t_1 = t_2 = t$ in each region, the efficient spatial allocation of capital K^* is achieved, as is also true, of course, at the untaxed equilibrium. But a tax cut from $t_1 = t$ to $t_1 = 0$ by

[58] See references cited in n. 52 above.

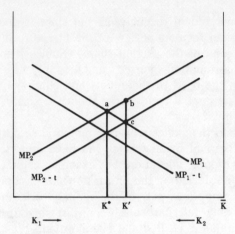

FIGURE 9   Elimination of the tax on capital in jurisdiction 1 creates a loss of output equal to *abc*.

region 1 will result in an inefficient inflow of capital, resulting in a final equilibrium K' and a deadweight loss (i.e., reduction in aggregate output) equal to *abc*. Of course, the magnitude of this loss depends positively on the elasticity of demand for the final output of both regions, and on the elasticity of substitution between capital and fixed factors.

This point is obvious enough, but it is worth emphasizing because many studies which examine the efficiency effects of the property tax do so from the perspective of a single, small jurisdiction. In Figure 10, small locality 1 starts, let us suppose, with a tax rate t equal to that of the rest of the economy. Locality 1 takes the net return on capital, $MP_2 - t$, as exogenously given. Now consider an elimination of the tax in locality 1. The capital stock in locality 1 increases, which appears to result in a reduction in excess burden equal to *acd*. However, this is more than offset by the loss of output in the rest of the economy, which results, as before, in a net loss of *abc*. The partial equilibrium or "local view" excess burden measure *acd* can thus be quite misleading. The reason is that the allocative effects of the tax in one locality cannot be evaluated irrespective of the distortions obtaining elsewhere in the economy. This familiar second-best problem necessitates an economy-wide general equilibrium perspective on policy changes in one jurisdiction—

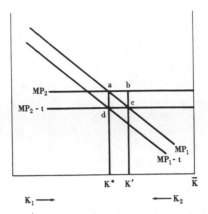

FIGURE 10 Seen from locality 1, elimination of the capital tax generates a net benefit of *acd*, while producing a net loss to society of *abc*.

assuming, that is, that one wishes to evaluate the welfare effects of property taxes from the viewpoint of the whole economy. From the viewpoint of locality 1 alone, the tax reduction in Figure 10 does indeed result in a welfare gain of *acd*.[59]

In concluding this section, we mention a study by Arnott and MacKinnon [8], who compute the general equilibrium impact of property taxation in a hypothetical monocentric city, including both allocative and incidence effects.[60] They suppose a fixed metropolitan population, a variable urban/rural boundary with a fixed price

[59] We are not being very precise here. The welfare gain to "locality 1," *acd*, may actually accrue to landowners, shareholders of firms, or consumers who reside outside of locality 1. This sort of issue is discussed further in the next section.

[60] Sullivan [346] also presents a general equilibrium computational analysis of industrial property taxation in an explicitly spatial framework. Sullivan considers both a small open (utility-taking) jurisdiction, in which landowners bear the full burden of the tax, and a closed system of cities in which households throughout the system and landowners in the taxing jurisdiction are made worse off while landowners in the other cities are made better off.

Another recent computational general equilibrium model of interest is presented by Kimbell and Harrison [199]. Their framework is suitable for inter-regional incidence and resource allocation analysis. It allows for a complex structure of inter-regional inter-industry trade, and for a number of factors with varying degrees of sectoral specificity and inter-regional mobility. They use this model to explore the effects of a reduction of capital income taxation in California (a la Proposition 13), and its implications for the rest of the U.S. economy.

of agricultural land, Cobb-Douglas preferences for housing and other goods, and a CES "production" or "aggregator" function for housing as a function of land and structure inputs. Arnott and MacKinnon present two variants of the basic model, depending on how one wants to model the disadvantages of an increasing ratio of structures to land. In one variant, attributed to Muth [257], households have a taste for land *per se*, so that doubling the amount of structure on a lot less than doubles the amount of housing service it provides. In the other variant, attributed to Grieson [151], households do not have a taste for land *per se*, but the marginal cost of adding structure to a lot is increasing. This presumably reflects the technology of housing construction. In either case, forces are at work to keep the population from concentrating at the city center in properties of infinite density.

The rest of the model is fairly standard: all households commute to the city center, incurring a constant transportation cost per mile, and all households have fixed incomes. (There is no congestion in transportation.) The property tax is assessed against housing. Arnott and MacKinnon simulate both the Muth and Grieson cities, with effective tax rates (as a percentage of net rents) of 0, 0.24, 0.25, and 0.26. The 0.25 rate is a sort of benchmark case, to be compared with the no-tax situation and to provide a level around which to evaluate an incremental tax change.

In this model, the property tax distorts the housing market, depressing the equilibrium amount of structures and, since the city boundary is endogenous, causing the city radius to fall. Equilibrium utility for city residents falls, as do land rents (and thus the welfare of absentee landlords). The excess burden of the 25 percent tax, compared to the no-tax equilibrium, is 8.5 percent.[61] The marginal excess burden, that is, the excess burden resulting from an increase in the property tax rate from 24 percent to 26 percent, is 18.3 percent.

As far as tax incidence is concerned, the model can determine the effect of the property tax on land rents and housing prices. It is found that while land rents do fall, landlords bear a share of the

---

[61] Excess burden is measured either in the compensating or equivalent variation sense, for both the Muth and Grieson cities. The results of the welfare analysis do not depend significantly on which welfare measure, or which type of city, one considers.

property tax that is less than the share of land in house value, or, put another way, the tax on structures is borne entirely by renters and, in addition, the renters bear part of the tax on land. (As Arnott and MacKinnon note, this reflects the fact that land is in variable supply to the metropolitan area.) Unfortunately, this model does not explicitly incorporate a capital market, so that the effect of the property tax on the return to capital is not directly evaluated. In fact, however, it would appear that the model is best interpreted as one with a fixed net return to capital, since the cost of structures depends only on density of development, not on the total amount of structures built. The model could therefore portray a single metropolitan area with perfect capital mobility but no labor mobility. Alternatively, it could portray a representative member of an entire system of urban areas in an economy with fixed total population. In this case, however, the entire economy must be seen as small and open with respect to world capital markets. This might be accurate for a country such as Canada, but might be less accurate for the U.S. In any case, it is clear that the new view of property tax incidence cannot be valid in such a model, since the new view requires that the economy be closed and the net return to capital endogenously determined. It is also clear that the welfare perspective in the analysis must be that of the "small" economy being modeled (whether an individual metropolitan area or an entire national economy), since the welfare effects of capital flows to or from other regions are not evaluated.

5.3. Land taxation

The classic view on the taxation of land is that, since land is inelastically supplied, a land tax is borne entirely by landowners and produces no incentives for inefficient resource allocation. While both of these conclusions are correct within the context of certain models, both can also be challenged. Interestingly, the challenges in both instances have to do with the role of land in an intertemporal setting.

Feldstein [121] questions the traditional view of land tax incidence by supposing that land and produced capital are assets held by life-cycle utility-maximizing households in an overlapping generations model. Suppose output is a linear homogeneous function of aggregate capital, labor, and land $F(K, L, T)$, that this output can be either consumed or added to the capital stock, that each generation is of the same size, and that each saves a proportion σ of its net (wage) income when young in order to consume in old age. The tax rate on land rents (the only taxed commodity) is t, and the price of land is r. The condition for equilibrium in the asset markets is that the value of assets sold by the old, $K + rT$, is equal to the value of assets demanded by the young, $\sigma F_L L$, where F_L is the marginal product of labor, equal to the wage. The portfolio equilibrium condition, insuring that households will be willing to hold both assets, is that the net returns to capital and labor be equated, i.e., letting subscripts denote marginal products,

$$F_K = \frac{F_T(1-t)}{r}. \qquad (5.19)$$

Substituting into the asset market equilibrium condition yields

$$\sigma F_L L = K + \frac{F_T(1-t)T}{F_K}. \qquad (5.20)$$

This condition determines K implicitly as a function of t, given that L and T are fixed. Since the derivative of the right-hand side with respect to t is non-zero, it follows that changes in the rate of land rent taxation cannot leave K unaffected. In fact, provided that the asset market is stable, one can easily see that an increase in t causes an increases in K. This reduces the gross (and net) return to capital, and, assuming complementarity, raises the gross returns to labor and land. This cushions the fall in net land rents, resulting in some shifting of the tax to capital. (Indeed, it is possible for net land rents actually to increase, as Feldstein shows in an example.) Thus land, though inelastically supplied, does not bear the entire burden of the land rent tax.

The shifting of the tax on land rents in this model is crucially dependent, however, on an implicit intergenerational transfer. The nature of this transfer is best appreciated by noting that, discounted at the initial equilibrium level of the interest rate, the owners of land at the time that the tax is (unexpectedly) imposed experience a capital loss of $tF_T T/F_K$, as all future taxes are capitalized into land values. Even if tax revenues are handed back in lump-sum form to old individuals, the initial generation only receives one period's taxes, with a present value of only $tF_T T/(1 + F_K)$, which does not compensate it for its capital loss. Fane [118] observes, however, that if the government were to issue a bond paying $tF_T T$ in perpetuity, and were to endow initial landowners with these bonds, the intergenerational transfer effect of the tax increase would be cancelled: such consols would be worth precisely $tF_T T/F_K$, and would exactly offset the capital loss to landowners. They would then have no incentive to change their savings behavior, the wealth of succeeding generations would be unaffected, and the intertemporal real equilibrium of the economy would be unchanged. Gross factor prices would be constant, so that the net rent of land falls by the amount of the tax, and no shifting occurs.

Even without issuing bonds to offset this intergenerational transfer, the real equilibrium of the economy may be unaffected by a land rent tax if there are private intergenerational transfers, as in Barro [19]. Calvo et al. [84] analyze a land rent tax in an economy where each generation derives utility from its children's utility and is able to carry out intergenerational transfers (bequests) as desired. In this model it is assumed that tax revenues are returned lump-sum either to old or young individuals, and it is shown that the value of bequests changes in a way that leaves each generation's equilibrium consumption path (i.e., the intertemporal real equilibrium of the economy) unchanged. Exactly as suggested by traditional theory, the value of land falls by precisely the capitalized value of future taxes, with no change in any equilibrium factor prices. The easiest way to see this result is to observe that interlocking generations behave like a single "dynastic" intergenerational utility maximizer, optimizing subject to a budget constraint requiring the present value of consumption to be no greater than the present value of wages. In Calvo et al. the tax-transfer scheme does not change the feasible intergenerational consumption set. Since the real equilibrium is therefore undisturbed, full capitalization follows from (5.19) (i.e., F_K and F_T are tax-invariant).

One may conclude that the traditional results on the incidence of a land tax need not necessarily be overturned, even in an explicitly dynamic setting. However, this conclusion is sensitive to the precise way in which intertemporal consumption/savings behavior is modeled, and on the disposition of tax revenues through associated

118   D. E. WILDASIN

expenditure/debt policies. Analysts may disagree on the appropriate assumption to make in either or both cases.
We now turn to the possible allocative effects of land taxation. Traditionally, it has been argued that the taxation of land rent is non-distortionary because land is inelastically supplied. This has led to proposals to shift from general property taxation, under which the returns to both capital and land are taxed, to site value taxation, which would exclude capital from the tax base. The expected consequence of such a tax reform would be an increase in the capital intensity of land use, and an improvement in the efficiency of resource allocation. Brueckner [70] provides a recent formal demonstration of this result, as well as an analysis of the implications of a move toward site value taxation for land values.

This traditional view of the neutrality of land taxation is based on static efficiency analysis, however. By contrast, Bentick [26] and Mills [244] argue that land value taxation creates incentives for more rapid development of land, and is thus dynamically non-neutral. This result is already suggested by Eq. (5.16), showing how the value of an investment is affected by a property tax. Provided that the net rate of return at which future income is discounted remains unchanged, an increase in the tax rate in effect raises the discount rate. This, in turn, ought to discourage projects that yield returns in the more distant future.

To establish this conclusion more explicitly, consider two possible uses of a parcel of land, A and B, one of which yields a return R^A beginning in period 0 and continuing until period T (rapid development), the second which yields no return until period $T' > 0$ and then yields R^B until period T (speculative land use). Let $V_t(A, \tau)$ be the market value of the parcel in period t when committed to project A, given a tax rate on land value of τ. We have

$$V_t(A, \tau) = \sum_{s=t}^{T} \frac{R^A - \tau V_{s-1}(A, \tau)}{(1+r)^{s-t}}$$

$$= \sum_{s=t}^{T} \frac{R^A}{[(1+r)(1+\tau)]^{s-t}}, \qquad (5.21)$$

where we assume a constant discount rate of r and that the tax on land value in period $s - 1$ is paid at the end of the period. The tax has the same effect on the value of the parcel as an equal increase in the discount rate.

For project B, we similarly have

$$V_t(B, \tau) = \sum_{s=T'}^{T} \frac{R^B}{[(1+r)(1+\tau)]^{s-t}}. \qquad (5.22)$$

Now suppose that $V_0(A, 0) = V_0(B, 0)$, i.e., both projects are equally attractive in the absence of a tax. Since the income stream from A exceeds that from B until T', whereupon that of B exceeds that of A (i.e., B is unambiguously "later" than A), we must have $V_0(A, \tau) > V_0(B, \tau)$ for any $\tau > 0$. In other words, the tax works against projects yielding benefits relatively farther in the future.

The above argument does not necessarily controvert the neutrality of other possible land value taxation schemes. As discussed in greater detail in Wildasin [372], the above tax scheme, because it is based on the current market value of a parcel, results in a stream of taxes that is use-dependent. In particular, if projects A and B are equally attractive in the absence of a tax, i.e., $V_0(A, 0) = V_0(B, 0)$, the value of the parcel in project B must rise more rapidly (or fall more slowly) over time than that for project A, i.e., $V_t(A, 0) < V_t(B, 0)$ for $t > 0$. This is because intertemporal arbitrage would require capital gains on the parcel in use B to compensate for holding it with no cash flow, until $t = T'$. Hence, since taxes are tied to current V_t's, they must be higher on the parcel in use B. This explains the non-neutrality result. However, if the land tax were calculated in some use-independent fashion, for example, as a tax per acre that is invariant with respect to current market values, the classical neutrality result is restored. One possibility is to calculate a "standard value" for a parcel, in the spirit of Vickrey [355]. Thus, not all forms of land value taxation introduce non-neutralities.[62]

In studying the effects of taxation on the dynamic allocation of land, it is interesting to consider other taxes in addition to a simple land value tax. For example, Markusen and Scheffman [216] analyze the effects of capital gains taxes on the conversion of land from rural to urban (residential) use. In the Markusen–Scheffman two-period model, the capital gains tax is levied on a realization

---

[62] For more discussion of this and related issues, see Bentick [24, 25, 27], Skouras [328], Arnott and Lewis [7], Tideman [348, 349], Mills [245], and Eckart [106].

basis, and only applies to land that is converted from rural to urban use between the first and second periods. This tax causes more first-period development of land to occur. Kanemoto [197] generalizes the Markusen–Scheffman model by considering a continuous-time analysis in which land is gradually converted from rural to urban use. In contrast to Markusen-Scheffman, Kanemoto finds that if the capital gains tax is levied only at the time of conversion, the rate of conversion slows down and the stock of residential housing at each time is reduced. In this model, capital is used along with land to produce housing, and although the capital gains tax reduces the amount of housing, it need not reduce the amount of housing capital. In fact, if capital is highly substitutable for land in housing production, and if the demand for housing is relatively inelastic, the amount of housing capital may actually increase under capital gains taxation. This is not surprising, since tax-induced substitution toward capital and away from land may increase the demand for capital, if the overall reduction in the equilibrium quantity of housing is restrained by inelastic demand. Kanemoto also analyzes a property tax, assessed at a uniform rate on housing capital and on land in both rural and urban uses. This tax also results in a reduction in the amount of housing capital. Again, if land and capital are sufficiently substitutable and the demand for housing is sufficiently inelastic, the use of the differentially less heavily taxed factor in the housing sector, which in this case is land, may increase. Since taxes are levied at rates that differ across uses in the Kanemoto model, neutrality is of course not to be expected. Kanemoto's analysis confirms that the allocative effects of these taxes work in the directions that intuition would suggest.

6. INTERGOVERNMENTAL FISCAL RELATIONS

6.1. Introduction

This section discusses issues that arise because the decisions of one government influence the economic environment faced by another government. In some cases, these issues involve governments at the same level: e.g., library services provided by one city are used by residents from another city, or taxes levied by one state or province are partly borne by residents in another state. (We may refer to these as *horizontal* interactions.) In other cases, relations between different levels of government are involved (*vertical* interactions). Particularly of interest here are transfers (grants) from higher levels of government to lower levels, a very important source of financing for local government expenditures in many countries. These are often closely related in the literature, since oftentimes grants or other "vertical" policies are invoked as potential remedies for some sort of breakdown at the horizontal level. The discussion here begins with a treatment of horizontal issues including, where appropriate, their vertical remedies. To some extent, the focus will shift to vertical issues as we proceed.[63]

6.2. Interjurisdictional benefit spillovers

One sort of intergovernmental fiscal interaction that attracted early attention is the benefit "spillover." There are numerous examples: sewage treatment by an upstream city reduces the need for purification by downstream cities, the capture of criminals in one locality prevents them from committing crimes elsewhere, benefits from education provided by one jurisdiction may be enjoyed by households elsewhere if educated invididuals decide to relocate, income maintenance in one city helps eradicate poverty which benefits households in other places. Naturally one anticipates inefficiency to result from such externalities. If the population of each jurisdication is exogenously fixed, and if each chooses a level of public expenditure that is "locally optimal," i.e., such that the marginal benefits to residents are equated to marginal cost, the external benefit is ignored and Pareto efficiency is not achieved. (Everything runs in reverse, of course, for external diseconomies.) This point was established in contributions by Boskin [52], Brainard and Dolbear [61], Pauly [273], and Williams [381].

The parallel with standard externality theory can be pushed further. A Pigovian subsidy could internalize the externality. It

---

[63] Maxwell and Aronson [218], Break [62] and Gramlich [143] provide excellent surveys of and introductions to a number of the topics discussed in this chapter. In addition, these authors provide much greater attention to U.S. institutional structure than is possible here. Starrett [341] also treats many of the issues discussed in this section, especially Section 6.4.

would be provided by a higher-level government to the lower-level government in the form of a grant that lowers the relative price of the externality-producing good. A lump-sum grant does not, of course, achieve this end. Rather, some per unit subsidy is required. In the U.S., this is often achieved by a "matching" arrangement such that each dollar spent by the local government is matched by a contribution of x by the higher-level government. Then the effective price of a dollar of public spending falls from $1 to $(1 - m)$ where $m = x/(1 + x)$. By suitable choice of a matching rate, then, a higher level government could internalize the benefit spillover generated by a lower level government. (See, e.g., Breton [63] and Oates [264] for more discussion.)

Note that this simple analysis depends heavily on the assumption that lower-level governments act in a locally-optimizing fashion, given a fixed population. (Indeed, in the literature, a locality is often modeled as a single household, as discussed in Section 3.2.) Only on the basis of such a hypothesis can one infer that the public good generating the spillover is underprovided, and that a grant with a matching rate that just internalizes the externality will restore efficiency. But the extensive discussion in Sections 3 and 4 shows how problematic the assumption of locally-optimizing behavior is. Median voter equilibria, Romer–Rosenthal equilibria, profit-maximizing developer equilibria, and wealth-maximizing voter equilibria are all efficient only under special assumptions. One cannot say in general whether localities tend to overspend or underspend on local public goods. Thus, the argument that goods providing spillovers result in market (or, rather, political) failure is somewhat tenuous, as is, of course, the argument for the proposed remedy.

One should not over-emphasize these difficulties. Strong simplifications are sometimes necessary to focus attention on essential aspects of an issue. Nonetheless, the problem of modeling local government behavior is ultimately a critical one for understanding possible resource misallocation arising from intergovernmental fiscal interactions, and for the design of remedies. This issue will recur in succeeding sections.

While the possible underprovision of local public goods is by far the best known aspect of the benefit spillover phenomenon, spillovers can be important for other reasons as well. For example, they affect the distributional impact of government policies, as when a poor central city provides services to a workforce that consists, to a significant degree, of commuters from wealthy suburbs. The phrase "central city exploitation hypothesis" has been used to describe such a situation, and some authors, including Bradford and Oates [60], Greene, et al. [150], and Neenan [258] have attempted to quantify the value of the benefit flows across juridisdictional boundaries in selected U.S. metropolitan areas.[64] This is a highly challenging research problem. For example, as Bradford and Oates discuss, it is not entirely obvious whether one ought to measure benefits in "total" terms, or whether the value imputed to each unit of exported benefits should be the value of the marginal unit. (The choice presumably depends on the precise question one wishes to answer.)

Above all, however, attempts to make such estimates face the major difficulty that demands for local public goods, whether by residents or non-residents, cannot be directly observed. Greene *et al.*, for example, assume identical additively separable utility functions of the form $u(x, z) = \phi_1(x) + \phi_2(z)$, where x is net (private) income and z is the level of public good provision. The marginal benefit of the public good is then $MRS(x, z) = \phi_2'(z)/\phi_1'(x)$ which, for households in a given jurisdiction, will vary only with x. Relative marginal benefits (across income levels) thus depend only on the marginal utilities of income, about which some evidence may be available. If, finally, it is assumed that the public good is provided at a level such that $\sum MRS = MC$, and if the marginal cost is known (e.g., $MC = \$1$ by choice of units), the actual magnitude of the marginal benefit can be assessed for households in various income classes. The faster the marginal utility of income declines, the higher will be the imputed marginal benefit of the public good to high income households. Greene *et al.* consider two cases, one with a constant marginal utility of income, and one with the marginal utility of income inversely proportional to income. They find that the imputation of benefits across income classes, and across jurisdictional boundaries, is quite sensitive to

---

[64] These studies also estimate cost spillovers, in the form of exported taxes, among jurisdictions. Tax spillovers are discussed in detail in Section 6.3.

this assumption, but that their central city—Washington, DC—does generate fiscal benefits for suburbs in the metropolitan area in either case.[65] Evidently, these results must be interpreted with considerable caution. There is clearly scope here for further research.

In addition to distributional issues, benefit spillovers from central cities to suburbs may also be important for urban spatial structure. Schweizer [321] considers a system of metropolitan areas, among and within which households are freely mobile. The flow of households into any one jurisdiction is limited by the rising per capita cost of public services. In a given metropolitan area, the central city provides a public good that benefits both own-residents and the residents of suburban areas. The problem is to determine what happens to the spatial structure of a metropolitan area, specifically, the population density gradient, as central government public good provision increases.

Though the results hold more generally, the analysis is simplest when the metropolitan area is a utility-taker relative to the whole economy. Increasing the level of public good in the central city will attract residents to suburbs, since utilities there would rise at unchanged populations. If the public good is initially provided at an efficient level, central city utility and therefore population will be unaffected by a change in public spending. Overall, then, an increase in the level of public good flattens the density gradient in the metropolitan area.

There remains scope for further analysis of benefit spillovers along these lines. It would be useful, for example, to examine the implications of spillovers for equilibrium wages, land rents, and other important variables characterizing the equilibrium urban structure. These are problems in positive economics that might also be important for the normative analysis of these externalities.

6.3. Tax exporting, tax competition, and optimal local taxation

Just as local public spending can generate benefits for non-residents, so might local taxation generate costs for non-residents. The shifting

---

[65] Interestingly, when allowance for cost spillovers is made, it appears that the central city produces net benefits for the suburbs in the case of declining marginal utility of income, but the reverse is true when the marginal utility of income is constant.

of the burden of lower-level government taxation to non-residents is generally referred to as *tax exporting*. It is sometimes argued that the incentive to tax-export distorts local tax structures and that tax exporting induces higher-than-efficient levels of local public expenditure. In addition to these possible allocative effects, tax exporting is also important from the viewpoint of tax incidence analysis. As one might expect, tax exporting is often related to the market power that a jurisdiction has. A tax on corn in a small corn-producing locality would not raise the equilibrium price of corn at all, and therefore could not be shifted to non-residents. This might not be the case, however, for a tax on hotel services in Florida in the winter, since in this case the taxing jurisdiction is fairly large relative to the market for a good that may not have highly perfect substitutes. These considerations indicate that the tax exporting capability of a jurisdiction will depend on constraints imposed by the market environment. Indeed, some studies emphasize only the constraints and focus on attempts by states or localities to attract industry by offering tax rebates on property taxes (or possibly other inducements such as publicly-provided infrastructure). This sort of behavior, which is generally referred to as *tax competition,* presumably reflects a highly elastic supply of factors (e.g., capital) to a locality, such that the locality is unable to impose a burden on non-resident factor owners. Tax competition is sometimes thought to distort the local tax structure, and to induce lower-than-efficient levels of local public expenditure.

It would appear that tax exporting and tax competition are simply different aspects of the same general problem. How does a locality determine an optimal tax policy in a given economic environment, taking interjurisdictional commodity and factor flows into account? Are locally-optimal policies efficient in a broader context? Do such considerations distort the local public expenditure decision? And, finally, what are the implications of such policies for the distribution of income and economic welfare? These are the fundamental issues to be discussed in this section.

In an early insightful analysis of tax exporting, McLure [227] demonstrated how a local tax on an exported commodity could raise its equilibrium price, depending on the elasticity of net demand facing the jurisdiction. A simple partial equilibrium model can illustrate the forces at work. Suppose S and D denote supply and demand for a good, with subscripts L and N referring to local and non-local. If p is the price of the good on the national market, and a per unit tax t is imposed on suppliers in a locality, the equilibrium condition for p is

$$D_L(p) + D_N(p) - S_L(p - t) - S_N(p) = 0,   \tag{6.1}$$

which determines p implicitly in terms of t. If σ_L^D, σ_L^S denote the local share in total demand and supply (e.g., $\sigma_L^D = D_L/(D_L + D_N)$), and if ε_L^D, ε_L^S, etc. denote local and non-local demand and supply elasticities, then one has[66]

$$\frac{dp}{dt} = \frac{-\dfrac{p}{p-t}\,\sigma_L^S \varepsilon_L^S}{\sigma_L^D \varepsilon_L^D + (1 - \sigma_L^D)\varepsilon_N^D - \dfrac{p}{p-t}\,\sigma_L^S \varepsilon_L^S - (1 - \sigma_L^S)\varepsilon_N^S}.   \tag{6.2}$$

Hence, the equilibrium price is not affected at all if $\varepsilon_L^S = 0$, or if any other demand or supply elasticities are infinite. Also $dp/dt \to 0$ as $\sigma_L^S \to 0$. Under any of these conditions, the locality is a price taker: a "small open economy." If $dp/dt > 0$, however, one expects that at least some tax burden is shifted to outsiders. Indeed, this idea is familiar from the optimal tariff literature in international trade theory, going back to Bickerdike [39].[67] The essential point is easily demonstrated. The loss of real income to local consumers from an incremental increase in t is $D_L(dp/dt)$, and the loss to local producers is $-S_L(d[p - t]/dt)$. The increase in tax revenue is $S_L + tS_L'(d[p - t]/dt)$, where S_L' is the derivative of S_L. The net gain to the locality is then

$$tS_L'\frac{d(p-t)}{dt} + (S_L - D_L)\frac{dp}{dt}.   \tag{6.3}$$

If $t > 0$, the first term is negative because $d(p - t)/dt < 0$. The second term is positive if the locality can affect the equilibrium price of the good. For t sufficiently small, the second term dominates the first, and a positive tax rate therefore raises local welfare.[68]

---

[66] See McLure [234] for a similar derivation.

[67] See, e.g., Bhagwati and Srinivasan [38] for a recent presentation of optimal tariff theory.

[68] This discussion assumes that changes in the profits of local producers accrue to local residents, and that the aggregate local real income change is a meaningful measure of local welfare change. (If local production occurs in firms not locally-owned, the welfare gain is of course larger.)

Note that this shows that localities definitely may have incentives to use taxes that are not optimal from a national perspective. Implicitly, the above analysis assumes that local tax revenues can be returned, lump-sum, to local residents. Imagine, then, an economy in which each jurisdiction can impose a non-distorting lump-sum tax, e.g., a land tax. In the absence of household mobility (more specifically, in the absence of congestion externalities arising from such mobility), such taxes would permit a first-best optimum to be achieved, conditional on whatever level of public expenditure might be selected in each locality. This would be Pareto-efficient for the economy as a whole. However, each jurisdiction that is able to influence equilibrium prices for exported goods would find it advantageous to tax exports, rebating the tax revenue in the form of land tax reductions. The net result, of course, is that welfare falls in at least some jurisdictions, and it may fall in all. This conclusion is well-known in the theory of retaliatory tariffs in international trade, e.g., Johnson [195].

Tax exporting, then, can result in inefficient taxation. Suppose we now consider a somewhat different situation. Let each jurisdiction be a price-taker in all traded-goods markets. Suppose also that there is some non-traded commodity in each locality that can be taxed, such as labor, and that labor has non-zero demand and supply elasticities. Then, in general, the locally-optimal tax policy (see below for more detail) would require non-zero tax rates on labor and on traded goods, resulting of course in a departure from first-best efficiency, since both the local labor markets and the traded goods markets are tax-distorted.[69] Suppose, however, that there is some traded good for which the demand, at the national level, is perfectly inelastic, or that there is some factor which is inelastically supplied. Clearly, if all localities jointly increase their taxes on such a good, the net effect would be to ease the distortions in the local labor markets without exacerbating the distortion of the market for the traded good or factor. (This argument is found in Gordon [137] and Wilson [383].)

Indeed, such a case was illustrated in Figure 10, in which each

---

[69] This general conclusion is familiar from the optimal taxation literature. See, e.g., Atkinson and Stiglitz [12] and Tresch [353] for textbook expositions. Dasgupta and Stiglitz [97] discuss the optimal tax and tariff structure for an open economy.

jurisdiction finds it advantageous to reduce its tax on perfectly mobile capital even though capital is fixed in supply for the economy as a whole. This situation seems to exemplify the phenomenon of tax competition: highly elastic demand or supply of traded commodities causes localities to drive down their taxes. The net effect, obviously, can be welfare-reducing for all or some localities. Just as tax exporting may induce jurisdictions to depart from highly efficient taxes on non-traded inelastically supplied or demanded commodities, so tax competition may induce localities to depart from highly efficient taxes on traded goods that are inelastically supplied or demanded at the national level. In the first case, taxing traded goods imposes a negative externality on outsiders, while in the second case it generates a positive externality.

General equilibrium analysis of tax exporting and tax competition. While the above general considerations shed light on the possible welfare effects of taxation of traded commodities, the discussion so far has implicitly abstracted from a number of relevant complexities. For example, suppose that an exported good is also locally consumed. An increase in the tax on this good might partly be borne by non-residents. It will also fall partly on local residents and will create some "local" excess burden in the sense that local consumer and producer prices are driven apart. (We assume here that the tax is assessed against both residents and non-residents, at uniform rates.) Suppose the locality must finance its expenditures using a combination of such taxes on traded and (possibly) non-traded goods. There may then be some tradeoff between higher taxation of traded vs. non-traded goods, or between traded goods for which the proportion of local vs. non-local consumption differs.

A discussion of such tradeoffs requires a general equilibrium analysis, as presented by Arnott and Grieson [6], for example.[70] The essence of the analysis is as follows. Let $x = (x_1, \ldots, x_n)$ be a net consumption bundle of traded and non-traded commodities for the single household residing in a jurisdiction. Let the producer price vector p for these commodities be fixed, which implies that the production technology (local or external) is linear. Consumer prices equal $(p + t)$, where t is a vector of tax rates and where t_i may be

---

[70] See also Arnott [5] and Wiegard [364].

constrained to equal zero for some commodities (i.e., some commodities may be untaxed). There are no profits or other lump-sum incomes. The consumer optimizes subject to a budget constraint, generating an indirect utility function $v(p + t, z)$ where z is a vector of public goods. The locally optimal tax policy, conditional on a given vector of public goods z, is found by maximizing v subject to a revenue constraint

$$tX = C(z), \tag{6.4}$$

where X is the vector of taxable net consumer demand, including both domestic demand x and foreign demand $x' = X - x$. Associating a multiplier λ with the budget constraint (6.4), the first-order conditions characterizing the maximum of v subject to (6.4) are, using Roy's formula,

$$-v_I x_i + \lambda \left(X_i + t \frac{\partial X}{\partial t_i} \right) = 0 \tag{6.5}$$

for all taxable commodities i.

In the special case where $x_i = 0$, (6.5) simply becomes a condition characterizing the collection of maximal tax revenue from foreigners: the locality exploits its monopoly power by choosing t_i so that

$$x_i' + t \frac{\partial x'}{\partial t_i} = 0. \tag{6.6}$$

In the more general case where $x_i > 0$, (6.5) shows that the *local* real income loss per dollar's worth of incremental tax revenue collected from an increase in the tax rate is equated across all taxed goods i and j, i.e.,

$$\frac{x_i}{X_i + t \dfrac{\partial X}{\partial t_i}} = \alpha = \frac{x_j}{X_j + t \dfrac{\partial X}{\partial t_j}} \tag{6.7}$$

where $\alpha = \lambda v_I^{-1}$. Except for cross-price effects, (6.7) shows that the tax rate on a commodity is higher, the greater the fraction of foreign demand and the lower the demand elasticity. This is seen by supposing $\partial X_k / \partial t_i = 0$ for all $k \neq i$, and for all i. Letting $\varepsilon_i = \partial \log X_i / \partial \log(p_i + t_i)$ denote the total demand elasticity for i, $\sigma_i = x_i / X_i$ the local share of demand for i, and $\tau_i = t_i / (p_i + t_i)$ the proportionate tax rate on i, (6.7) yields

$$\frac{\tau_i}{\tau_j} = \frac{\varepsilon_j}{\varepsilon_i} \frac{1 - \alpha\sigma_i}{1 - \alpha\sigma_j}. \tag{6.8}$$

This is just the inverse elasticity rule, modified to show that tax rates are also inversely related to local consumption shares. (This expression reduces to the inverse elasticity formula when $\sigma_i = \sigma_j = 1$.)

The analysis culminating in (6.7) and (6.8) shows that an optimal tax structure will in general require non-zero tax rates on both traded and non-traded commodities. In each case, there is a balancing of the revenue gains against the *local* real income loss, and it is obvious from (6.8) that the opportunity to export taxes, by shifting the real income loss to outsiders, shifts the tax structure toward heavier taxation of traded goods for which the jurisdiction has some market power. This general equilibrium analysis has also revealed, as one would expect, that cross-price effects should, in general, be taken into account in the evaluation of local tax policy.

Although the discussion so far has focused on the incentive for localities to exploit monopoly power to influence the terms of trade with the rest of the economy, the choice of optimal tax policy for an open economy has a number of interesting aspects even when the terms of trade are fixed. This issue could be studied in a quite general framework, allowing for many commodities and factors and unlimited flexibility in the choice of tax instruments. For present purposes, however, it is more interesting to look at specialized models which are designed with the policy regimes of typical local governments in mind, such as Beck [22] or McDonald [219]. Beck, for example, examines a locality that imports capital at an exogenously fixed net rate of return, and uses this capital to produce a non-traded good, such as residential housing or local services, and a traded (export) good. Labor, which is immobile, is used only in the production of the traded good. The locality provides two public goods, one which benefits households and one which benefits firms, and finances these outlays by a property tax, i.e., a tax on capital. Effective tax rates on capital in the non-traded and traded goods sectors are allowed to differ, however, as would occur with a uniform nominal rate and differential assessment of each type of property. Assuming Cobb–Douglas preferences and technology, Beck is able to present numerical simulations which indicate that it is advantageous, from the viewpoint of the representative household, for the locality to tax non-traded goods capital at a differentially higher rate. Such a policy attracts more capital to the traded goods sector than a uniform tax, and thus could be interpreted as a form of tax competition. Beck also considers optimal tax policy when there is an exogenously-specified minimum wage that is sufficiently high to create unemployment, at least when both categories of capital are taxed at equal rates. Preferential treatment of traded goods capital creates new employment opportunities in this case and the advantage derived from differential capital taxation is accordingly higher than in the full employment version of the model.

A limitation of simulation techniques, of course, is that they do not clearly reveal why the structural parameters of the economy interact to produce certain results. Subsequent work by Wilson [383] presents a general theoretical analysis of optimal differential taxation of business and residential property that does not require specific functional representations of preferences and technology. Wilson also considerably generalizes the Beck model by allowing labor to be used as an input in the non-traded goods industry. Now it is no longer invariably true that traded goods capital is optimally taxed at a lower rate than capital used to produce non-traded goods. Instead, the optimal rates depend on elasticities of production and consumption, factor shares, and other parameters. If both sectors have identical technologies, then capital used in the traded goods sector ought to be more lightly taxed. The general intuition behind this result appears to hinge on the fact that there is an infinitely elastic demand for exports but a finite elasticity of demand for non-traded goods. This suggests that, *cet. par.*, the welfare loss from taxation of capital is higher in the traded goods sector, and hence the tax rate there should be lower. However, Wilson shows that a lower tax rate on non-traded goods capital is sometimes optimal, and is more likely, when the elasticity of substitution in production in the non-traded (traded) goods sector is high (low), when the non-traded goods sector is labor intensive, and when the elasticity of substitution in consumption is high. Under these conditions, the elasticity of demand for capital in the non-traded goods sector tends to be high, and/or a tax reduction in the non-traded goods sector tends to increase the equilibrium amount of capital in the traded goods sector. Traditional optimal taxation theory leads one to expect a lower tax rate on non-traded goods capital under these conditions.

Tax exporting, tax competition, and public spending. Let us now consider the expenditure implications of tax exporting and tax competition. A popular view, found, e.g., in Bird and Slack [40], Hogan and Shelton [180], Ladd [205], McLure [228], Oates [264], and Zimmerman [392], is that tax exporting lowers the effective marginal cost of local public goods, inducing inefficient expansion of the local public sector. Alternatively, Mieszkowski and Toder [241] have argued that tax exporting only lowers the average price of local spending, not the marginal price. This issue is examined formally in Wildasin [376], where it is demonstrated that if a locality chooses its tax structure optimally, as in the Arnott–Grieson analysis sketched above, the possibility of exporting taxes does not affect the evaluation of public expenditure at the margin. The result follows by a simple application of the envelope theorem: given an optimizing tax structure, incremental revenues can as well be raised entirely from taxes on local residents as from those on traded commodities. Hence, the possibility of exporting taxes is of no special value at the margin, and the marginal cost of public spending is no different than it would be if incremental funding came only from internal sources.

This argument assumes that localities optimize their tax structures, and, in particular, that the range of tax instruments is not too restricted. In some cases, this assumption might be inappropriate. For example, localities might be required to use only uniform property taxes to finance their spending. If a non-negligible part of the tax could always be exported, such as some portion of the tax on industrial property, then the community would have an incentive to spend more than it otherwise would.

Actually, it would seem to be empirically rather unlikely that much of the local property tax can be exported, at least in the long run.[71] It is much more plausible that individual jurisdictions see the net cost of capital as exogenously fixed, with no exporting possibility. The question in this case is not whether localities have an incentive to spend "more" because they can shift costs to outsiders, but whether they have an incentive to spend "less" for fear of overtaxing mobile capital which is then driven away. "More" or "less" comparisons require some reference level of public good provision, however, and it is not exactly clear what the appropriate level is. For example, one might demonstrate that localities would wish to spend more on property-tax-financed local public goods if all local capital could be held fixed in the face of higher taxes. But if this hypothetical situation could never arise in practice because the mobility of capital cannot be effectively restrained, of what relevance is the comparison? The economy, after all, could be assumed to be different in any number of ways, resulting in many different hypothetical levels of local spending. Why should this particular one be of interest?

Several approaches to this problem have been followed in the literature. For example, Zodrow and Mieszkowski [395] examine the incentive to provide a local public good to households and/or firms when incremental spending must be financed either by a property tax or by a head tax. For the case of public goods provided to households, but financed by a tax on freely mobile capital used in production, they find that incremental public spending is always less attractive than it would be if financed via a head tax, and that the property tax on mobile capital therefore induces "underprovision" of the local public good.

An alternative approach is taken by Wilson [384], who compares public goods levels in terms of the welfare effects of hypothetical changes in the amounts provided. Wilson imagines an economy with many small identical jurisdictions, each relying on a uniform property tax to provide a local public good and each facing an

---

[71] This statement does not contradict the Mieszkowski–Zodrow [243] argument (mentioned in Section 5.2) that the local tax falls on capital as a whole, even for a small jurisdiction. From the viewpoint of the spending decision of the individual locality, the key question is whether local tax policy perceptibly influences the net return to capital in the economy as a whole. This effect will still be small for a small jurisdiction, even if external capital, in the aggregate, bears a non-trivial fraction of the local property tax.

exogenously given net return to capital. Capital is fixed in supply to the economy as a whole. Wilson infers that tax competition results in too little public good provision if all households would be made better off by a simultaneous small increase in the amount of public good provided in all jurisdictions, given that each community is initially at a locally-optimal policy. The idea here is that decentralized localities may find themselves in a prisoner's dilemma, having driven taxes and spending too low in an effort to attract mobile capital at the expense of others. The relevant comparison, then, is with the outcome where all jurisdictions play cooperative strategies.

Wilson finds that local spending is too low in the above sense whenever incremental spending, and the accompanying balanced budget tax changes, would cause an outflow of capital. To see the intuition behind this result, consider an economy where local public goods are produced using a single all-purpose private good. Given the fixed supply of capital to the economy as a whole, the tax on capital is, in the aggregate, an ideal non-distorting tax. Local public goods should be provided at the point there the Samuelsonian $\sum MRS = MC$ condition is satisfied. For an individual locality, however, the local property tax is a distortionary tax, and it may well restrict the public good to a level such that $\sum MRS > MC$ because of the perceived marginal excess burden of the local tax.[72] In such an economy, each jurisdiction sees a local tax/spending increase as causing a loss of local capital, satisfying Wilson's condition, and each would benefit from a simultaneous expansion of public good provision.[73]

Tax incidence in an open economy.   We now turn to the distribu-

---

[72] Certain additional assumptions concerning the effect of public good provision on the demand for private goods are required to guarantee $\sum MRS > MC$. See Wildasin [370, 374] for discussion. Also see the references of n. 45 above.

[73] Wilson's model is actually somewhat more complex than this, because he explicitly analyses the local public good production process. He assumes that capital and labor are the inputs to this process, and finds that these inputs will not be chosen in a production-efficient manner. Given this inefficiency, however, he finds that a sufficient condition for underprovision of local public goods is that public production is more labor intensive than private production. This accords with the above intuitive argument. The labor intensity condition insures that an expansion of local public good provision does not bring in so much capital that the local capital stock rises as taxes and spending increase.

tional implications of tax exporting. We have seen that a tax in one jurisdiction can influence the price of a taxed good or factor in other jurisdictions. But this is, of course, only part of the effect of the tax. For example, a tax in one jurisdiction on an exported good will not only raise the good's price. It will also, by contracting output, cause factors to be released from the export industry. These must be absorbed either in other industries in the taxing jurisdiction or in other localities. Such intersectoral and/or interjurisdictional factor flows generally necessitate changes in factor prices, which can be important for the functional and interregional distribution of income.

The types of considerations that come into play here are well-known in tax incidence theory: factor proportions and demand and substitution elasticities are important determinants of the effect of a tax on equilibrium factor and output prices. In addition, interjurisdictional factor (and commodity) mobility is important and adds a new dimension to the usual non-spatial tax incidence analysis. A number of studies, including McLure [229, 230, 231], Homma [182], and Gerking and Mutti [135] have extended the Harberger two-sector model by assuming two regions, two traded goods, and two factors, one of which (generally labor) is immobile, the other of which is mobile. McLure and Homma assume that each region is completely specialized in the production of one good, while Gerking and Mutti allow one region to produce both goods.

There are many tax policies that one can study in such a setting, and we cannot enumerate or discuss all the possibilities here. The flavor of the analysis, however, can easily be illustrated by examination of a representative case, drawn from Gerking and Mutti. Suppose region A exports good 1 and imports good 2. A produces both 1 and 2, while B produces only 2. Capital is mobile, labor is immobile. Consider now a tax on output of good 1 in region A. The tax causes the gross price of good 1 to rise, to an extent that depends on the elasticity of demand for good 1, as we have seen. In addition, the net price of good 1 falls, as does its output. This results in a flow of factors from production of good 1 to production of good 2, as the output of good 2 expands. If industry 1 is capital intensive in A relative to industry 2, industry 2 cannot absorb all of the released capital at unchanged factor prices, and the price of capital is therefore depressed. Consequently capital flows to region

B. Wages rise in both regions. If industry 1 is labor intensive, contraction of the industry drives up the return to capital in *A,* causing an inflow of capital from *B.* Wages then fall in both regions. These conclusions contrast with those of McLure and Homma, who assume that each region is completely specialized. In such a case, a tax on *A*'s export necessarily causes a capital flow from *A* to *B,* causing the wage in *A* to fall and that in *B* to rise.

In addition to illuminating the distributional effect of tax policy in a spatial context, these general equilibrium analyses show that it may not be welfare-enhancing for a region to tax an exported commodity, even if the terms of trade can be affected. The reason, essentially, is that an increase in the price of an exported good may be accompanied by a more-than-offsetting increase (decrease) in the price of an imported (exported) factor.

In any application, therefore, it is important to evaluate the complete impact of a change in tax policy, including all relevant price changes. One may be able to justify certain special assumptions in some cases. For example, one might wish to assume that each jurisdiction is small relative to the markets for mobile factors but large relative to some output markets. Considerations of this sort might make it possible to reach some judgment about the amount of exporting of various taxes in practice. (See, for example, McLure [228], Phares [277], and Pogue [283] for estimates of tax exporting.) Ultimately, of course, detailed empirical study would be required to ascertain precisely the general equilibrium impact of a tax change. As suitable empirical information becomes available, applications of general equilibrium computational algorithms a la Shoven and Whalley [327], perhaps using a model such as that of Kimball and Harrison [199], would clearly be valuable.

Game-theoretic considerations. The analysis so far has been implicitly based on the assumption that strategic interactions between governments can be ignored. Thus, in raising the tax on an exported good, we assume that a jurisdiction is constrained only by the external net demand for its exports. The response of other jurisdictions could be important in some applications, however (McLure [235]). Kolstad and Wolak [202], for instance, consider the case of severance taxes on coal by the states of Montana and Wyoming, noting that the policy of one state may influence the optimal policy of the others. Kolstad and Wolak examine the hypothesis that states will find Nash equilibria in tax rates, and show that the amount of exporting under this non-cooperative behavior is significantly greater than zero but less than one would find with complete cooperation. They also illustrate that when either state is a Stackelberg leader, it chooses a higher tax rate for itself, inducing also a higher tax rate for the follower.

Mintz and Tulkens [248] present a detailed analysis of the interactions between two jurisdictions, each of which taxes a traded good and provides a local public good. Each locality's optimal tax/expenditure policy is determined, conditional on the other's policy, and reaction functions are derived. Reaction functions are discontinuous, which implies that Nash equilibria may not exist. When equilibria do exist, they are not, in general, Pareto optimal. Essentially, a tax change in one locality affects both the price faced by consumers, and the amount of tax revenue collected, in the other jurisdiction. Both of these effects are ignored by the self-interested policymakers, resulting in inefficiency.

6.4. Household mobility and intergovernmental fiscal interactions

One aspect of horizontal fiscal interactions that deserves special consideration concerns household mobility. As discussed by many authors (see, e.g., Oates [262, 264], Buchanan [77], Gramlich [141], Gramlich and Laren [144], and Brown and Oates [64]), poor households may be attracted, and rich households repelled, by (pro-poor) local redistribution, whether through taxes, transfers, or the provision of public services, and the scope for redistributive programs at the local government level may therefore be very limited. On reflection, it is apparent that this problem is related to the locational efficiency problem discussed in Section 2. A redistributive program causes fiscal externalities to be associated with migration: entry of a wealthy household generates net benefits for a jurisdiction, and entry of a poor household generates net costs. Locational efficiency clearly requires that such redistribution not be carried out. (If it is undertaken nonetheless, it may be possible for intergovernmental grants to prevent some of the resulting efficiency losses, as discussed in the next section.) In addition, it has been recognized that potential adverse migratory flows may provide a disincentive for redistributive policy at the local level. Indeed, in the limiting case where a jurisdiction is a utility taker, redistribution can only increase (decrease) the number of poor (rich) households, without increasing their welfare at all. Many models of local government behavior would imply that no redistribution would occur in this case.[74]

This raises the general question of the implications of household mobility for the determination of local public expenditure (and also for tax policy). For example, if an increase in public services (and taxes) is expected to result in an increase in local population, does this provide an incentive (or disincentive) to carry out the marginal expenditure? Several possibilities come to mind. Immigration can lead to congestion. (In the particular case of redistributive transfers, the congestion cost of a poor migrant would just be the resulting extra transfer payment.) On the other hand, immigration can increase equilibrium land values, which would be advantageous to landowners. Other prices might also be affected.

Section 4 has already discussed some of the implications of household mobility for public expenditure determination. There we saw that, under some circumstances, land value- or profit-maximizing behavior leads to fully efficient outcomes. Migration, in these cases, does not distort the public expenditure margin. In these cases, however, it is also true that locational efficiency is achieved, through appropriate combinations of assumptions about congestibility of local public goods and their financing. What happens in more general cases?

Starrett [337, 338, 340] and Boadway [45] address this issue. Starrett evaluates the welfare effect of incremental public expenditure in a jurisdiction from the perspective of the households initially residing there. While Starrett's model is quite general, the essential ideas can be understood using variants of the simple model of Section 2. Suppose first that there are just two classes of households in the economy, one of which is immobile and holds all land endowments (class 1) and the other of which consists of freely

---

[74] Pauly [274] shows, however, that there will be at least some local redistribution in cases where local policy can affect equilibrium utilities. Also, Oakland [261] emphasizes that mobility among regions may be much more restricted than mobility among localities within an urban area. Oakland in fact develops a model of lower-level government redistribution with completely immobile households.

mobile workers (class 2). Suppose that community i taxes land at rate τ_{ir}, and imposes a head tax of τ_{in}. Assume for simplicity that there is no agricultural sector, and no production of the all-purpose good. Each class has an endowment $\bar{x}^k$ of this good. Also for simplicity, assume no interpersonal crowding effects. The immobile households in jurisdiction i enjoy utility $v^1(r_i, \tau_{ir}, \tau_{in}, z_i)$, obtained by maximizing $u_i^1(x_i^1, t_i^1, z_i)$ subject to the budget constraint

$$x_i^1 + r_i t_i^1 = \bar{x}^1 + (r_i - \tau_{ir})T_i - \tau_{in}. \tag{6.9}$$

The immobile households in jurisdiction i obtain utility $v_i^2(r_i, \tau_{in}, z_i)$ after maximizing $u_i^2(\cdot)$ subject to

$$x_i^2 + r_i t_i^2 = \bar{x}^2 - \tau_{in}. \tag{6.10}$$

Suppose jurisdiction i is small and open in the sense that the utility offered to type-2 households must be equal to some exogenously-given $\bar{v}^2$. Local policy cannot then affect the welfare of migrants and we therefore imagine that it is selected by immobile households, subject to a local government budget constraint

$$\tau_{ir}T_i + \tau_{in}(n_i^2 + 1) = C_i(n_i^2 + 1, z_i) \tag{6.11}$$

to maximize v_i^1. (Here we normalize $n_i^1 = 1$ without loss of generality.) To keep the analysis simple suppose that τ_{in} is fixed, so that incremental expenditures are financed by land taxation.

A change in z_i will now affect the utility of the immobile decisionmaker in three ways: directly, through the effect on land rents, and through the effect on the land tax. The equilibrium condition

$$v_i^2 = \bar{v}^2 \tag{6.12}$$

can be used to solve for r_i in terms of z_i. The land market equilibrium condition

$$t_i^1 + n_i^2 t_i^2 = T_i \tag{6.13}$$

and the government budget constraint (6.11) can then be used to solve for n_i^2 and τ_{ir} in terms of z_i. One can then differentiate v_i^1 with respect to z_i to determine whether an incremental unit of z_i will be welfare-enhancing or not.[75] We find

$$(v_{il}^1)^{-1} \frac{dv_i^1}{dz_i} = MRS_i^1 + (T_i - t_i^1) \frac{\partial r_i}{\partial z_i} - T_i \frac{\partial \tau_{ir}}{\partial z_i}$$

$$= MRS_i^1 + n_i^2 MRS_i^2 - C_{iz} - (C_{in} - \tau_{in}) \frac{\partial n_i^2}{\partial z_i} \quad (6.14)$$

where v_{il}^1 is the marginal utility of income for immobile households in i and MRS_i^k is the marginal valuation of the public good in i by households of type k.

It is clear from (6.14) that the locality will choose efficient levels of public good provision if congestion effects are internalized at the margin $(C_{in} = \tau_{in})$. If this is not the case, however, the locality has an incentive to distort its expenditure decision, either to attract $(\tau_{in} > C_{in})$ or repel $(\tau_{in} < C_{in})$ migrant households. Thus, the problems of locational efficiency and expenditure efficiency are closely related.

It should be noted, however, that the utility-taking assumption is central to this result.[76] Boadway [45] varies the Starrett model by supposing that there is only one class of households in the entire economy and that land rents in all jurisdictions are shared equally among them. Obviously, a jurisdiction cannot be regarded as utility-taking in this framework, since local residents would then be indifferent to policy and no determinate theory of local government behavior could be derived. Thus, Boadway assumes that each jurisdiction maximizes the utility of its residents, subject to an equal utility constraint, and that the jurisdiction perceives the effect of its own policies on the true equilibrium level of utility in the economy as a whole. In effect, then, the locality is open but not small. But since each jurisdiction is then effectively choosing policies that maximize the common level of utility throughout the entire economy, its policies will be chosen in an efficient way. Boadway

---

[75] The details of the argument are easily worked out. See also Wildasin [373] for a similar model.

[76] Actually, this assumption is not clearly spelled out in Starrett. In fact, the equilibrium condition that determines how population changes with local policy is left unspecified. Thus, the foregoing analysis, though consistent with Starrett, makes certain explicit assumptions not found in the original discussion.

concludes, therefore, that migration does not induce localities to distort their expenditure decisions.

The varying conclusions reached by Starrett and Boadway thus seem clearly dependent on differing assumptions. One might wish to use one approach or the other, depending on the application in hand. Of course, in both cases the political decision-making mechanism that determines local behavior is quite simple. In more complex models, there may be little reason to expect efficient locally-optimizing policies. The implications of household mobility for the efficiency of local policy remain to be examined in such a context.

6.5. Intergovernmental transfers

Let us now turn to a discussion of the effect of higher-level government policies on localities and other lower-level governments. The discussion will focus on intergovernmental grants, since these have been widely studied. However, it is worth mentioning that intergovernmental transfers are not the only federal government policies that are important for urban economies and the local public sector. For example, federal tax policy can influence capital formation and thus urban growth, as discussed by Courant [91]. More specifically, some features of the tax law may favor owner-occupied housing, or may favor housing in general as against other forms of investment. (See, e.g., Rosen, [303].) As another example, a tax on wage income reduces the relative value of time and thus the cost of commuting, which distorts urban spatial structure (see Wildasin, [378]). These aspects of federal tax policy would be relevant, for instance, in any complete analysis of the efficiency effects of the property tax. For brevity, however, we do not discuss these issues further.

A. Modeling recipient government response to aid. For many purposes, one wishes to be able to predict the effect of transfers from higher level governments on the spending and other policies of recipient governments. For example, how much do lump-sum grants stimulate local spending compared with matching grants? Does a given lump-sum transfer to a locality cause local public spending to increase by the amount of the grant, or might the grant take the place of some local financing and, in effect, be rebated to residents in the form of a tax reduction? Also, does it matter whether or not the funds received are specifically designated for a particular function, such as police protection, or are such designations economically irrelevant?

All of these questions have been examined at some length, theoretically and empirically, in the literature. The easiest way to approach them is through the "community preference" model discussed in Section 3.2. Certain theoretical results, noted there, are easily established: Matching grants stimulate recipient government spending more (per dollar of grant funds received) than lump-sum grants. Government spending increases in response to lump-sum grants by an amount given by the income elasticity of demand for public goods, and responds identically to equal increases in private income. (If the income elasticity of demand for private goods is positive, this implies that some lump-sum aid is used to reduce taxes.) Finally, consider lump-sum categorical aid, that is, lump-sum transfers that are to be spent only on a particular governmental function. If the amount of such aid is no greater than the otherwise desired amount of expenditure on the specified function, it will be equivalent, in its effects on recipient government spending and on welfare, to an equal but unrestricted lump-sum transfer.[77] These well-known results appear, e.g., in Oates [264], and in other studies mentioned in Section 3.2.

These propositions also have their counterparts in the median voter model. For example, Bradford and Oates [58, 59] show how the stimulative effects of matching relative to lump-sum grants reappear in a simple majority-voting framework. To see their result, suppose that initially a matching rate m is offered to a jurisdiction. Let w^k, x^k, and t^k be the income, private good consumption, and local tax share of household k in the locality. Then, if $C(z)$ represents the level of public good expenditure, this household faces the budget constraint

$$x^k + t^k(1 - m)C(z) = w^k, \qquad (6.15)$$

---

[77] This conclusion follows because the recipient can reduce the budget for the specified function, using the savings to support other functions or to cut taxes: the fungibility argument. If the size of the grant is greater than otherwise desired expenditure on the function, the funds will not be completely fungible and expenditure on the aided function will be correspondingly higher.

and the median voter chooses, say, the level z_m of public good provision, resulting in x_m^k units of private good consumption for voter k. The total transfer to the locality is $mC(z_m)$. Now suppose the locality receives an equal lump-sum grant of $L = mC(z_{\hat{m}})$. Voter k's budget constraint becomes

$$x^k + t^k C(z) = w^k + t^k L, \tag{6.16}$$

which passes through the consumption bundle (x_m^k, z_m) but which has a higher relative price of z at that point. Clearly this grant substitution will induce the median voter to demand less than z_m units of the public good. Moreover, any voter who was initially below-median will remain below median. (The rotation of the budget line through the point (x_m^k, z_m) ensures this, by revealed preference.) Thus, a majority of voters favors a reduction in spending under the lump-sum grant.

Not all implications of the community preference model necessarily extend to the median voter model, however. For example, an increase in total or median income in a jurisdiction need not have the same effect on local public spending as an equivalent increase in lump-sum aid. A dollar increase in total community income will increase spending more or less than a dollar of aid, according as the median voter's share of the income increase is greater or less than that voter's tax share. If, however, tax shares are based on property shares, and property ownership is proportional to income, this equal share condition would be met. It is plausible, therefore, that expenditure responses to income and lump-sum aid would be similar in magnitude in a median voter model.

Empirical results seem to be generally consistent with many of the implications of the community preference and median voter models. For example, intergovernmental aid seems to increase recipient government expenditures, more so for matching than lump-sum grants, higher private income leads to higher public expenditures, etc. One puzzling result, however, is the finding that a dollar's worth of lump-sum aid increases public spending more than a dollar's worth of private income—the so-called flypaper effect.

This finding has led to a number of attempts to revise the simple theory. One approach, suggested by Courant, et al. [92] and by Oates [267], is to suppose that households experience a fiscal illusion when the jurisdiction in which they reside receives a grant. (A similar argument appears in Winer [385].) A lump-sum grant lowers the cost to the locality of any given level of public good provision, and this may incorrectly be perceived as lowering the per unit price of local public goods. Lump-sum grants would then have substitution as well as income effects, and would stimulate spending more than equal increases in private income, as seems to be observed. Note, however, that any actual adjustments that the locality makes in response to lump-sum grants will surprise its residents: increases in government spending will cost more than expected, i.e., the perceived budget constraint differs from the true one, and this may be noticed as the community tries to move along the perceived constraint.

An alternative explanation for a flypaper effect can be developed by hypothesizing, as in Oates [266, 268], that public services are more cheaply provided to higher-income residents. (The standard example is education: it is held that educational output, for a given amount of publicly-provided inputs, depends heavily on the socio-economic characteristics of children, and in turn on their parents' income.) Hamilton [161] argues that, in a cross-section of jurisdictions, higher-income jurisdictions will spend less per unit of (say) education because they effectively substitute private inputs for public ones. The income elasticity of demand for education will thus be higher than the estimated income elasticity of demand for educational expenditure. An increase in lump-sum aid does not directly improve the socio-economic variables that substitute for public inputs in education. A cross-section regression would therefore be expected to show that, per incremental dollar, grants result in greater increases in public *expenditure* on education than equal increments to income—even though the opposite might be true of the effect on units of education *per se*. Hamilton finds that at least part of the empirical discrepancy between income and grant effects on local spending can be explained in this way, for reasonable assumptions about substitutability between public and private inputs and other parameters.

A third possible explanation for the flypaper effect can be based on the observation (see Fisher, [124, 125, 126] that many grants that appear to be lump-sum are actually allocated according to formulae that have implicit matching features. For instance, grant size can be positively dependent on "tax effort," i.e., some measure of recipient government tax rates, perhaps relative to tax rates in other jurisdictions. In such a case, an increase in expenditures financed from own-sources will increase tax effort and hence grant aid, thus lowering the effective marginal cost of public expenditures to the recipient jurisdiction. Statistical analyses that fail to account for such implicit matching would obviously tend to exhibit higher expenditure responsiveness to grants than to income.[78]

Still another illusion argument has been advanced by Filimon et al. [122]. They suggest that voters are not aware of the amount of grant funds received by a jurisdiction, so that the possibility of using grants to reduce own-source financing and increase private consumption may never arise. This could be the result, in part, of behavior by bureaucrats who seek to maximize local spending and who therefore try to disguise or conceal any grant aid. In their empirical work, Filimon et al. find support for this hypothesis.

Of course, despite all of these considerations, it is quite possible that the flypaper effect presents a problem for the standard community preference and median voter models because those models are fundamentally invalid. As the discussion of Sections 3 and 4 indicates, there are many possible alternative models of local government behavior that could be used to analyze the effects of grants. Romer and Rosenthal [297], for example, use a budget-maximizing bureaucrat model to show how grants may interact with reversion levels to influence spending in ways quite different from those predicted by the standard median voter model. (Filimon et al. find some empirical support for this approach to the analysis of grants.) Most of the other models discussed in Sections 3 and 4 however, especially those in which household mobility is important,

---

[78] See also Chernick [86] for a discussion of the process by which the terms of a grant are sometimes negotiated between donor and recipient, and the implications for recipient behavioral response to grant programs. In related work, McGuire [222, 223, 224] has also emphasized that the terms under which grant funds are received may be subject to negotiation, and that there can in general be both price and income effects that are not explicit features of the actual transfer. McGuire supposes that the community has made utility-maximizing choices and then infers a preference structure, and share of grants received in lump-sum form, that are compatible with the data. McGuire also, however, allows for an "illusion" parameter, and finds that even the lump-sum components of grants stimulate spending more than private income.

have not been used to analyze recipient government response to intergovernmental transfers. Whether the effects of grants on spending might depend on household mobility remains largely an unexplored issue, worth careful consideration in future research.[79]

B. Normative aspects of intergovernmental transfers. As a matter of accounting identity, all grant funds received by a jurisdiction must be used either to augment spending or to reduce taxes. The allocative and distributional effects of such grants obviously will depend on exactly how the recipient government behaves under this constraint. For this reason the foregoing positive analysis is ultimately of crucial importance for normative issues of grant design or reform.

This subsection discusses several efficiency and equity aspects of intergovernmental transfers. We begin with seminal papers by Buchanan [72, 73], who was concerned with the problems of horizontal equity and efficiency in federal systems.[80] Buchanan argued that, on net, local fiscal systems tend to treat unequally households who are alike in all respects except that they reside in different jurisdictions, even if localities are horizontally equitable in the treatment of households *within* their jurisdictional boundaries. Of course, if households are freely mobile, horizontal inequities cannot persist in equilibrium: migration serves as a spatial arbitrage mechanism to ensure that equals are everywhere equally well off. As a consequence, however, households may be responding to fiscal incentives that induce inefficient location patterns. This is relevant for the problem of locational efficiency discussed in Section 2.

To illustrate, consider two jurisdictions 1 and 2. Initially, let us suppose neither jurisdiction collects taxes or provides public services. Suppose that all households are identical except for income, and that in an initial equilibrium we have three type 1 individuals with $30,000 incomes and three type 2 with $10,000 incomes. Suppose this equilibrium has two wealthy individuals and one poor

[79] See the discussion in the next subsection. Also, for an interesting attempt to integrate the locational choices of households, the determination of property values, and the decisionmaking of a decisive voter in an empirically-workable predictive model, see Inman [185, 186, 188].

[80] The Buchanan argument is restated and expanded in Boadway and Flatters [46, 47].

TABLE I
Real income distribution with proportional local income taxes

Household type	Jurisdiction 1		Jurisdiction 2	
	Pure public goods	Per capita benefits	Pure public goods	Per capita benefits
1	$0.9 \times \$30{,}000$ $+ G^1(\$7{,}000)$	$0.9 \times \$30{,}000$ $+ \$7{,}000/3$	$0.9 \times \$30{,}000$ $+$ $G^1(\$5{,}000)$	$0.9 \times \$30{,}000$ $+ \$5{,}000/3$
2	$0.9 \times \$10{,}000$ $+ G^2(\$7{,}000)$	$0.9 \times \$10{,}000$ $+ \$7{,}000/3$	$0.9 \times \$10{,}000$ $+$ $G^2(\$5{,}000)$	$0.9 \times \$10{,}000$ $+ \$5{,}000/3$

Note: Total tax revenue $C_1 = \$7{,}000$, $C_2 = \$5{,}000$.

individual in locality 1, with the other households in 2. Suppose the jurisdictions are equivalent in other respects, so that no household has an incentive to move.

Now let each jurisdiction impose a 10% tax, and suppose that the benefits of the resulting local expenditure, C_i in locality i, are either purely public, valued at, say, $G^k(C_i)$ to households of type k, or that benefits are equal to total outlays and are allocated on a per capita basis, giving $C_i/(n_i^1 + n_i^2)$ to each household. The real income distribution is now as shown in Table I.

If households are immobile, the net effect of the local policies is to make households in jurisdiction 1 better off than those in 2, whether local public goods are purely public or not. One might regard this as a horizontally inequitable outcome, as Buchanan argues.

Another way of looking at this problem of horizontal inequity is in terms of the tax rates required to finance public services. A jurisdiction can finance a given level of public spending with a lower tax rate if its tax base is greater: in our example, $5,000 worth of public spending can be achieved in jurisdiction 1 with a tax rate of less than 10%.[81]

Now suppose instead that households are freely mobile. Under a 10% tax in each jurisdiction, both rich and poor households will

---

[81] Partly as a result of important court decisions on local school finance in the U.S., this issue has attracted considerable attention in recent years. See Inman and Rubinfeld [194] and Rubinfeld [308] for discussion.

wish to move from poor jurisdiction 2 to rich jurisdiction 1. In fact, if the relocation of households did not affect private incomes, jurisdiction 2 would, in equilibrium, be completely empty.[82] Of course, this would not occur in practice because of the presence of immobile factors of production, which would cause wages to rise (fall) in the sending (receiving) jurisdiction, until income differentials are created which would be sufficient to compensate for the fiscal advantages of the rich jurisdiction. At this point, there are no horizontal inequities, in the sense that households of each type are equally well off in either jurisdiction. This fiscally-induced migration may result in locational inefficiency, however.[83] Indeed, recalling the analysis of Section 2, it is quite clear that the tax-expenditure policies portrayed in Table I do produce inefficient locational choices. Pure public goods should not be financed by taxes on mobile labor, and public expenditures yielding per capita benefits are, in effect, providing perfectly congestible or purely private goods, and should be financed with a uniform head tax.[84] In neither case is an income tax optimal.

One possible way that these problems could be corrected would be for lower-level government tax structures to be revised. As Section 2's discussion makes clear, this could at least solve the locational inefficiencies that arise in the free-mobility case. However, in some contexts (for example, from the perspective of a policymaker in a higher-level government), it may be appropriate to take lower-level tax structures as given.

In such a context, many authors have examined the use of intergovernmental transfers as a method for dealing with these problems of horizontal inequity or locational inefficiency. The usual proposal involves "equalizing" grants, which allow all jurisdictions to achieve a representative level of public spending (usually per capita) at a representative tax rate.[85] In the example above, a

---

[82] This sort of unrestricted migration occurs in the model of Wheaton [359], because there are no locationally-fixed factors of production.

[83] For recent discussions of fiscally-induced migration in Canada see Winer and Gauthier [386] and Watson [356].

[84] Also, congestible public goods should not be financed by taxes on the returns to immobile factors. Boadway and Flatters [48] discuss this issue.

[85] The literature on this topic is large, and we only mention a few examples here: Boadway and Flatters [46, 47, 48], Bradbury et al. [56], Buchanan [72, 73], Buchanan and Wagner [79], Feldstein [120], Flatters, et al. [127], Hartwick [164], LeGrand [206], LeGrand and Reschovsky [207], and Yinger [391].

spatially-uniform proportional federal income tax could be levied and used to transfer $2,000 to locality 2. Both jurisdictions would then be able to sustain $7,000 of expenditure at a 10% local tax rate, and the horizontal inequity or locational efficiency problem would seem to disappear.

Several possible complications arise with such equalization programs, however. Suppose, for example, that upon receiving an equalizing transfer, jurisdiction 2 keeps C_2 constant at $5,000, and reduces its income tax rate (to 6%). Is the outcome now horizontally equitable? In the per capita benefits case, a type 1 individual in jurisdiction 2 now has a real income (gross of federal tax[86]) of $0.94 \times \$30,000 + \$5,000/3 = 0.9 \times \$30,000 + \$1,200 + \$5,000/3 > 0.9 \times \$30,000 + \$7,000/3$. Thus, horizontal inequities persist in the high income class—now favoring, however, the type 1 individual in the poor jurisdiction. On the other hand, a simple calculation shows that the type 2 individuals in jurisdiction 2 are still worse off than those in jurisdiction 1. Furthermore, in the case where local public goods benefits are not equal to expenditures per capita, the situation is even more complex. With a reduction of the tax rate in jurisdiction 2 to 6% and constant public expenditure, experimentation easily demonstrates that individuals of either (or both or neither) type may be better or worse off in locality 2 than in jurisdiction 1, depending on the functions G^k.

Thus, whether equalizing grants actually reduce, eliminate, reverse, or even exacerbate existing horizontal inequities or locational inefficiencies depends very much on the behavioral response of recipient jurisdictions and on the nature and distribution of the benefits from local government spending. As noted originally, the locational inefficiencies themselves arise from the interaction between the local public good production technology (crowding) and local tax structure. It is difficult, therefore, to propose one particular type of intergovernmental transfer program as a solution to lapses in equity or efficiency in all cases.

Given these complexities, it seems appropriate to study the welfare effects of intergovernmental transfers under a variety of

---

[86] For simplicity, we calculate gross-of-federal-tax incomes because the spatially-uniform federal tax can be ignored for horizontal equity or locational efficiency purposes.

hypotheses about local tax structure, local government expenditure determination, mobility/immobility of households, congestibility of local public goods, etc. Wildasin [373], for example, considers an economy (like that discussed in Section 6.4 above) in which each locality contains some immobile landowning households and in which there is a class of freely mobile non-landowning households. Immobile households are assumed to control local expenditures. (In fact, each jurisdiction takes the utility of mobile households as given, so that mobile households have no incentive to vote or otherwise influence local policy.) If only a local land tax is used to finance local spending, and if local public goods are purely public, then an efficient level of local public spending will be achieved in each locality, and from Section 2 we also know that locational efficiency is achieved. Intergovernmental grants which are conditioned either on population or on public spending will introduce distortions in such an economy. On the other hand, if local public goods are congestible, and if immobile households are able to impose head taxes as well as using land taxes to finance local spending, it turns out that optimal local taxes will in fact be chosen so that efficient locational choices again emerge. Expenditure efficiency is also achieved, and grants again have no efficiency role to play.

Grants have a more important function when local taxes are not optimal, however. If localities are restricted to land taxes when local public goods are impure, i.e., if optimal head taxes cannot be used, then inefficient locational choices will be made. Immobile households will then manipulate local spending so as to deter entry of congestion-generating mobile households. Given these two distorted margins, grants can indeed improve welfare. For example, a per capita grant program can eliminate the incentive to distort the local expenditure decision. It will also, of course, change the equilibrium locational pattern of the mobile households, in a way which might or might not improve locational efficiency. Matching grants could also improve expenditure efficiency. Essentially, the usefulness of any grant program depends on the general equilibrium response of the spending and locational decisions in all jurisdictions, and these in turn depend on several empirical parameters.

This analysis confirms that optimal grant policy depends sensitively on the characteristics of local public services, and on local tax structures.[87] It is limited, however, by the assumption that local taxes fall only on non-produced goods (land or heads). A further issue arises when lower-level governments tax produced structures or variably-supplied labor. How might these tax distortions be relevant for the evaluation of grant policy? An analysis which explores this issue is presented in Wildasin [377]. A local "distortionary factor" is derived that depends on demand and supply elasticities for a taxed good or factor, and that reflects the marginal excess burden of local taxation. Other things the same, a net welfare gain can be had by transferring resources toward jurisdictions with high distortionary factors. For example, an incremental increase in matching grants, starting from zero, will be welfare-enhancing if (equity-weighted) distortionary factors are positively correlated with local spending levels, even though matching grants might themselves distort the local expenditure decision.[88]

These considerations suggest that the determination of optimal grant policy depends on many factors in addition to wealth or income, the focus of much of the equalization literature.[89] The discussion here has only indicated a few possible approaches to the welfare evaluation of grants in an economy with expenditure, locational, and tax distortions. We may conclude our discussion by drawing attention, once again, to the critical problem of modeling

---

[87] An extension of the analysis to the case where the utility of migrant households is not regarded as exogenous appears in Bucovetsky [81]. This extension permits an explicit strategic interdependence among lower-level governments.

[88] Wildasin [377] focuses mainly on interjurisdictional variation in marginal excess burdens, which is relevant for the allocation of a *given* amount of grant funds among a set of recipients. If one asks instead whether an increase in the scale of the grant program is desirable, one must trade off the distortions at the central (donor) government level against the distortions at the recipient government level. The analysis in Wildasin addresses this question only in the special case where recipient and donor tax the same base (e.g., income). By contrast, Sheshinski [326] shows the possible advantages of grants when the central government has access to less distortionary taxes than the recipient government.

[89] This is not to say that equalizing grants are necessarily sub-optimal among feasible alternatives. Indeed, the discussion of tax distortions mentioned above may provide further support for equalizing transfers. For given demand and supply elasticities, it is shown in Wildasin [377] that distortionary factors will be higher in high tax rate jurisdictions. If jurisdictions with limited tax bases impose higher tax rates (higher "fiscal effort"), equalizing grants might serve quite effectively to reduce the most serious local tax distortions. A careful evaluation of equalizing or other grant formulae from this perspective remains to be done, however.

recipient government behavioral response to grants. This remains one of the chief challenges to the successful analysis of resource allocation through the local public sector.

Acknowledgements

In preparing this study I have accumulated a lengthy list of debts. First, I thank R. Arnott not only for editorial help but for reading the entire manuscript and making numerous suggestions for improvement. J. Brueckner, P. Hobson, Y. Kanemoto, W. Oates, and E. Olsen made specific comments and suggestions for which I am especially grateful. In addition to those already mentioned, I thank E. Berglas, D. Epple, E. Gramlich, J. V. Henderson, P. Hobson, R. Inman, P. Mieszkowski, D. Pines, T. Romer, D. Rubinfeld, U. Schweizer, J. Sonstelie, D. Starrett, T. N. Tideman, J. Wilson, J. Yinger, and G. Zodrow for bringing to my attention or providing access to important published and unpublished work, as well as comments. Undoubtedly their help will lengthen the shelf life of this product. None of the above bears any responsibility for errors or omissions, however.
R. Harvey and S. Ziss read through the initial manuscript, suggesting many stylistic improvements and noting numerous minor blemishes. So did K. Wildasin, who also helped in many other ways as well. S.-W. Chung, D. Johnston, and T.-W. Ch assisted in preparation of the references. My thanks to all.

References

[1] Aaron, H. J., *Who Pays the Property Tax?* Washington, D.C.: Brookings, 1975.
[2] Anderson, R. J., Jr., and T. D. Crocker, "Air Pollution and Residential Property Values," *Urban Studies,* **8** (1971), 171–180.
[3] Anderson, R. J. Jr., and T. D. Crocker, "Air Pollution and Property Values: A Reply," *Review of Economics and Statistics,* **54** (1972), 470–473.
[4] Arnott, R. J., "Optimal City Size in a Spatial Economy," *Journal of Urban Economics,* **6** (1979), 65–89.
[5] Arnott, R. J., "Optimal Taxation in a Spatial Economy with Transport Costs," *Journal of Public Economics,* **11** (1979), 307–334.
[6] Arnott, R. J., and R. E. Grieson, "Optimal Fiscal Policy for a State or Local Government," *Jorunal of Urban Economics,* **9** (1981), 23–48.
[7] Arnott, R. J., and F. D. Lewis, "The Transition of Land to Urban Use," *Journal of Political Economy,* **87** (1979), 161–170.
[8] Arnott, R. J., and J. G. MacKinnon, "The Effects of the Property Tax: A General Equilibrium Simulation," *Journal of Urban Economics,* **4** (1977), 389–407.
[9] Arnott, R. J., and J. E. Stiglitz, "Aggregate Land Rents, Expenditure on Public Goods, and Optimal City Size," *Quarterly Journal of Economics,* **93** (1979), 471–500.
[10] Arrow, K. J., *Social Choice and Individual Values.* New York: Wiley, 1963.
[11] Atkinson, A. B., and N. H. Stern, "Pigou, Taxation and Public Goods," *Review of Economic Studies,* **41** (1974), 119–128.

[12] Atkinson, A. B., and J. E. Stiglitz, *Lectures on Public Economics*. New York: McGraw-Hill, 1980.

[13] Aumann, R. J., "Existence of Competitive Equilibria in Markets with a Continuum of Traders," *Econometrica*, **34** (1966), 1–17.

[14] Bailey, M. J., "Note on the Economics of Residential Zoning and Urban Renewal," *Land Economics*, **35** (1959), 288–292.

[15] Barlow, R., "A Comment on Alternative Federal Policies for Stimulating State and Local Expenditures," *National Tax Journal*, **22** (1969), 282–285.

[16] Barlow, R., "Efficiency Aspects of Local School Finance," *Journal of Political Economy*, **78** (1970), 1028–1040.

[17] Barlow, R., "Efficiency Aspects of Local School Finance: Reply," *Journal of Political Economy*, **81** (1973), 199–202.

[18] Barr, J. L., and O. A. Davis, "An Elementary Political and Economic Theory of the Expenditures of Local Governments," *Southern Economic Journal*, **22** (1966), 149–165.

[19] Barro, R. J., "Are Government Bonds Net Wealth?" *Journal of Political Economy* **82** (1974), 1095–1118.

[20] Barro, R. J., "On the Determination of the Public Debt," *Journal of Political Economy* **87** (1979), 940–971.

[21] Barzel, Y., "Private Schools and Public School Finance," *Journal of Political Economy*, **81** (1973), 174–186.

[22] Beck, J. H., "Tax Competition, Uniform Assessment, and the Benefit Principle," *Journal of Urban Economics*, **13** (1983), 127–146.

[23] Beck, J. H., "Nonmonotonic Demand for Municipal Services: Variation Among Communities," *National Tax Journal* **37** (1984), 55–68.

[24] Bentick, B. L., "Improving the Allocation of Land Between Speculators and Users: Taxation and Paper Land," *Economic Record* **48** (1972), 18–41.

[25] Bentick, B. L., "The Allocation of Land Between Speculators and Users Under a Land Ownership Tax: Reply," *Economic Record* **50** (1974), 451–452.

[26] Bentick, B. L., "The Impact of Taxation and Valuation Practices on the Timing and Efficiency of Land Use," *Journal of Political Economy*, **87** (1979), 859–868.

[27] Bentick, B. L., "A Tax on Land Value is Neutral," *National Tax Journal*, **35** (1982), 113.

[28] Berglas, E., "Distribution of Tastes and Skills and the Provision of Local Public Goods," *Journal of Public Economics* **6** (1976), 409–423.

[29] Berglas, E., "User Charges, Local Public Services, and Taxation of Land Rents," *Public Finance*, **37** (1982), 178–188.

[30] Berglas, E., "Quantities, Qualities, and Multiple Public Services in the Tiebout Model," *Journal of Public Economics* **25** (1984), 299–322.

[31] Berglas, E., and D. Pines, "Clubs, Local Public Goods, and Transportation Models: A Synthesis," *Journal of Public Economics*, **15** (1981), 141–162.

[32] Berglas, E., and D. Pines, "Resource Constraint, Replicability and Mixed Clubs: A Reply," *Journal of Public Economics* **23** (1984), 391–397.

[33] Bergstrom, T. C., "A Note on Efficient Taxation," *Journal of Political Economy*, **81** (1973), 187–191.

[34] Bergstrom, T. C., and R. P. Goodman, "Private Demands for Public Goods," *American Economic Review*, **63** (1973), 280–296.

[35] Bergstrom, T. C., D. L. Rubinfeld, and P. Shapiro, "Micro-based Estimates of Demand Functions for Local School Expenditures," *Econometrica* **50** (1982), 1183–1205.

[36] Berliant, M., "Equilibrium Models with Land: A Criticism and an Alternative," *Regional Science and Urban Economics*, **15** (1985), 325–340.

[37] Bewley, T. F., "A Critique of Tiebout's Theory of Local Public Expenditures," *Econometrica*, **49** (1981), 713–740.
[38] Bhagwati, J. N., and T. N. Srinivasan, *Lectures on International Trade*. Cambridge: MIT Press, 1983.
[39] Bickerdike, C. F., "The Theory of Incipient Taxes," *The Economic Journal*, **16** (1906), 529–535.
[40] Bird, R., and E. Slack, *Urban Public Finance in Canada*. Toronto: Butterworth's, 1983.
[41] Bishop, G. A., "Stimulative Versus Substitute Effects of State School Aid in New England," *National Tax Journal*, **17** (1964), 133–143.
[42] Black, D., "On the Rationale of Group Decision-Making," *Journal of Political Economy*, **56** (1948), 23–34.
[43] Black, D., *The Theory of Committees and Elections*. Cambridge: Cambridge University Press, 1958.
[44] Bloom, H. S., H. F. Ladd, and J. Yinger, "Are Property Taxes Capitalized into House Values?" in *Local Provision of Public Services: The Tiebout Model After Twenty-Five Years*, ed. by G. R. Zodrow, 145–164. New York: Academic Press, 1983.
[45] Boadway, R, "On the Method of Taxation and the Provision of Local Public Goods: Comment," *American Economic Review*, **72** (1982), 846–851.
[46] Boadway, R., and F. Flatters, "Efficiency and Equalization Payments in a Federal System of Government: A Synthesis and Extension of Recent Results," *Canadian Journal of Economics*, **15** (1982), 613–633.
[47] Boadway, R., and F. Flatters, *Equalization in a Federal State*. Ottawa: Economic Council of Canada, 1982.
[48] Boadway, R., and F. Flatters, "Efficiency, Equity, and the Allocation of Resource Rents," in *Fiscal Federalism and the Taxation of National Resources*, ed. by C. E. McLure, Jr. and P. Mieszkowski, 99–123. Lexington: Lexington Books, 1983.
[49] Boadway, R. W., and D. E. Wildasin, *Public Sector Economics*, 2nd edition. Boston: Little, Brown, 1984.
[50] Borcherding, T. E., W. C. Bush, and R. M. Spann, "The Effects on Public Spending of the Divisibility of Public Outputs in Consumption, Bureaucratic Power, and the Size of the Tax-Sharing Group," in *Budgets and Bureaucrats*, ed. by T. E. Borcherding, 211–228. Durham: Duke University Press, 1977.
[51] Borcherding, T. E., and R. T. Deacon, "The Demand for the Services of Non-Federal Governments," *American Economic Review*, **62** (1972), 891–901.
[52] Boskin, M. J., "Local Government Tax and Product Competition and the Optimal Provision of Public Goods," *Journal of Political Economy*, **81** (1973), 203–210.
[53] Bosworth, B. P., *Tax Incentives and Economic Growth*. Washington, D.C.: Brookings, 1984.
[54] Bowen, H. R., "The Interpretation of Voting in the Allocation of Economic Resources," *Quarterly Journal of Economics*, **58** (1943), 27–48.
[55] Bowman, J., "Tax Exportability, Intergovernmental Aid, and School Finance Reform," *National Tax Journal*, **27** (1974), 163–173.
[56] Bradbury, K., H. Ladd, M. Perrault, A. Reschovsky, and J. Yinger, "State Aid to Offset Fiscal Disparities Across Communities," *National Tax Journal* **37** (1984), 151–170.
[57] Bradford, D. F., "Factor Prices May Be Constant but Factor Returns Are Not," *Economics Letters* **1** (1978), 199–203.
[58] Bradford, D. F., and W. E. Oates, "The Analysis of Revenue Sharing in a

New Approach to Collective Fiscal Decisions," *Quarterly Journal of Economics*, **85** (1971), 416–439.

[59] Bradford, D. F., and W. E. Oates, "Towards a Predictive Theory of Intergovernmental Grants," *American Economic Review*, **61** (1971), 440–448.

[60] Bradford, D. F., and W. E. Oates, "Suburban Exploitation of Central Cities and Governmental Structure," in *Redistribution Through Public Choice*, ed. by H. Hochman and G. Peterson, 43–92. New York: Columbia University Press, 1974.

[61] Brainard, W. C., and F. T. Dolbear, Jr., "The Possibility of Oversupply of Local 'Public' Goods: A Critical Note," *Journal of Political Economy*, **75** (1967), 86–90.

[62] Break, G., *Financing Government in a Federal System*. Washington D.C.: Brookings, 1980.

[63] Breton, A., "A Theory of Government Grants," *Canadian Journal of Economics and Political Science*, **31** (1965), 175–187.

[64] Brown, C. C., and W. E. Oates, "Assistance to the Poor in a Federal System," unpublished, 1985.

[65] Brueckner, J. K., "Equilibrium in a System of Communities with Local Public Goods," *Economics Letters*, **2** (1979), 387–393.

[66] Brueckner, J. K., "Property Values, Local Public Expenditure, and Economic Efficiency," *Journal of Public Economics*, **11** (1979), 223–246.

[67] Brueckner, J. K., "Labor Mobility and the Incidence of the Residential Property Tax," *Journal of Urban Economics*, **10** (1981), 173–182.

[68] Brueckner, J. K., "A Test for Allocative Efficiency in the Local Public Sector," *Journal of Public Economics*, **19** (1982), 311–331.

[69] Brueckner, J. K., "Property Value Maximization and Public Sector Efficiency," *Journal of Urban Economics*, **14** (1983), 1–16.

[70] Brueckner, J. K., "A Modern Analysis of the Effects of Site Value Taxation," *National Tax Journal* (forthcoming).

[71] Brueckner, J. K., and T. L. Wingler, "Public Intermediate Inputs, Property Values, and Allocative Efficiency," *Economics Letters* **14** (1984), 245–250.

[72] Buchanan, J. M., "Federalism and Fiscal Equity," *American Economic Review*, **40** (1950), 583–599.

[73] Buchanan, J. M., "Federal Grants and Resource Allocation," *Journal of Political Economy*, **60** (1952), 208–217.

[74] Buchanan, J. M., "Fiscal Institutions and Efficiency in Collective Outlay," *American Economic Review*, **54** (1964), 227–235.

[75] Buchanan, J. M., "An Economic Theory of Clubs," *Economica* **33** (1965), 1–14.

[76] Buchanan, J. M. *The Demand and Supply of Public Goods*. Chicago: Rand-McNaly, 1968.

[77] Buchanan, J. M., "Principles of Urban Fiscal Strategy," *Public Choice*, **11** (1971), 1–16.

[78] Buchanan, J. M., and C. J. Goetz, "Efficiency Limits of Fiscal Mobility: An Assessment of the Tiebout Model," *Journal of Public Economics*, **1** (1972), 25–43.

[79] Buchanan, J. M., and R. E. Wagner, "An Efficiency Basis for Federal Fiscal Equalization," in *The Analysis of Public Output*, ed. by J. Margolis, 139–158. New York: Columbia University Press, 1970.

[80] Bucovetsky, S., "Optimal Jurisdictional Fragmentation and Mobility," *Journal of Public Economics*, **16** (1981), 171–192.

[81] Bucovetsky, S., "Exit, Voice and Mobility: Towards a Positive Theory of Federalism," unpublished, 1983.

[82] Burstein, N. R., "Voluntary Income Clustering and the Demand for Housing and Local Public Goods," *Journal of Urban Economics*, 7 (1980), 175–185.

[83] Bush, W. C., and A. T. Denzau, "The Voting Behavior of Bureaucrats and Public Sector Growth," in *Budgets and Bureaucrats* ed. by T. E. Borcherding, 90–99. Durham: Duke University Press, 1977.

[84] Calvo, G. A., L. J. Kotlikoff, and C. A. Rodriguez, "The Incidence of a Tax on Pure Rent: A New (?) Reason for an Old Answer," *Journal of Political Economy*, 87 (1979), 869–874.

[85] Carlton, D. W., "The Spatial Effects of a Tax on Housing and Land", *Regional Science and Urban Economics*, 11 (1981), 509–528.

[86] Chernick, H. A., "An Economic Model of the Distribution of Project Grants," in *Fiscal Federalism and Grants-in-Aid*, ed. by P. Mieszkowski and W. H. Oakland, 81–103. Washington, D.C.: The Urban Institute, 1979.

[87] Church, A. M., "Capitalization of the Effective Property Tax Rate on Single Family Homes," *National Tax Journal*, 28 (1974), 113–122.

[88] Coen, R. M., and B. J. Powell, "Theory and Measurement of the Incidence of Differential Property Taxes on Rental Housing," *National Tax Journal*, 25 (1972), 211–222.

[89] Coughlin, P. J., and M. J. Hinich, "Necessary and Sufficient Conditions for Single-Peakedness in Public Economic Models," *Journal of Public Economics*, 25 (1984), 161–180.

[90] Courant, P. N., "A General Equilibrium Model of Heterogeneous Local Property Taxes," *Journal of Public Economics*, 8 (1977), 313–328.

[91] Courant, P. N., "On the Effects of Federal Capital Taxation on Growing and Declining Areas," *Journal of Urban Economics*, 14 (1983), 242–261.

[92] Courant, P. N., E. M. Gramlich, and D. L. Rubinfeld, "The Stimulative Effects of Intergovernmental Grants: or Why Money Sticks Where It Hits," in *Fiscal Federalism and Grants-in-Aid*, ed. by P. Mieszkowski and W. H. Oakland, 5–21. Washington, D.C.: The Urban Institute, 1979.

[93] Courant, P. N., E. M. Gramlich, and D. L. Rubinfeld, "Public Employee Market Power and the Level of Government Spending," *American Economic Review*, 69 (1979), 806–817.

[94] Cowing, T. G., "Real Property Taxes, Local Public Services and Residential Property Values: Comment," *Southern Economic Journal*, 41 (1974), 325–329.

[95] Craig, S. G., and R. P. Inman, "Federal Aid and Public Education: An Empirical Look at the New Fiscal Federalism," *Review of Economics and Statistics* 64 (1982), 541–552.

[96] Cushing, B. J., "Capitalization of Interjurisdictional Fiscal Differentials: An Alternative Approach," *Journal of Urban Economics*, 15 (1984), 317–326.

[97] Dasgupta, P., and J. E. Stiglitz, "Benefit-Cost Analysis and Trade Policies," *Journal of Political Economy*, 82 (1974), 1–33.

[98] Davis, O. H., and G. A. Haines, Jr., "A Political Approach to a Theory of Public Expenditures: The Case of Municipalities," *National Tax Journal*, 19 (1966), 259–275.

[99] Devarajan, S., D. Fullerton, and R. A. Musgrave, "Estimating the Distribution of Tax Burdens: A Comparison of Different Approaches," *Journal of Public Economics* 13 (1980), 155–182.

[100] Diamond, P. A., and J. A. Mirrlees, "Optimal Taxation and Public Production I: Production Efficiency," *American Economic Review*, 61 (1971), 8–27.

[101] Diamond, P. A., and J. A. Mirrlees, "Optimal Taxation and Public Production II: Tax Rules," *American Economic Review*, 61 (1971), 261–278.

[102] Diamond, D. B. Jr., and G. S. Tolley, *The Economics of Urban Amenities.* New York: Academic Press, 1982.
[103] Downs, A., *An Economic Theory of Democracy.* New York: Harper, 1957.
[104] Dusansky, R., M. Ingber, and N. Karatjas, "The Impact of Property Taxation on Housing Values and Rents," *Journal of Urban Economics,* 10 (1981), 240–255.
[105] Eberts, R. W., and T. J. Gronberg, "Jurisdictional Homogeneity and the Tiebout Hypothesis," *Journal of Urban Economics,* 10 (1981), 227–239.
[106] Eckart, W., "The Neutrality of Land Taxation in an Uncertain World," *National Tax Journal,* 36 (1983), 237–242.
[107] Edel, M., and E. Sclar, "Taxes, Spending, and Property Values: Supply Adjustment in a Tiebout-Oates Model," *Journal of Political Economy,* 82 (1974), 941–954.
[108] Edelson, N. M., "Efficiency Aspects of Local School Finance: Comments and Extensions," *Journal of Political Economy,* 81 (1973), 158–173.
[109] Ellickson, B., "A Generalization of the Pure Theory of Public Goods," *American Economic Review,* 63 (1973), 417–432.
[110] Ellickson, B., "The Politics and Economics of Decentralization," *Journal of Urban Economics,* 4 (1977), 135–149.
[111] Enelow, J. M., and M. J. Hinich, *The Spatial Theory of Voting: An Introduction.* New York: Cambridge University Press, 1984.
[112] Epple, D., R. Filimon, and T. Romer, "Housing, Voting, and Moving: Equilibrium in a Model of Local Public Goods with Multiple Jurisdictions," *Research in Urban Economics,* 3 (1983), 59–90.
[113] Epple, D., R. Filimon, and T. Romer, "Equilibrium Among Local Jurisdictions: Toward an Integrated Treatment of Voting and Residential Choice," *Journal of Public Economics* 24 (1984), 281–308.
[114] Epple, D., and K. Schipper, "Municipal Pension Funding: A Theory and Some Evidence," *Public Choice* 37 (1981), 141–178.
[115] Epple, D., and A. Zelenitz, "The Implications of Competition Among Jurisdictions: Does Tiebout Need Politics?" *Journal of Political Economy,* 89 (1981), 1197–1217.
[116] Epple, D., and A. Zelenitz, "The Roles of Jurisdictional Competition and of Collective Choice Institutions in the Market for Local Public Goods," *American Economic Review,* May 1981, 87–92.
[117] Epple, D., A. Zelenitz, and M. Visscher, "A Search for Testable Implications of the Tiebout Hypothesis," *Journal of Political Economy,* 86 (1978), 405–426.
[118] Fane, G., "The Incidence of a Tax on Pure Rent: The Old Reason for the Old Answer," *Journal of Political Economy,* 92 (1984), 329–333.
[119] Feldman, A. M., *Welfare Economics and Social Choice Theory,* Boston: Martinus Nijhoff, 1980.
[120] Feldstein, M., "Wealth Neutrality and Local Choice in Public Education," *American Economic Review,* 65 (1975), 75–89.
[121] Feldstein, M., "The Surprising Incidence of a Tax on Pure Rent: A New Answer to an Old Question," *Journal of Political Economy,* 85 (1977) 349–360.
[122] Filimon, R., T. Romer, and H. Rosenthal, "Asymmetric Information and Agenda Control: The Bases of Monopoly Power in Public Spending," *Journal of Public Economics,* 17 (1982), 51–70.
[123] Fischel, W. A., "Fiscal and Environmental Considerations in the Location of Firms in Suburban Communities," in *Fiscal Zoning and Land Use Controls,* ed. by E. S. Mills and W. E. Oates, 119–173. Lexington: Lexington Books, 1975.

[124] Fisher, R. C., "Theoretical View of Revenue Sharing Grants," *National Tax Journal*, 32 (1979), 173–184.

[125] Fisher, R. C., "Expenditure Incentives of Intergovernmental Grants: Revenue Sharing and Matching Grants," *Research in Urban Economics*, 1 (1981), 201–218.

[126] Fisher, R. C., "Income and Grant Effects on Local Expenditure: The Flypaper Effect and Other Difficulties," *Journal of Urban Economics* 12 (1982), 324–345.

[127] Flatters, F., V. Henderson, and P. Mieszkowski, "Public Goods, Efficiency and Regional Fiscal Equalization," *Journal of Public Economics*, 3 (1974), 99–112.

[128] Foley, D., "Resource Allocation and the Public Sector," *Yale Economic Essays*, 7 (1967), 43–98.

[129] Freeman, A. M., "Air Pollution and Property Values: A Methodological Comment," *Review of Economics and Statistics*, 53 (1971), 415–416.

[130] Freeman, A. M., "On Estimating Air Pollution Control Benefits from Land Value Studies," *Journal of Environmental Economics and Management*, 1 (1974), 74–83.

[131] Freeman, A. M., "Air Pollution and Property Values: A Further Comment," *Review of Economics and Statistics*, 56 (1974), 554–556.

[132] Freeman, A. M., "Spatial Equilibrium, the Theory of Rents, and the Measurement of Benefits from Public Programs: Comment," *Quarterly Journal of Economics*, 89 (1975), 470–473.

[133] Freeman, A. M., *The Benefits of Environmental Improvement: Theory and Practice*. Baltimore: Johns Hopkins University Press, 1979.

[134] George, H., *Progress and Poverty*. New York: Robert Schalkenbach Foundation, 1955.

[135] Gerking, S. D., and J. H. Mutti, "Possibilities for the Exportation of Production Taxes: A General Equilibrium Analysis," *Journal of Public Economics*, 16 (1981), 233–252.

[136] Goldstein, G. S., and M. V. Pauly, "Tiebout Bias on the Demand for Local Public Goods," *Journal of Public Economics*, 16 (1981), 131–144.

[137] Gordon, R. H., An Optimal Taxation Approach to Fiscal Federalism," *Quarterly Journal of Economics*, 98 (1983), 567–586.

[138] Gramlich, E. M., "Alternative Federal Policies for Stimulating State and Local Expenditures," *National Tax Journal*, 21 (1968), 119–129.

[139] Gramlich, E. M., "A Clarification and a Correction," *National Tax Journal*, 22 (1969), 286–290.

[140] Gramlich, E. M., "Intergovernmental Grants: A Review of the Empirical Literature," in *The Political Economy of Fiscal Federalism*, ed. by W. E. Oates, 219–240. Lexington: Lexington Books, 1977.

[141] Gramlich, E. M., "An Econometric Examination of the New Federalism," *Brookings Papers on Economic Activity*, 2 (1982), 327–360.

[142] Gramlich, E. M., "Models of Excessive Government Spending: Do the Facts Support the Theories?" in *Public Finance and Public Employment*, Proceedings of the 36th Congress of the International Institute of Public Finance, 289–308. Detroit: Wayne State University Press, 1982.

[143] Gramlich, E. M., "Reforming U.S. Fiscal Federalism Arrangements," in *American Domestic Priorities*, ed. by J. M. Quigley and D. L. Rubinfeld, 34–69. Berkeley: University of California Press, 1985.

[144] Gramlich, E. M., and D. S. Laren, "Migration and Income Redistribution Responsibilities," *Journal of Human Resources* 19 (1984), 488–511.

[145] Gramlich, E. M., and D. L. Rubinfeld, "Micro Estimates of Public Spending

Demand Functions and Tests of the Tiebout and Median Voter Hypothesis," *Journal of Political Economy*, **90** (1982), 536–560.

[146] Gramlich, E. M., and D. L. Rubinfeld, "Voting on Public Spending: Differences Between Public Employees, Transfer Recipients, and Private Workers," *Journal of Policy Analysis and Management* **1** (1982), 516–533.

[147] Greenberg, J., "Existence of an Equilibrium with Arbitrary Tax Schemes for Financing Local Public Goods," *Journal of Economic Theory*, **16** (1977), 137–150.

[148] Greenberg, J., "Local Public Goods with Mobility: Existence and Optimality of a General Equilibrium," *Journal of Economic Theory*, **30** (1983), 17–33.

[149] Greenberg, J., and S. Weber, "Tiebout Equilibrium Under Restricted Preferences Domain," *Journal of Economic Theory* (forthcoming).

[150] Greene, K. V., W. B. Neenan, and C. D. Scott, *Fiscal Interactions in a Metropolitan Area*. Lexington: Lexington Books, 1977.

[151] Grieson, R. E., "The Economics of Property Taxes and Land Values: The Elasticity of Supply of Structures," *Journal of Urban Economics*, **1** (1974), 367–381.

[152] Guesnerie, R., and C. Oddou, "On Economic Games Which are Not Necessarily Superadditive: Solution Concepts and Application to a Local Public Good Problem with Few Agents," *Economics Letters*, **3** (1979), 301–306.

[153] Guesnerie, R., and C. Oddou, "Second-Best Taxation as a Game," *Journal of Economic Theory*, **25** (1981), 67–91.

[154] Gustely, R. D., "Local Taxes, Expenditures and Urban Housing: A Reassessment of the Evidence," *Southern Economic Journal*, **42** (1976), 651–665.

[155] Hamilton, B., and J. Whalley, "Tax Treatment of Housing in a Dynamic Sequenced General Equilibrium Model," University of Western Ontario WP 8425C (1984).

[156] Hamilton, B. W., "Property Taxes and the Tiebout Hypothesis: Some Empirical Evidence," in *Fiscal Zoning and Land Use Controls*, ed. by E. S. Mills and W. E. Oates, 13–29. Lexington: Lexington Books, 1975.

[157] Hamilton, B. W., "Zoning and Property Taxation in a System of Local Governments," *Urban Studies*, **12** (1975), 205–211.

[158] Hamilton, B. W., Capitalization of Intrajurisdictional Differences in Local Tax Prices," *American Economic Review*, **66** (1976), 743–753.

[159] Hamilton, B. W., "The Effects of Property Taxes and Local Public Spending on Property Values: A Theoretical Comment," *Journal of Political Economy*, **84** (1976), 647–650.

[160] Hamilton, B. W., "A Review: Is the Property Tax a Benefit Tax?" in *Local Provision of Public Services: The Tiebout Model After Twenty-Five Years*, ed. by G. R. Zodrow, 85–108. New York: Academic Press, 1983.

[161] Hamilton, B. W., "The Flypaper Effect and Other Anomalies," *Journal of Public Economics*, **22** (1983), 347–362.

[162] Hamilton, B. W., E. S. Mills, and D. Puryear, "The Tiebout Hypothesis and Residental Income Segregation," in *Fiscal Zoning and Land Use Controls*, ed. by E. S. Mills and W. E. Oates, 101–118. Lexington: Lexington Books, 1975.

[163] Harberger, A. C., "The Incidence of the Corporation Income Tax," *The Journal of Political Economy*, **70** (1962), 215–240.

[164] Hartwick, J. M., "The Henry George Rule, Optimal Population, and Interregional Equity," *Canadian Journal of Economics*, **13** (1980), 695–700.

[165] Haurin, D. R., "The Effect of Property Taxes on Urban Areas," *Journal of Urban Economics* **7** (1980), 384–396.

160   D. E. WILDASIN

[166] Heinberg, J. D., and W. E. Oates, "The Incidence of Differential Property Taxes on Urban Housing: A Comment and Some Further Evidence," *National Tax Journal*, **23** (1970), 92–98.

[167] Helpman, E., D. Pines, and E. Borukhov, "The Interaction Between Local Government and Urban Residential Location: Comment," *The American Economic Review* **66** (1976), 961–967.

[168] Henderson, J. M., "Local Government Expenditures: A Social Welfare Analysis," *Review of Economics and Statistics*, **50** (1968), 156–163.

[169] Henderson, J. V., *Economic Theory and the Cities*. New York: Academic Press, 1977.

[170] Henderson, J. V., "Theories of Group, Jurisdiction, and City Size," in *Current Issues in Urban Economics*, ed. by P. Mieszkowski and M. Straszheim, 235–269. Baltimore: Johns Hopkins University Press, 1979.

[171] Henderson, J. V., "Community Development: The Effects of Growth and Uncertainty," *The American Economic Review* **70** (1980), 894–910.

[172] Henderson, J. V., "The Tiebout Model: Bring Back the Entrepreneurs" *Journal of Political Economy* **93** (1985), 248–264.

[173] Hildenbrand, W., *Core and Equilibria of a Large Economy*. Princeton: Princeton University Press, 1974.

[174] Hirsch, W., *The Economics of State and Local Government*. New York: McGraw-Hill, 1970.

[175] Hobson, P., "The Incidence of Heterogeneous Residential Property Taxes," *Journal of Public Economics*, forthcoming.

[176] Hobson, P., "The Economic Effects of the Property Tax," unpublished, 1985.

[177] Hochman, O., "Land Rents, Optimal Taxation and Local Fiscal Independence in an Economy with Local Public Goods," *Journal of Public Economics*, **15** (1981), 59–85.

[178] Hochman, O., "Congestable Local Public Goods in an Urban Setting," *Journal of Urban Economics*, **11** (1982), 290–310.

[179] Hochman, O., "Clubs in an Urban Setting," *Journal of Urban Economics*, **12** (1982), 85–101.

[180] Hogan, T. D., and R. B. Shelton, "Interstate Tax Exportation and States' Fiscal Structures," *National Tax Journal*, **26** (1973), 553–564.

[181] Hogan, T. D., and R. B. Shelton, "A Note on Barlow's Local School Finance," *Journal of Political Economy*, **81** (1973), 192–198.

[182] Homma, M., "On The Theory of Interregional Tax Incidence," *Regional Science and Urban Economics*, **7** (1977), 377–392.

[183] Hyman, D. N., and E. C. Pasour, Jr., "Property Tax Differentials and Residential Rents in North Carolina," *National Tax Journal*, **26** (1973), 303–307.

[184] Hyman, D. N., and E. C. Pasour, Jr., "Real Property Taxes, Local Public Services and Residential Property Values: Reply," *Southern Economic Journal*, **41** (1974), 329–331.

[185] Inman, R. P., "Grants in a Metropolitan Economy—A Framework for Policy," in *Financing the New Federalism*, ed. by W. E. Oates, 88–114. Baltimore: The Johns Hopkins University Press, 1975.

[186] Inman, R. P., "Micro-Fiscal Planning in the Regional Economy: A General Equilibrium Approach," *Journal of Public Economics*, **7** (1977), 237–260.

[187] Inman, R. P., "Testing Political Economy's 'as if' Proposition; Is the Median Voter Really Decisive?" *Public Choice*, **33** (1978), 45–65.

[188] Inman, R. P., "Optimal Fiscal Reform of Metropolitan Schools," *American Economic Review* **68** (1978), 107–122.
[189] Inman, R. P., "The Fiscal Performance of Local Governments: An Interpretative Review," in *Current Issues in Urban Economics*, ed. by P. Mieszkowski and M. Straszheim, 270–321. Baltimore: Johns Hopkins University Press, 1979.
[190] Inman, R. P., "Wages, Pensions, and Employment in the Local Public Sector," in *Public Sector Labor Markets*, ed. by P. Mieszkowski and G. E. Peterson (eds), 11–57. Washington: Urban Institute, 1981.
[191] Inman, R. P., "'Municipal Pension Funding: A Theory and Some Evidence': A Comment," *Public Choice* **37** (1981), 179–187.
[192] Inman, R. P., "Public Employee Pensions and the Local Labor Budget," *Journal of Public Economics* **19** (1982), 49–71.
[193] Inman, R. P., "The Economic Case for Limits to Government," *American Economic Review* **72** (1982), 176–183.
[194] Inman, R. P., and D. L. Rubinfeld, "The Judicial Pursuit of Local Fiscal Equity," *Harvard Law Review* **92** (1979), 1662–1750.
[195] Johnson, H. G., "Optimum Tariffs and Retaliation," *The Review of Economic Studies*, **21** (1953–54), 142–153.
[196] Kanemoto, Y., *Theories of Urban Externalities*. Amsterdam: North-Holland, 1980.
[197] Kanemoto, Y., "Housing as an Asset and the Effects of Property Taxation on the Residential Development Process," *Journal of Urban Economics* **17** (1985), 145–166.
[198] Kanemoto, Y., "Externalities in Space," *Fundamentals of Pure and Applied Economics*, forthcoming.
[199] Kimball, L. J., and G. W. Harrison, "General Equilibrium Analysis of Regional Fiscal Incidence," in *Applied General Equilibrium Analysis*, ed. by H. E. Scarf and J. B. Shoven, 275–313. Cambridge: Cambridge University Press.
[200] King, A. T., *Property Taxes, Amenities, and Residential Land Values*. Cambridge: Ballinger, 1973.
[201] King, A. T., "Estimating Property Tax Capitalization: A Critical Comment," *Journal of Political Economy*, **85** (1977), 425–431.
[202] Kolstad, C. D., and F. A. Wolak, Jr., "Competition in Interregional Taxation: The Case of Western Coal," *Journal of Political Economy*, **91** (1983), 443–460.
[203] Kotlikoff, L. J., "Taxation and Savings: A Neoclassical Perspective," *Journal of Economic Literature* **22** (1984), 1576–1629.
[204] Kramer, G., "On a Class of Equilibrium Conditions for Majority Rule," *Econometrica* **41** (1973), 285–297.
[205] Ladd, H. F., "Local Education Expenditures, Fiscal Capacity, and the Composition of the Property Tax Base," *National Tax Journal*, **28** (1975), 145–158.
[206] LeGrand, J., "Fiscal Equity and Central Government Grants to Local Authorities," *Economic Journal*, **85** (1975), 531–547.
[207] LeGrand, J., and A. Reschovsky, "Concerning the Appropriate Formulae for Achieving Horizontal Equity Through Federal Revenue Sharing," *National Tax Journal*, **24** (1971), 475–486.
[208] LeRoy, S. F., "Urban Land Rent and the Incidence of Property Taxes, *Journal of Urban Economics*, **3** (1976), 167–179.

[209] Lin, C., "A General Equilibrium Analysis of Property Tax Incidence" unpublished (1985).

[210] Lind, R. C., "Spatial Equilibrium, the Theory of Rents and the Measurement of Benefits from Public Progress," *Quarterly Journal of Economics*, **87** (1973), 188–207.

[211] Lind, R. C., "Spatial Equilibrium, the Theory of Rents, and the Measurement of Benefits from Public Programs: A Reply," *Quarterly Journal of Economics* **89** (1975), 474–476.

[212] Lindhal, E., "Just Taxation: A Positive Solution" in *Classics in the Theory of Public Finance*, ed. by R. A. Musgrave and A. T. Peacock, 168–176. New York: St. Martin's Press, 1967.

[213] Mackay, R. J., and C. L. Weaver, "Commodity Bundling and Agenda Control in the Public Sector," *Quarterly Journal of Economics* **98** (1983), 611–635.

[214] Malinvaud, E., *Lectures on Microeconomic Theory*. Amsterdam: North-Holland, 1973.

[215] Margolis, J., "The Demand for Urban Public Services," in *Issues in Urban Economics*, ed. by H. S. Perloff and L. Wingo, Jr., 527–565. Baltimore: The Johns Hopkins University Press, 1968.

[216] Markusen, J. R., and D. T. Scheffman, "The Timing of Residential Land Development: A General Equilibrium Approach," *Journal of Urban Economics*, **5** (1978), 411–424.

[217] Martinez-Vazquez, J., "Selfishness versus Public 'Regardingness' in Voting Behavior," *Journal of Public Economics* **15** (1981), 349–361.

[218] Maxwell, J. A., and J. R. Aronson, *Financing State and Local Governments*. Washington: Brookings, 1977.

[219] McDonald, J. E., "An Economic Analysis of Local Inducements for Business," *Journal of Urban Economics*, **13** (1983), 322–336.

[220] McDougall, G. S., "Local Public Goods and Residential Property Values: Some Insights and Extensions," *National Tax Journal*, **29** (1976), 436–447.

[221] McGuire, M., "Group Segregation and Optimal Jurisdictions," *Journal of Political Economy*, **82** (1974), 112–132.

[222] McGuire, M., "An Econometric Model of Federal Grants and Local Fiscal Response," in *Financing the New Federalism*, ed. by W. E. Oates, 115–138. Baltimore: Johns Hopkins University Press, 1975.

[223] McGuire, M., "A Method for Estimating the Effects of a Subsidy on the Receiver's Resource Constraint," *Journal of Public Economics*, **10** (1978).

[224] McGuire, M., "The Analysis of Federal Grants into Price and Income Components," in *Fiscal Federalism and Grants-in-Aid*, ed. by P. Mieszkowski and W. H. Oakland, 31–50. Washington: The Urban Institute, 1979.

[225] McKelvey, R. D., "Intransitivities in Multidimensional Voting Models and Some Implications for Agenda Control," *Journal of Economic Theory*, **12** (1976), 472–482.

[226] McKelvey, R. D., "General Conditions for Global Intransitivities in Formal Voting Models," *Econometrica* **47** (1979), 1085–1112.

[227] McLure, C. E. Jr., "Commodity Tax Incidence in Open Economies," *National Tax Journal*, **17** (1964), 187–204.

[228] McLure, C. E. Jr., "The Interstate Exporting of State and Local Taxes: Estimates for 1962," *National Tax Journal*, **20** (1967), 49–77.

[229] McLure, C. E. Jr., "The Inter-Regional Incidence of General Regional Taxes," *Public Finance/Finances Publiques*, **24** (1969), 457–483.

[230] McLure, C. E. Jr., "Taxation, Substitution, and Industrial Location," *Journal of Political Economy*, **78** (1970), 112–132.

[231] McLure, C. E. Jr., "The Theory of Tax Incidence With Imperfect Factor Mobility," *Finanzarchiv*, **30** (1971), 24–48.

[232] McLure, C. E. Jr., "General Equilibrium Incidence Analysis: The Harberger Model After Ten Years," *Journal of Public Economics* **4** (1975), 125–161.

[233] McLure, C. E. Jr., "The New View of the Property Tax: A Caveat," *National Tax Journal*, **30** (1977), 69–76.

[234] McLure, C. E. Jr., "Market Dominance and the Exporting of State Taxes," *National Tax Journal*, **34** (1981), 483–486.

[235] McLure, C. E. Jr., "Tax Exporting and the Commerce Clause," in *Fiscal Federalism and the Taxation of Natural Resources*, ed. by C. E. McLure, Jr. and P. Mieszkowski, 169–192. Lexington: Lexington Books, 1983.

[236] Meadows, G. R., "Taxes, Spending, and Property Values: A Comment and Further Results," *Journal of Political Economy*, **84** (1976), 869–880.

[237] Mieszkowski, P. M., "On the Theory of Tax Incidence," *The Journal of Political Economy* **75** (1967), 250–262.

[238] Mieszkowski, P. M., "The Property Tax: An Excise Tax or a Profits Tax?" *Journal of Public Economics*, **1** (1972), 73–96.

[239] Mieszkowski, P., "The Distributive Effects of Local Taxes: Some Extensions," in *Public and Urban Economics*, ed. by R. E. Grieson, 293–312. Lexington: Heath, 1976.

[240] Mieszkowski, P., and A. M. Saper, "An Estimate of the Effects of Airport Noise on Property Values," *Journal of Urban Economics* **5** (1978), 425–440.

[241] Mieszkowski, P. M., and E. Toder, "Taxation of Energy Resources," in *Fiscal Federalism and the Taxation of Natural Resources*, ed. by C. McLure and P. Mieszkowski, 65–92. Lexington: Heath, 1983.

[242] Mieszkowski, P. M., and G. R. Zodrow, "The New View of the Property Tax: A Reformulation," NBER Working Paper No. 1481 (1984).

[243] Mieszkowski, P. M., and G. R. Zodrow, "The Incidence of the Local Property Tax: A Re-evaluation," NBER Working Paper No. 1485 (1984).

[244] Mills, D. E., The Non-Neutrality of Land Taxation," *National Tax Journal*, **34** (1981), 125–130.

[245] Mills, D. E., "Reply to Tideman," *National Tax Journal*, **35** (1982), 115.

[246] Mills, E. S., "Economic Analysis of Urban Land-Use Controls," in *Current Issues in Urban Economics*, ed. by P. Mieszkowski and M. Straszheim, 511–541. Baltimore: Johns Hopkins University Press, 1979.

[247] Mills, E. S., and W. E. Oates, "The Theory of Local Public Services and Finance: Its Relevance to Urban Fiscal and Zoning Behavior," in *Fiscal Zoning and Land Use Controls*, ed. by E. S. Mills and W. E. Oates, 1–12. Lexington: Lexington Books, 1975.

[248] Mintz, J., and H. Tulkens, "Commodity Tax Competition Between Member States of a Federation: Equilibrium and Efficiency," CORE Discussion Paper No. 8427 (1984).

[249] Mohring, H., "Land Values and the Measurement of Highway Benefits," *Journal of Political Economy*, **69** (1961), 236–249.

[250] Mueller, D. C., *Public Choice*. Cambridge: Cambridge University Press, 1979.

[251] Mumy, G. E., "The Economics of Local Government Pensions and Pension Funding," *Journal of Political Economy* **86** (1978), 517–528.

[252] Musgrave, R. A., *The Theory of Pubic Finance: A Study in Public Economy*. New York: McGraw-Hill, 1959.

[253] Musgrave, R. A., "Provision for Social Goods," in *Public Economics*, ed. by J. Margolis and H. Guitton, 124–144. London: Macmillan, 1969.

[254] Musgrave, R. A., "Theories of Fiscal Federalism," *Public Finance*, **24** (1969), 521–532.
[255] Musgrave, R. A., "Economics of Fiscal Federalism," *Nebraska Journal of Economics and Business*, **10** (1971), 3–13.
[256] Musgrave, R. A., and P. B. Musgrave: *Public Finance in Theory and Practice*, 4th ed. New York: McGraw-Hill, 1984.
[257] Muth, R. F., *Cities and Housing*. Chicago: The University of Chicago Press, 1969.
[258] Neenan, W. B., *Political Economy of Urban Areas*. Chicago: Markham Publishing Company, 1972.
[259] Negishi, T., "Public Expenditure Determined by Voting with One's Feet and Fiscal Profitability," *Swedish Journal of Economics*, **74** (1972), 452–458.
[260] Niskanen, W. A. Jr., *Bureaucracy and Representative Government*. Chicago: Aldine, Atherton, 1971.
[261] Oakland, W. H., "Income Redistribution in a Federal System," in *Local Provision of Public Services: The Tiebout Model After Twenty-Five Years*, ed. by G. R. Zodrow, 131–143. New York: Academic Press, 1983.
[262] Oates, W. E., "The Theory of Public Finance in a Federal System," *Canadian Journal of Economics*, **1** (1968), 37–54.
[263] Oates, W. E., "The Effects of Property Taxes and Local Public Spending on Property Values: An Empirical Study of Tax Capitalization and the Tiebout Hypothesis," *Journal of Political Economy*, **77** (1969), 957–971.
[264] Oates, W. E., *Fiscal Federalism*. New York: Harcourt Brace Jovanovich, 1972.
[265] Oates, W. E., "The Effects of Property Taxes and Local Public Spending on Property Values: A Reply and Yet Further Results," *Journal of Political Economy*, **81** (1973), 1004–1008.
[266] Oates, W. E., "The Use of Local Zoning Ordinances to Regulate Population Flows and the Quality of Local Services," in *Essays in Labor Market Analysis*, ed. by O. C. Ashenfelter and W. E. Oates, 201–219, New York: John Wiley & Sons, 1977.
[267] Oates, W. E., "Lump-Sum Intergovernmental Grants Have Price Effects," in *Fiscal Federalism and Grants-in-Aid*, ed. by P. Mieszkowski and W. H. Oakland, 23–30. Washington, D.C., The Urban Institute, 1979.
[268] Oates, W. E., "On Local Finance and the Tiebout Model," *American Economic Review*, May 1981, 93–98.
[269] Ochs, J., and T. Merz, "On Testing the Hypothesis that Myopia Is a Cause of Municipal Pension Underfunding," *Journal of Urban Economics* **15** (1984), 371–377.
[270] Orr, L. L., "The Incidence of Differential Property Taxes on Urban Housing," *National Tax Journal*, **21** (1968), 253–262.
[271] Orr, L. L., "The Incidence of Differential Property Taxes: A Response," *National Tax Journal*, **23** (1970), 99–101.
[272] Ott, M., "Bureaucracy, Monopoly, and the Demand for Municipal Services," *Journal of Urban Economics*, **8** (1980), 362–382.
[273] Pauly, M. V., "Optimality, 'Public' Goods and Local Governments: A General Theoretical Analysis," *Journal of Political Economy*, **78** (1970), 572–584.
[274] Pauly, M. V., "Income Redistribution as a Local Public Good," *Journal of Public Economics*, **2** (1973), 35–58.
[275] Pauly, M. V., "A Model of Local Government Expenditure and Tax Capitalization," *Journal of Public Economics*, **6** (1976), 231–242.
[276] Pestieau, P., "Fiscal Mobility and Local Public Goods; A Survey of the

Empirical and Theoretical Studies of the Tiebout Model," in *Locational Analysis of Public Facilities*, ed. by J. F. Thisse and H. G. Zoller, 11–41. Amsterdam: North-Holland, 1983.

[277] Phares, D., *Who Pays State and Local Taxes?* Cambridge: Oelgeschlager, Gunn and Hain, Publishers, Inc., 1980.

[278] Pines, D., "On the Capitalization of Land Improvement Projects", *Economics Letters*, 15 (1984), 377–384.

[279] Pines, D., "Profit Maximizing Developers and the Optimal Provision of Local Public Goods in a Closed System of a Few Cities," *La Revue Economique*, 36 (1985), 45–62.

[280] Pines, D., and Y. Weiss, "Land Improvement Projects and Land Values," *Journal of Urban Economics*, 3 (1976), 1–13.

[281] Pines, D., and Y. Weiss, "Land Improvements Projects and Land Values: An Addendum," *Journal of Urban Economics*, 11 (1982), 199–204.

[282] Plott, C. R., "Equilibrium and Majority Rule," *American Economic Review*, 57 (1967), 787–806.

[283] Pogue, T., "Tax Exporting and the Measurement of Fiscal Capacity," in *Proceedings of the Sixty-Ninth Annual Conference* National Tax Association-Tax Institute of America (1976), 79–89.

[284] Polinsky, A. M., and D. L. Rubinfeld, "The Long-Run Effects of a Residential Property Tax and Local Public Services," *Journal of Urban Economics*, 5 (1978), 241–262.

[285] Polinsky, A. M., and S. Shavell, "The Air Pollution and Property Value Debate," *Review of Economics and Statistics*, 57 (1975), 100–104.

[286] Polinsky, A. M., and S. Shavell, "Amenities and Property Values in a Model of an Urban Area," *Journal of Public Economics*, 5 (1976), 119–129.

[287] Pollakowski, H. O., "The Effects of Property Taxes and Local Public Spending on Property Values: A Comment and Further Results", *Journal of Political Economy*, 81 (1973), 994–1003.

[288] Pommerehne, W. W., "Institutional Approaches to Public Expenditure: Empirical Evidence from Swiss Municipalities," *Journal of Public Economics*, 9 (1978), 255–280.

[289] Richter, D. K., "Existence of a General Equilibrium in Multiregional Economies with Public Goods," *International Economic Review*, 16 (1975), 201–221.

[290] Richter, D. K., "Existence and Computation of a Tiebout General Equilibrium," *Econometrica*, 46 (1978), 779–805.

[291] Richter, D. K., "Weakly Democratic Regular Tax Equilibria in a Local Public Goods Economy with Perfect Consumer Mobility," *Journal of Economic Theory*, 27 (1982), 137–162.

[292] Ridker, R. B., and J. A. Henning, "The Determinants of Residential Property Values With Special Reference to Air Pollution," *Review of Economics and Statistics*, 49 (1967), 246–257.

[293] Roback, J., "Wages, Rents, and the Quality of Life," *Journal of Political Economy*, 90 (1982), 1257–1278.

[294] Romer, T., and H. Rosenthal, "Political Resource Allocation, Controlled Agendas, and the Status Quo," *Public Choice*, 33 (1978), 27–43.

[295] Romer, T., and H. Rosenthal, "Bureaucrats vs. Voters: On the Political Economy of Resource Allocation by Direct Democracy," *Quarterly Journal of Economics*, 93 (1979), 563–588.

[296] Romer, T., and H. Rosenthal, "The Elusive Median Voter," *Journal of Public Economics*, 12 (1979), 143–170.

[297] Romer, T., and H. Rosenthal, "An Institutional Theory of the Effect of

166   D. E. WILDASIN

Intergovernmental Grants," *National Tax Journal*, **33** (1980), 451–458.
[298] Romer, T., and H. Rosenthal, "Median Voters or Budget Maximizers: Evidence from School Expenditure Referenda," *Economic Inquiry*, **20** (1982), 556–578.
[299] Romer, T., and H. Rosenthal, "Voting and Spending: Some Empirical Relationships in the Political Economy of Local Public Finance," in *Local Provision of Public Services: The Tiebout Model After Twenty-Five Years*, ed. by G. R. Zodrow, 165–183. New York: Academic Press, 1983.
[300] Romer, T., H. Rosenthal, and K. Ladha, "If at First You Don't Succeed: Budgeting by a Sequence of Referenda," in *Public Finance and the Quest for Efficiency*, Proceedings of the 38th Congress of the International Institute of Public Finance, 87–108. Detroit: Wayne State University Press, 1984.
[301] Rose-Ackerman, S., "Market Models of Local Government: Exit, Voting, and the Land Market," *Journal of Urban Economics*, **6** (1979), 319–337.
[302] Rose-Ackerman, S., "Beyond Tiebout: Modeling the Political Economy of Local Government," in *Local Provision of Public Services: The Tiebout Model After Twenty-Five Years*, ed. by G. R. Zodrow, 55–84. New York: Academic Press, 1983.
[303] Rosen, H. S., "Housing Decisions and the U.S. Income Tax: An Econometric Analysis," *Journal of Public Economics*, **11** (1979), 1–23.
[304] Rosen, H. S., and D. J. Fullerton, "A Note on Local Tax Rates, Public Benefit Levels, and Property Values," *Journal of Political Economy*, **85** (1977), 433–440.
[305] Rosen, K. T., "The Impact of Proposition 13 on House Prices in Northern California: A Test of the Interjurisdictional Capitalization Hypothesis," *Journal of Political Economy*, **90** (1982), 191–200.
[306] Rosen, S., "Hedonic Prices and Implicit Markets: Product Differentiation in Pure Competition," *Journal of Political Economy*, **82** (1974), 34–55.
[307] Rosen, S., "Wage-based Indexes of Urban Quality of Life," in *Current Issues in Urban Economics*, ed. by P. Mieszkowski and M. Straszheim, 74–104. Baltimore: Johns Hopkins University Press, 1979.
[308] Rubinfeld, D. L., "Judicial Approaches to Local Public-Sector Equity," in *Current Issues in Urban Economics*, ed. by P. Mieszkowski and M. Straszheim, 542–576. Baltimore: Johns Hopkins University Press, 1979.
[309] Rubinfeld, D. L., "The Economics of the Local Public Sector," in *Handbook of Public Economics*, ed. by A. Auerbach and M. Feldstein, forthcoming.
[310] Rufolo, A. M., "Efficient Local Taxation and Local Public Goods," *Journal of Public Economics*, **12** (1979), 351–376.
[311] Sacks, S., and R. Harris, "The Determinants of State and Local Government Expenditures and Intergovernmental Flow of Funds," *National Tax Journal*, **17** (1964), 75–85.
[312] Samuelson, P. A., "The Pure Theory of Public Expenditure," *Review of Economics and Statistics*, **36** (1954), 387–389.
[313] Samuelson, P. A., "Diagrammatic Exposition of a Theory of Public Expenditure," *Review of Economics and Statistics*, **37** (1955), 350–356.
[314] Samuelson, P. A., "Pure Theory of Public Expenditure and Taxation," in *Public Economics*, ed. by J. Margolis and H. Guitton 98–123. London: Macmillan, 1969.
[315] Sandler, T., and J. T. Tschirhart, "The Economic Theory of Clubs: An Evaluative Survey," *Journal of Economic Literature* **18** (1980), 1481–1521.
[316] Sandler, T., and J. T. Tschirhart, "Mixed Clubs: Further Observations," *Journal of Public Economics* **23** (1984), 381–389.

[317] Schweizer, U., "Edgeworth and the Henry George Theorem: How to Finance Local Public Projects," in *Locational Analysis of Public Facilities*, ed. by J. F. Thisse and H. G. Zoller, 79–83. Amsterdam: North-Holland, 1983.

[318] Schweizer, U., "Efficient Exchange with a Variable Number of Consumers," *Econometrica*, **51** (1983), 575–584.

[319] Schweizer, U., "Fiscal Decentralization Under Free Mobility," *Regional Science and Urban Economics* **14** (1984), 317–330.

[320] Schweizer, U., "General Equilibrium in Space and Agglomeration," *Fundamentals of Pure and Applied Economics*, forthcoming.

[321] Schweizer, U., "Fiscal Federalism, Spillovers, and Residential Choice," *Papers and Proceedings of the Regional Science Association* (forthcoming).

[322] Schweizer, U., P. Varaiya, and J. Hartwick, "General Equilibrium and Location Theory," *Journal of Urban Economics*, **3** (1976), 285–303.

[323] Scott, A. D., "The Evaluation of Federal Grants," *Economica*, **19** (1952), 377–394.

[324] Sen, A. K., *Collective Choice and Social Welfare*. San Francisco: Holden-Day, 1970.

[325] Shepsle, K. A., and B. R. Weingast, "Structure-induced Equilibrium and Legislative Choice," *Public Choice*, **37** (1981), 503–519.

[326] Sheshinski, E., "The Supply of Communal Goods and Revenue Sharing," in *The Economics of Public Services*, ed. by M. S. Feldstein and R. P. Inman, 253–273. London: Macmillan, 1977.

[327] Shoven, J. B., and J. Whalley, "A General Equilibrium Calculation of the Effects of Differential Taxation of Income From Capital in the U.S.," *Journal of Public Economics*, **1** (1972), 281–321.

[328] Skouras, T., "The Allocation of Land Between Speculators and Users under a Land Ownership Tax: A Comment," *Economic Record* **50** (1974), 449–450.

[329] Slutsky, S. M., "A Voting Model for the Allocation of Public Goods: Existence of an Equilibrium," *Journal of Economic Theory*, **14** (1977), 299–325.

[330] Smith, A. S., "Property Tax Capitalization in San Francisco", *National Tax Journal*, **23** (1970), 177–193.

[331] Sonstelie, J. C., "The Incidence of a Classified Property Tax," *Journal of Public Economics*, **12** (1979), 75–86.

[332] Sonstelie, J. C., "The Welfare Cost of Free Public Schools," *Journal of Political Economy*, **90** (1982), 794–808.

[333] Sonstelie, J. C., and P. R. Portney, "Profit Maximizing Communities and the Theory of Local Public Expenditure," *Journal of Urban Economics*, **5** (1978), 263–277.

[334] Sonstelie, J. C., and P. R. Portney, "Gross Rents and Market Values: Testing the Implications of Tiebout's Hypothesis," *Journal of Urban Economics*, **7** (1980), 102–118.

[335] Sonstelie, J. C., and P. R. Portney, "Take the Money and Run: A Theory of Voting in Local Referenda," *Journal of Urban Economics*, **8** (1980), 187–195.

[336] Stahl, K., and P. Varaiya, "Local Collective Goods: A Critical Re-examination of the Tiebout Model," in *Locational Analysis of Public Facilities*, ed. by J. F. Thisse and H. G. Zoller, 45–53. Amsterdam: North Holland, 1983.

[337] Starrett, D. A., "Measuring Externalities and Second Best Distortions in the Theory of Local Public Goods," *Econometrica*, **48** (1980), 627–642.

[338] Starrett, D. A., "On the Method of Taxation and the Provision of Local Public Goods," *American Economic Review*, **70** (1980), 380–392.

[339] Starrett, D. A., "Land Value Capitalization in Local Public Finance," *Journal of Political Economy*, **89** (1981), 306–327.

[340] Starrett, D. A., "On the Method of Taxation and the Provision of Local Public Goods: Reply," *The American Economic Review*, **72** (1982), 852–853.

[341] Starrett, D. A., *Foundations of Public Economics*, forthcoming.

[342] Stiglitz, J. E., "The Demand for Education in Public and Private School Systems," *Journal of Public Economics*, **3** (1974), 349–385.

[343] Stiglitz, J. E., "The Theory of Local Public Goods," in *The Economics of Public Services*, ed. by M. Feldstein and R. P. Inman, 274–333. London: Macmillan, 1977.

[344] Stiglitz, J. E., "Public Goods in Open Economies with Heterogeneous Individuals," in *Locational Analysis of Public Facilities*, ed. by J. F. Thisse and H. G. Zoller, 55–78. Amsterdam: North-Holland, 1983.

[345] Stiglitz, J. E., "The Theory of Local Public Goods Twenty-Five Years After Tiebout: A Perspective," in *Local Provision of Public Services: The Tiebout Model After Twenty-Five Years*, ed. by G. R. Zodrow, 17–54. New York: Academic Press, 1983.

[346] Sullivan, A. M., "The General Equilibrium Effects of the Industrial Property Tax: Incidence and Excess Burden," *Regional Science and Urban Economics*, **14** (1984), 547–564.

[347] Thirsk, W. R., "Political Sensitivity versus Economic Sensitability: A Tale of Two Property Taxes," in *Tax Policy Options in the 1980's*, ed. by W. Thirsk and J. Whalley, 384–401. Canadian Tax Foundation, 1982.

[348] Tideman, T. N., "A Tax on Land Value is Neutral," *National Tax Journal*, **35** (1982), 109–111.

[349] Tideman, T. N., "A Rehabilitation of the Neutrality of a Tax on Land Value," unpublished, 1982.

[350] Tiebout, C. M., "A Pure Theory of Local Expenditures," *Journal of Political Economy*, **64** (1956), 416–424.

[351] Topham, N., "A Reappraisal and Recalculation of the Marginal Cost of Public Funds," *Public Finance/Finances Publiques* **39** (1984), 394–405.

[352] Topham, N., "Excess Burden and the Marginal Cost of Public Funds," *Economics Letters* **17** (1985), 145–148.

[353] Tresch, R. W., *Public Finance: A Normative Theory*, Texas: Business Publications, Inc., 1981.

[354] Usher, D., "An Instructive Derivation of the Expression for the Marginal Cost of Public Funds," *Public Finance/Finances Publiques* **39** (1984), 406–411.

[355] Vickrey, W., "Defining Land Value for Tax Purposes," in *The Assessment of Land Value*, ed. by D. M. Holland, 25–36. Madison: University of Wisconsin Press, 1970.

[356] Watson, W. G., "Equalization Is About Equity, Not Efficiency," unpublished (n.d.).

[357] Westhoff, F., "Existence of Equilibria in Economies with a Local Public Good," *Journal of Economic Theory*, **14** (1977), 84–112.

[358] Westhoff, F., "Policy Inferences from Community Choice Models: A Caution," *Journal of Urban Economics*, **6** (1979), 535–549.

[359] Wheaton, W. C., "Consumer Mobility and Commodity Tax Bases: The Financing of Local Public Goods," *Journal of Public Economics*, **4** (1975), 377–384.

[360] Wheaton, W. C., "The Incidence of Interjurisdictional Differences in Commercial Property Taxes," *National Tax Journal* **37** (1984), 515–528.

[361] White, M. J., "Fiscal Zoning in Fragmented Metropolitan Areas," in *Fiscal*

Zoning and Land Use Controls, ed. by E. S. Mills and W. E. Oates, 31–100. Lexington: D. C. Heath, 1975.

[362] White, M. J., "Firm Location in a Zoned Metropolitan Area," in *Fiscal Zoning and Land Use Controls*, ed. by E. S. Mills and W. E. Oates, 175–202. Lexington: D. C. Heath, 1975.

[363] Wicks, J. H., R. A. Little, and R. A. Beck, "A Note on Capitalization of Property Tax Changes," *National Tax Journal*, **21** (1968), 263–265.

[364] Wiegard, W., "Distortionary Taxation in a Federal Economy," *Zeitschrift fuer Nationaloekonomie*, **40** (1980), 183–206.

[365] Wijkander, H., "Provision of Public Goods in Congested Cities," *Journal of Public Economics* **25** (1984), 127–142.

[366] Wildasin, D. E., *Theoretical Issues in Local Public Finance*, unpublished Ph.D. dissertation, 1976.

[367] Wildasin, D. E., "Local Government Decisions and the Market for Property: Some implications for Welfare and the Theory of Public Choice—Abstract," *Journal of Economics*, **2** (1976), 160.

[368] Wildasin, D. E., "Public Expenditures Determined by Voting With One's Feet and Public Choice," *Scandinavian Journal of Economics*, **79** (1977), 889–898.

[369] Wildasin, D. E., "Local Public Goods, Property Values, and Local Public Choice," *Journal of Urban Economics*, **6** (1979), 521–534.

[370] Wildasin, D. E., "Public Good Provision with Optimal and Non-optimal Commodity Taxation: The Single-Consumer Case," *Economics Letters*, **4** (1979), 59–64.

[371] Wildasin, D. E., "Locational Efficiency in a Federal System," *Regional Science and Urban Economics*, **10** (1980), 453–471.

[372] Wildasin, D. E., "More on the Neutrality of Land Taxation," *National Tax Journal*, **35** (1982), 105–115.

[373] Wildasin, D. E., "The Welfare Effects of Intergovernmental Grants in an Economy with Independent Jurisdictions," *Journal of Urban Economics*, **13** (1983), 147–164.

[374] Wildasin, D. E., "On Public Good Provision with Distortionary Taxation," *Economic Inquiry*, **22** (1984), 227–243.

[375] Wildasin, D. E., "Tiebout-Lindahl Equilibrium," unpublished, 1984.

[376] Wildasin, D. E., "Tax Exporting and the Marginal Cost of Public Expenditure," unpublished, 1984.

[377] Wildasin, D. E., "The Welfare Effects of Intergovernmental Grants with Distortionary Local Taxes," *Journal of Public Economics* **25** (1984), 103–126.

[378] Wildasin, D. E., "Income Taxes and Urban Spatial Structure," *Journal of Urban Economics* **18** (1985), 313–333.

[379] Wilde, J. A., "The Expenditure Effects of Grant-In-Aid Programs," *National Tax Journal*, **21** (1968), 340–348.

[380] Wilde, J. A., "Grants-In-Aid: The Analytics of Design and Response," *National Tax Journal*, **24** (1971), 143–155.

[381] Williams, A., "The Optimal Provision of Public Goods in a System of Local Government," *Journal of Political Economy*, **74** (1966), 18–33.

[382] Wilson, J. D., "The Excise Tax Effects of the Property Tax," *Journal of Public Economics*, **24** (1984), 309–330.

[383] Wilson, J., "Optimal Property Taxation in the Presence of Inter-Regional Capital Mobility," *Journal of Urban Economics*, **18** (1985), 73–89.

[384] Wilson, J., "A Theory of Inter-Regional Tax Competition," *Journal of Urban Economics* (forthcoming).

170   D. E. WILDASIN

[385] Winer, S. L., "Some Evidence on the Effect of the Separation of Spending and Taxing Decisions," *Journal of Political Economy*, **91** (1983), 126–140.
[386] Winer, S. L., and D. Gauthier, *Internal Migration and Fiscal Structure*. Ottawa: Economic Council of Canada, 1982.
[387] Yinger, J., "Prejudice and Discrimination in the Urban Housing Market," in *Current Issues in Urban Economics*, ed. by P. Mieszkowski and M. Straszheim, 430–468. Baltimore: Johns Hopkins University Press, 1979.
[388] Yinger, J., "Capitalization and the Median Voter," *American Economic Review*, **71** (1981), 99–103.
[389] Yinger, J., "Capitalization and the Theory of Local Public Finance," *Journal of Political Economy*, **90** (1982), 917–943.
[390] Yinger, J., "Inefficiency and the Median Voter: Property Taxes, Capitalization, Heterogeneity, and the Theory of the Second Best," *Research in Urban Economics* (forthcoming).
[391] Yinger, J., "On Fiscal Disparities Across Cities," *Journal of Urban Economics* (forthcoming).
[392] Zimmerman, D., "Resource Misallocation from Interstate Tax Exportation: Estimates of Excess Spending and Welfare Loss in a Median Voter Framework," *National Tax Journal*, **36** (1983), 183–202.
[393] Zodrow, G. R., "The Tiebout Model After Twenty-Five Years: An Overview," in *Local Provision of Public Services: The Tiebout Model After Twenty-Five Years*, ed. by G. R. Zodrow, 1–16. New York: Academic Press, 1983.
[394] Zodrow, G. R., and P. Mieszkowski: "The Incidence of the Property Tax: The Benefit View Versus the New View," in *Local Provision of Public Services: The Tiebout Model After Twenty-Five Years*, ed. G. R. Zodrow, 109–130. New York: Academic Press, 1983.
[395] Zodrow, G. R., and P. M. Mieszkowski: "Pigou, Property Taxation and the Under-Provision of Local Public Goods," *Journal of Urban Economics* (forthcoming).

INDEX

FUNDAMENTALS OF PURE AND APPLIED ECONOMICS

Additional volumes in preparation
ISSN: 0191-1708